Feasting with Shellfish in
the Southern Ohio Valley

Feasting with Shellfish in the Southern Ohio Valley

Archaic Sacred Sites and Rituals

Cheryl Claassen

The University of Tennessee Press / Knoxville

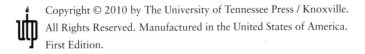
The paper in this book meets the requirements of American National Standards Institute /
National Information Standards Organization specification Z39.48-1992 (Permanence of
Paper). It contains 30 percent post-consumer waste and is certified by the Forest Steward-
ship Council.

Thanks to the Society for Historical Archaeology and editor J. W. Joseph for permission to
reuse the contents of Chapter 4, taken from "Washboards, Pigtoes, and Muckets: Historic
Musseling Industries of the Mississippi Watershed," by Cheryl Claassen in *Historical
Archaeology* 28 (2): 1–125, 1994.

Quotations from "The Essential Features of Adena Ritual and Their Implications," by
R. Berle Clay in *Southeastern Archaeology* 17(1):1–21, used by permission from editor
Charles Cobb.

Library of Congress Cataloging-in-Publication Data

Claassen, Cheryl, 1953–
Feasting with shellfish in the southern Ohio Valley: Archaic sacred sites and rituals /
Cheryl Claassen. — 1st ed.
    p. cm.
Includes bibliographical references and index.
ISBN-13: 978-1-57233-714-5 (hardcover: alk. paper)
ISBN-10: 1-57233-714-1 (hardcover: alk. paper)
    1. Indians of North America—Ohio River Valley—Antiquities.
    2. Indians of North America—Ohio River Valley—Rites and ceremonies.
    3. Kitchen-middens—Ohio River Valley.
    4. Shellfish—Social aspects—Ohio River Valley—History.
    5. Excavations (Archaeology)—Ohio River Valley.
    6. Sacred space—Ohio River Valley—History.
    7. Landscapes—Social aspects—Ohio River Valley—History.
    8. Ohio River Valley—Antiquities.
    9. Green River Valley (Ky.)—Antiquities.
    10. Tennessee River Valley—Antiquities. I. Title.

E78.O4C55 2010
977—dc22
2010011935

Patty Jo Watson
Jack Hofman
Ken Sassaman
Michael Russo
Karen Bassie-Sweat
Jill Furst
Robert L. Hall
James E. Brady

For inspiration derived from your writings and conversations.

David Anderson
Ken Sassaman
Patty Jo Watson
Evan Peacock
William Marquardt
Tom Whyte

For true support in my endeavors over the past 25 years. Never underestimate the power of a compliment or the honor derived from honest intellectual consideration.

CONTENTS

ILLUSTRATIONS

Figures

Tables

ACKNOWLEDGMENTS

A study like this, depending as I did on the literature rather than primarily reexamination of collections and field notes or excavation, owes much to diggers, authors, curators, and colleagues. I need to thank specifically those colleagues who dealt with my (frequent) e-mail inquiries, often sending me information: Anne Bader, Aaron Deter-Wolf, Lynne Sullivan, Ken Sassaman, Bob Mensforth, Russell Stafford, Chris Moore, Steve Mocas, Jon Lothrop, George Crothers, David Dye, Nancy O'Malley, Russell Stafford, Dick Jefferies, Ben Shields, Sheldon Burdin, Boyce Driskell, Kandace Hollenbach, Jennifer McDonough, Dan Allen, Matt Gage, Michael Anslinger, Sam Simmens, William Fox, Gary Crites, Pat Tench, Donald Cochran, Marie Danforth, Mary Bade, Homes Hogue, Sara Surface-Evans, Evan Peacock, Cheryl Munson, Jim Theler, Bill Marquardt, Pat Watson, Lora Lamarre, and Rodney Demott.

The following individuals sent theses, publications, or site files: Keith Little, Michael Anslinger, Ben Shields, Kyle Lubsen, Marie Danforth, Aaron Deter-Wolf, Anne Bader, Rodney Demott, Dan Allan, Lynne Sullivan, Chris Moore, and Nancy O'Malley.

Aaron Deter-Wolf told me about the Nashville Basin sites, discussed Ensworth with me, and gave me site locations, Ensworth material, contacts in the Falls area, and feedback on a 2007 SEAC paper. Anne Bader gave me the Falls of the Ohio contacts that I needed and her own unpublished papers and wisdom about KYANG, Meyer, and Panther Rock. She, Richard Stallings, Steve Mocas, and Phil DiBlasi answered numerous questions about Falls sites in general. Thanks to Matt Gage for Whitesburg Bridge dates and to Jonathon Lothrop for conversations about East Steubenville in the early years of this project.

In the course of writing this book and preparing an NSF proposal for radiocarbon dating many of these sites in spring 2009, I visited several repositories. Thanks to Nancy O'Malley for four days of help with the Green River collections at the Webb Museum, and for Figures 7.1, 7.2, and 7.3. Also, thanks to Chris Pappas for help most of one day at the

Webb Museum, and George Crothers for permission to peruse the Webb collections. Thanks to Phil DiBlasi for permission to visit the University of Louisville curatorial facility, help with collections, and copies of the KYANG files.

Thanks to Lynne Sullivan and Jeff Chapman for help and access to WPA paperwork and files for western Tennessee sites on two occasions. Michaelynn Harle helped me at the McClung Museum as well. At the University of Tennessee Department of Anthropology, I was helped by Jennifer Kirkmeyer on several occasions, and Rachel Black. Nicholas Herrmann gave help and access to Hayes paperwork. At the University of Alabama, Mary Body arranged for WPA photos (Figures 6.1, 6.2, and 6.3) and intervened on my behalf in efforts to get NAGPRA files. She located all of the boxes I needed on a visit to the collections. Eugene Futato also gave assistance and Sunday night admission to the trailer. Those trips were funded by a Graduate School University Research Grant, Appalachian State University. That grant also provided the money to acquire the Alabama WPA photos.

Several publications have influenced me strongly over the past 15 years: *An Archaeology of the Soul* (Robert Hall), *At the Edge of the World* (Karen Bassie Sweet), *The Natural History of the Soul* (Jill Furst), *Sacred Places in North America* (Courtney Milne), and books edited by James Brady. Articles that were instrumental to what I have written here were written by Jack Hofman (1985), Brian Hayden (2000), and Mike Russo (2004), influencing the entire project; Ken Sassaman (2004) influencing Chapter 1, Berle Clay (1998) influencing Chapter 9, Diane Warren's dissertation (2004) and John Blitz (Blitz and Livingood 2004) influencing Chapter 6, Patricia Lambert (2001) and Dominique Rissolo (2005) for the going-to-water ideas, and Jenny James (2006) on dogs, influencing Chapter 8. I have clearly relied heavily on the thinking/work of Dan Morse, Martha Rolingson, William Webb, and Pat Cridlebaugh and the Green River volume edited by Marquardt and Watson (2005). There were several bibliographies that I also mined—Bader 2007 and Sassaman 2004 stand out in my memory.

Thanks to Ken Sassaman, who not only answered various inquiries but wrote a very useful review of the manuscript (as did an anonymous reviewer). Thanks to Martha Rolingson for drawing all of those site maps in the 1960s, and to Andi Cockran (Appalachian State), who produced the regional and district maps. Finally, thanks to Gregory G. Reck, chair of the Anthropology Department, Appalachian State University, who gave me several course reductions to write, and whose praise means much to me.

CHAPTER 1
THINKING ABOUT ARCHAIC HUNTER-GATHERERS

The hunter-gatherer-shellfishers of the southern Ohio Valley, who are the focus of this study, like those living in other regions of the Americas were once viewed as so culturally simple that they cared little about their dead and were concerned only with food (Webb and Haag 1940:109). The sometimes 30-foot-thick piles of shell, rock, and ash and the seemingly jumbled bodies supported this impression. By 1983, however, groups living to the west of them, the Archaic hunter-gatherers of the central Mississippi River valley, were attributed far more complexity in their social organization. Archaic-aged burial mounds were identified in southern Illinois (Charles and Buikstra 1983) and in Missouri (Reid 1983) and ancient villages were located (e.g., Koster site), both implying sedentism rather than habitual wandering as a lifestyle. Since 1990, mound building by similarly aged cultures located on the Gulf coastal plain has been verified (e.g., *Southeastern Archaeology* 1994 13[2]), as have repetitively used feasting sites on the Atlantic Coast (e.g., Russo 2004). Clearly, people who lived in villages, built mounds, and feasted had far more things to think about than simply eating.

Back at the shell mounds, visions of cultural simplicity were fading as well in the 1980s. The large number of burials at many of the riverside sites allowed a number of researchers to conclude that cemeteries were present and that the presence of shells and "domestic" debris indicated villages (e.g., Janzen 1977). The sporadic distribution of exotic stone and marine shell items among the dead suggested social differentiation. The great size of several of the body-bearing shell heaps implied efforts to mark territory (Charles and Buikstra 1983). While the evidence for sedentism suggested complex social organization, and that domesticated plants would be found within these villages, sparking the Shell Mound Archeological Project (Marquardt and Watson 1983), a horticultural base failed to materialize (Marquardt and Watson 2005a). Furthermore, a surprising number of victims of violence were uncovered in the 1990s (Smith 1995). Sedentism, cemeteries, mounds, territory, violence, and exotic goods amount to a case for Archaic transegalitarian societies among the users of these burial sites (Crothers 2004). The present study will make the case for feasting as well. Just how complex were the shell-heap-using peoples of the southern Ohio Valley?

The Development of Social Complexity

The foundation of social complexity is widely expressed as environmental abundance coupled with high population densities—opportunity and need. Short of an extremely rich coastal setting, such as those available to the Pacific Coast cultures, southern California cultures, or Danish cultures, where chiefdoms could be found among hunter-gatherers, an "average" environment would need domesticated plants to support complex social life. Domesticated plants and the artificial packing of space that farmers performed were necessary to enrich the environment to the point of producing surpluses, it was reasoned, which would then create a need for storage facilities and virtually year-round tending. Storage and tending would require sedentary living that would give rise to villages, notions of resource ownership, territoriality, and trade for items needed but located outside the territory. Defense of these owned resources would result in warfare. In eastern North America a suite of domesticated plants was available to people by 3,500 years ago, which set the stage for the development of complex social life (transegalitarian or corporate social life) in the centuries that followed—the creation of ceremonial centers, the building of mounds, the harnessing of resources to support craft specialists, etc.

The definition of complexity and its recognition by archaeologists have been encapsulated in trait lists (covered in Sassaman 2004:233–235). The traits of a complex society are numerous but sort into a core group (traits named by most authors) and a less necessary group (traits named by a few anthropologists). The core traits are high population density, sedentism (at least half of the year), territoriality, food storage, and inherited status. Social complexity can also be seen in the less necessary traits of long-distance exchange, elaborate technology, craft specialization, standardized prestige goods or valuables, delayed returns through feasting and gifting obligations, and defense/warfare. Other traits have been specified as well, such as dog breeding (Hayden 1996). Southeastern

U.S. archaeologists have repeatedly queried how mounds and feasting could occur without the standard suite of traits: agriculture, pottery, craft specialization, sedentism, storage pits, trade, or social inequality (e.g., authors in Gibson and Carr eds. 2004).

Having a few of these traits would not make a society complex. What is required by the most strident theorists is persistent, systemic inequality of groups, factions, and individuals. The definition of complexity apparently at play in the southeastern United States is that of some having power over many, which is far more lenient a definition than that employed by Arnold (1996) for the Chumash of the southern California coast. She requires forced labor as well as inherited privileges. Gibson and Carr (1999) thought that power in the hands of a few individuals (specifically priests) was necessary before mounds would be built.

This formula for social complexity and its chain of consequences had dissolved by 1980 with the discovery of several North American examples of hunter-gatherers living in villages; building storage facilities at individual houses, building mounds, creating cemeteries, and engaging in warfare, all without the benefits or liabilities of a diet based on domesticated plants. Archaeologists, paleoethnobotanists, and zooarchaeologists searched the environmental evidence found in the precocious villages in minute detail for the required environmental trigger for these developments, the intensified harvest of some key resources, the requisite population pressure, and for still-older specimens of domesticates that could explain their social development. They were successful, identifying environmental triggers for these developments, such as the Hypsithermal climatic episode, keeping intact the cause and effect relationship of environment, resource pressure or scarcity, and social complexity.

To expose further the issues under debate in modern hunter-gatherer studies, and the potential to the reader for the case study that follows to bear on these issues, I turn now to an abbreviated presentation of thoughts about complex society among the Archaic mound builders of the lower Mississippi River valley.

Poverty Point culture of Louisiana is best known from the vantage point of the Poverty Point site, located south of the confluence of six rivers. Whether a socially complex society constructed its five sizable clusters of six arcuate berms and several mounds, which are estimated to amount to 750,000 m^3 of dirt (J. Saunders 2004:158), and those in neighboring sites, has been argued by authors in Gibson and Carr (2004).

In keeping with the long-held theory that social complexity develops from agriculture, the subsistence base for Poverty Point was once thought to be domesticated plants. We now know that it was constructed entirely by hunter-gatherers. Their sedentism was challenged in the early 1980s, and several traits of complexity are now known to be absent (pottery and craft specialization) or rare (burials, structures, storage pits, trade evidence) (J. Saunders 2004:146).

Earlier mound sites in Louisiana, such as Watson Brake, Frenchman's Bend, and Caney Mounds, which preceded Poverty Point culture by some 1,900 years, also fail to show evidence of the formulaic components of complex society, including social stratification. Joe Saunders (2004) found domesticated plants, structures, storage pits, craft specialization, burials, and even trade to be nonexistent at these three multimound sites. Equivocal evidence existed for feasting and sedentism (defined as year-round occupancy), leaving only mounds as evidence of social stratification. Instead, those data, and the high redundancy in artifact types between sites, strongly suggested to Saunders that dirt mounds were produced by egalitarian groups with voluntary labor. This was the conclusion for Poverty Point as well, by three of the authors in Gibson and Carr, eds. (2004) *Signs of Power* (Gibson 2004, J. Saunders 2004, White 2004), as well as for other regional records (Crothers 2004).

But other authors disagreed, seeing socially stratified creators of all the Archaic earthen mound and shell ring/shell works complexes. Russo (2004) argued that the feasting evident at shell rings on the coast and the differentiation of habitation loci on top of shell rings are inconsistent with the expectations for egalitarian communities. Widmer (2004) believed that mounds in general indicate ownership of resource-rich places.

Sassaman and Heckenberger (2004) also thought Poverty Point culture was orchestrated by social elites. The evidence consisted of the alignments of mound clusters with different cardinal directions and the arrangements of mounds within individual clusters in an equilateral triangular shape. Furthermore, they pointed out that the creation of plazas by these mound clusters created inside and outside space that typically mirrors social organization. The creation of inside performance space, the placing of mounds in any one site to conform to a preconceived plan, and the placing of mound clusters to address the four cardinal directions all seemed to be sufficient evidence of social hierarchy to these authors. This construction/siting program may have begun 6,000 years ago and been enacted over a 1,500-year period.

More significant than the alignments and planning to these authors, however, was the indication that this social hierarchy was not forced by impinging material conditions such as food supply or population pressure, but rather derived from an idea (Sassaman and Heckenberger 2004) about the cosmos and how human beings would interact with the powerful and mysterious forces that were evident around them.

These concerns about the cosmos and the forces about in the world no doubt occupied the minds of most prehistoric people at least some of the time. They surely created places to interact with those forces and objects to carry their thanks and prayers, as well as intangible means of praying. Archaeologists are just awakening to the evidence of ritual and spirituality that has been in the features, sites, and landscapes we have worked in and with for years (Sundstrom 2000). This study will further this project of elucidating the spiritual life of Archaic peoples in the southern Ohio Valley.

In this present study of hunter-gatherers living from 7,000 to 4,000 years ago in the southern Ohio Valley, I offer another litmus test for Archaic hunter-gatherer social complexity, while underscoring the diversity among people of the era. The Ohio Valley is part of the midcontinental United States, an area stretching from the Mississippi River on the western side of Illinois eastward to Pennsylvania and from the southern Great Lakes southward to the Tennessee River. This area contains many of the sites used in formulating the idea of the Archaic period (10,000 to 4,000 years ago), such as Russell Cave, Rodgers Shelter, Modoc Rock Shelter, Lamoka Lake, and the shell heaps of Eva, Indian Knoll, Perry, and Mulberry Creek. Here also were located some of the earliest test cases for the environmental determinism that invoked the Hypsithermal climatic event and social questions of the 1960s–1970s New Archaeology, questions that specifically addressed the rise of social complexity in the eastern United States (see papers in Philips and Brown, eds. 1983 and Price and Brown, eds. 1985).

Excavations at the Koster site in Illinois led to the identification of hunter-gatherer village life and an oft-repeated claim that Archaic village life was made possible by the intensified exploitation of the newly developed backwater lakes and waterways of the area. High human density at these backwater lakes led to expressions of territoriality and signs of ethnic identity, trade, and warfare (evident in various authors in Phillips and Brown eds. [1983]). But rather than enhancing the aquatic resources of the entire midcontinent, the Hypsithermal was understood to have resulted in resource-rich patches (e.g., Walthall 1990). Highly desirable spatially restricted resources, such as shellfish, brought about through both their richness and patchiness relatively and absolutely dense human populations. The shell heaps of central Kentucky marked another such place rich in aquatic resources and were believed to be year-round villages in 1932 (Webb and Funkhouser 1932).

The role of the Hypsithermal has been so basic to the conceptualization of social and technological development during the Archaic that entire cultural histories are contained within the period bracketed by this climatic era, and a book about complex Archaic hunter-gatherers was organized according to its west to east trending atmospheric moisture pattern (Phillips and Brown eds., 1983). Lest the reader think that environmental determinism has faded away in the era of postprocessualism, a recent volume about the Green River shell sites concluded that the Hypsithermal could explain this phenomenon (Marquardt and Watson 2005a).

Not everyone credits the Hypsithermal, population pressure, or material needs for the signs of complexity, however, as several voices have called for a more anthropologically centered understanding of change in human societies of the midcontinent and Southeast (e.g., Brown 1983, Crothers 2004) or have given a greater role to ideas, specifically religion/ ritual, than environmental change in causing social organization change (e.g., Brooks 2004, Sassaman 2004, Sassaman and Heckenberger 2004). New botanical and climatological information indicates that the social changes present in the southeast and elsewhere in the eastern United States were not the result of either environmental change or subsistence, leaving historical developments in a stronger explanatory role. Furthermore, ethnographic information for hunter-gatherers indicates that each of the elements on those trait lists can occur independently.

If social complexity is recognizable as a majority of traits to be found in a list, then the shell collectors fail the test. There is no pottery, no scarce resource, no intensification of a significant resource except for mollusks (also known as naiads and unios), no formal cemeteries, no year-round occupation. However, there are good reasons to see that feasting and mortuary functions were paramount at shell-bearing sites. I will argue that the environment was important to these people, but not for its edibles. I, too, see a concern with power, but it is not that between individuals.

The physical landscape held inexhaustible potential for the expression of mysterious powers (e.g., Irwin 1994). Archaic people were particularly attuned to the expression of powers from the Underworld at major shoals, caves, and karstic terrain in general. In these locations a human-made context for the dead was created that promised renewal. Most of the dead were interred in the shell heaps, rituals of renewal were enacted, and great feasts were held. These places were probably part of a visionary landscape that was cosmologically and topographically charged (Irwin 1994:22) for millennia and were long remembered. Rituals of renewal and rebalancing developed, which required a focus on particular places, the sacrificing of human life, feasting with kin and non-kin, and particular types of offerings. These religious concerns and practices apparently kept in check any aggrandizing sponsors and priests.

There are other reasons than just issues of complexity for pursuing a study of the Archaic shellfishers of the southern Ohio Valley. We really know very little about this type of site, and in this study I offer not only intra- and interregional comparisons of shell-bearing sites but comparisons with non–shell-bearing mortuary sites and a subdivision of sites with shells. In past publications I have stressed that this type of site is unexpectedly circumscribed geographically. In this study I offer some possible criteria for their location, both social and natural. These places also invoke a discussion of primary forest efficiency, mortuary theory, the function of mounds, the types of evidence for ritual, influence upon Adena and Hopewell ritual and ritual places, and social memory.

A number of natural places were known to be residences of powerful entities or places where one could hope to commune with them. From 8,000 to 4,000 years ago people initiated modifications and amplifications of their environment in ways that enhanced their access to the mysterious powers around them. These culturally enhanced places concentrated power and created social memories of human successes and failures in attempts to keep balance and to gain the favor of the spirits. The places, and the fires and burials held in them, were marked in the individual and collective memory, on the landscape, and on their surfaces. Each of the large shell heaps was used repeatedly, often for more than 1,500 years, with remarkably little disturbance of earlier fires and burials. Those memories continued to metamorphose, and over the next 4,000 years these places were acted upon by Woodland and then by Mississippian people. Pilgrimages were no doubt made to them. These later people placed mounds near Archaic heaps, incorporated Archaic shell deposits into their own mounds, placed bodies into Archaic mortuaries often carrying signs of violent death, built buildings upon them, rejuvenated the use of marine shell, and revitalized several uses for stone.

Recent Developments in the Study
of Archaic Shellfishers

Since Jack Hofman (1984) first proposed the idea of aggregation camps, which was received with excitement but little controversy, and I first presented the idea that these heaps were not villages at all but mortuaries (Claassen 1988), which was received with both enthusiasm and doubt, the shell-bearing sites of the southern Ohio Valley have become a dynamic research topic, spawning numerous articles, two books (Carstens and Watson eds. 1996, Marquardt and Watson eds. 2005), and several dissertations (Crothers 1999, Hensley 1994, Herrmann 2004, Mohney 2002, Powell 1995) and theses (e.g., Lubsen 2004, Shields 2003, Turner 2006). A large part of the Kentucky Heritage Council conference program of 2006 was devoted to this topic.

Contractual archaeology has been expanding the database of sites for the Falls of the Ohio region (e.g., Bader 2007, 2009; Mocas 2009; White 2004). It was also the context of the recent excavation at the Whitesburg Bridge site in Alabama (Gage 2008) and the East Steubenville site dig (GAI 2007). Most important for my task, the Archaic shell rings and shell mounds of the southern Atlantic and Gulf coastline and the mortuary mounds along the St. Johns River in Florida have moved to center stage in southeastern archaeology, with exciting new evaluations and theoretical perspectives that situate these sites as constructed ceremonial locations (e.g., Aten 1999, Russo 2004, R. Saunders 2004, Wheeler et al. 2000). Archaeologists and bioarchaeologists have returned to several sites excavated between 1929 and 1950, either via new excavation in contract settings or through collections research. NAGPRA inventories now available for Tennessee and Kentucky sites and recent bioarchaeological studies of skeletal material give us basic skeletal information that had been lacking. There are many new radiocarbon dates.

There also have been important new theoretical works of relevance to the shell-bearing sites of the eastern United States concerning feasting (e.g., Russo 2004, Sassaman 2006), warfare (e.g., Mensforth 2005, Smith 1996), and hunter-gatherers (Gibson and Carr eds. 2004). These works allow us, and even require us, to consider anew these shell-bearing sites. This task has been made smaller because of the wonderful work of colleagues considering the Florida mounds and the coastal rings and shell works.

My thinking has evolved since my most recent statement about these sites in 1996 and will continue to evolve beyond this work. What I will do in this project is consider the "explanations" of shell mounding and the research that has occurred in the past two decades, and persevere in developing the concept of shell heaps as camps for ritual feasting and renewal/mortuary rites. Although I began this project decades ago by challenging the explanations offered for the conspicuous occurrence of shellfish and its seemingly sudden demise, I had not dismantled the overharvesting and the Hypsithermal hypotheses in the detail that is called for. I continue to be guided by the historic musseling industries (Claassen 1994) in my understanding of what the Archaic period shell-fishing activities could and could not have entailed, and I now perceive shell and objects and accumulations made from shell to have a symbolic meaning for renewal (Claassen 2008). Stimulated by the proximity of several caves to several shell heaps, I have begun to explore the significance of caves as ritual sites (Claassen 2006a, 2006b), offering here, for the first time, explicit ideas about the association of shell heaps with caves. I will explore further the burial practices of the shell heap users by incorporating several new lines of analysis unique to this study, such as burial depths and burial positioning. I will consider for the first time the artifacts and the significance of the dog burials, and recast the significance of the lithics in a ritual role and the shells in a feasting role. Where before I had downplayed the importance of the food content of the shells (Claassen 1996), now I see that was a mistake and find the food content key to their presence and to understanding what occurred in these places.

I hope to convince the reader that these shell heaps were not villages but camps for the duration of rituals conducted in these places. Their demise did not owe to insufficient mollusks but to changes in ritual practice. Their biographies were not identical. This study will lay the foundation for their reconceptualization as major ritual and feasting locations where rituals involved human and dog sacrifices and burial for renewal, object offerings, and a sodality of river keepers. In the end I show that the strongest interpretation of the differences in shell density, artifact types, features, physical locations, and the people buried in these sites, particularly those on the Green River, Harpeth/Duck rivers, and Ohio River is as various parts of a sacred site system with public ceremonial centers, bluff-top camps, private mortuaries, and natural sacred places. Large shell feasts were held at shell heap mortuary centers and not at the hundred or so other riverside sites with mortuaries created during the period from 8,000 to 4,000 years ago. This particular kind of sacred site system dissolved on the Green, Wabash, and Ohio rivers because of a change in ritual practices that ended the ceremonial center concept and the large public feasts. Centuries later their descendants would reappear as Adena/Hopewell with several important aspects of ritual practice intact from the Archaic period. Conversely, the attention given the shell heaps of the upper Tennessee River continued uninterrupted. While the key ritual practices of the Archaic disappeared, those places remained a viable part of Woodland social life and Mississippian ritual life.

The ramifications of these conclusions are significant and at odds with much that has been written and is taught about the eastern Archaic. Where shellfish have been conceptualized as a food of last resort for families who were living in an environment that was deteriorating, I argue that there was no significant food stress and that their adoption was motivated by social excess. Where shellfish have been seen as a scarce resource that required defending, I demonstrate that they were abundant and resilient to the relatively low-level harvest pressures of Archaic populations. Where shell heaps have been forced into the role of mundane villages providing proof of sedentism, I highlight the evidence that they were occupied only sporadically and that sedentism was not characteristic of these people. Although some researchers argue that power over others was beginning to be wielded by some and was associated with territoriality, cemeteries, warfare, and exchange networks, which coalesced as complex society, I offer instead that ritual practices motivated the raiding for sacrifices and the movement of goods for offerings, and defined sacred spaces for foragers. The power that was the focus of these activities was that perceived to reside not in the hands of a socially distinct few, but in the cosmos. The power to be mediated was that of the deities and spirits, not the aggrandizing personalities of a few kin. There are then many reasons for revisiting the shell heaps of the southern Ohio Valley.

Chapter 2
Archaic Shell-Bearing Sites
of the Southern Ohio Valley

The so-called "Shell Mound Archaic," those shell-bearing sites found on the Tennessee River, Ohio River, and Green River, as well as elsewhere, is the best known, most poorly dated phenomenon in eastern United States prehistory. For sites that have been treated as a single phenomenon, they have radiocarbon dates ranging from 8586 BP to 1315 BP.

Viewing Table 2.1 (all dates given in this study have been calibrated by the author), one can see that calibrated radiocarbon dates greater than 8000 BP have been returned on samples from the shell-bearing sites of Anderson, Eva, Ervin, and Hermitage Springs on four Tennessee rivers, and Ward in Kentucky on a tributary of the Green, on a fifth river. Use of the Mulberry Mound locus on the Tennessee River may also have begun. (Equally old dates come from freshwater shell heaps on the St. Johns River and the Gulf Coast of Florida at Hontoon Dead Creek and Horr's Island.) Not until 6,500 years ago did accumulations begin on the Ohio and on the Green River proper. Shell heaps began on the Savannah River and the southeastern Atlantic Coast after 5,500 years ago. Finally, between 4,500 and 4,000 years ago, four thousand years after shell mounding began on Tennessee rivers and in Florida, this site type appears on the Wabash and resumes on the Cumberland River.

We have, then, a very slow-moving phenomenon that began in western and central Tennessee, spread to neighbors on the Green River, then to their neighbors lower on the Ohio River and eventually up the Ohio and back to the Wabash and Cumberland rivers. Though there were hundreds of rivers that offered up mollusks, only a very few of them were selected by some Archaic hunter-gatherers. There is the hint of a migrating set of practices that combined the accumulation of freshwater shells with burial of the dead in selected riverside locations and the accumulation of freshwater shells and some ritual items on bluff tops.

Text continues on page 18

Table 2.1 Radiocarbon Dates by River (listed downriver to upriver)[1,2]

Site	Provenience	BPcal 95%	Raw rcy	Reference to Raw
		Green River Tributaries		
Barrett, Ky.				
	Bu100 hb	6473–6309	5620+/-40	Marquardt/Watson 2005b
	Bu87 hb	5310–5017	4520+/-40	Marquardt/Watson 2005b
Ward, Ky.				
	Bu262 hb	8586–8415	7714+/-50	Marquardt/Watson 2005b
	Bu224 hb	6636–6213	5600+/-100	Marquardt/Watson 2005b
	Bu44 hb	6173–5652	5120+/-90	Marquardt/Watson 2005b
	Bu421 hb	5646–5326	4800+/-65	Marquardt/Watson 2005b
	Bu175 hb	4834–4522	4134+/-60	Marquardt/Watson 2005b
Kirkland, Ky., Shell free				
	Bu34 hb	8307–7990	7320+/-80	Marquardt/Watson 2005b
	Bu56 hb	7612–7330	6600+/-80	Marquardt/Watson 2005b
	Bu40 hb	6607–6298	5650+/-80	Claassen 1996
	Bu45b hb	5284–4426	4240+/-150	Marquardt/Watson 2005b
	Bu45c	4844–4086	3990+/-160	Marquardt/Watson 2005b
	Bu18 hb	4432–3998	3830+/-80	Marquardt/Watson 2005b
		Green River		
Indian Knoll, Ky.				
	79N3	5585–5086	4670+/-70	Marquardt/Watson 2005b
	Bu 612 hb	5467–4983	4570+/-75	Marquardt/Watson 2005b
	79N2	5306–4874	4460+/-90	Marquardt/Watson 2005b
	21N3	5211–4625	4300+/-70	Marquardt/Watson 2005b
	21N4	4958–4528	4230+/-80	Marquardt/Watson 2005b
	shell-free	4417–3981	3800+/-80	Marquardt/Watson 2005b
	Bu 827 hb	3962–3639	3500+/-60	Marquardt/Watson 2005b
Bowles, Ky.				
	A3-12	5033–3907	4060+/-220	Marquardt/Watson 2005b
	A3-11	3880–3481	3440+/- 80	Marquardt/Watson 2005b
	A3-7	2953–2065	2420+/-200	Marquardt/Watson 2005b
	A2-2	2447–1315	1820+/-300	Marquardt/Watson 2005b
Read, Ky.				
	Bu86 hb	4048–3378	3470+/-200	Marquardt/Watson 2005b
	Bu15A hb	3841–3447	3400+/-100	Marquardt/Watson 2005b
	Bu31b hb	3814–3448	3350+/- 70	Marquardt/Watson 2005b

(cont.)

Site	Provenience	BPcal 95%	Raw rcy	Reference to Raw
Haynes, Ky.				
	A1-19	5942–5603	5080+/-90	Marquardt/Watson 2005b
	A2-17	5716–5467	4850+/-60	Marquardt/Watson 2005b
	A2-9	5582–5284	4650+/-60	Marquardt/Watson 2005b
	A1-4	5445–4983	4520+/-60	Marquardt/Watson 2005b
Carlston Annis, Ky.				
	D14L1 9	6276–5940	5350+/-80	Marquardt/Watson 2005b
	D14L9	5918–5608	5030+/-85	Marquardt/Watson 2005b
	D14L13	5650–5313	4760+/-90	Marquardt/Watson 2005b
	D14L15	5591–5072	4670+/-85	Marquardt/Watson 2005b
	L12-100.02	5316–4968	4500+/-60	Marquardt/Watson 2005b
	D14L20	5287–4815	4350+/-85	Marquardt/Watson 2005b
	A1L10	5029–4569	4250+/-80	Marquardt/Watson 2005b
	A1L8	4952–4015	4040+/-180	Marquardt/Watson 2005b
	Shell-free low	4810–4441	4080+/-40	Marquardt/Watson 2005b
	Shell-free up	4783–4418	4030+/-40	Marquardt/Watson 2005b
	C-L5	3815–3393	3330+/-80	Marquardt/Watson 2005b
	C13-15	2760–2438	2515+/-80	Marquardt/Watson 2005b
DeWeese, Ky.				
	B1-4	5600–4950	4570+/-80	Marquardt/Watson 2005b
	B1-18	5595–5320	4760+/-70	Marquardt/Watson 2005b
	B1-13	5577–5295	4650+/-50	Marquardt/Watson 2005b
	B2-11	5050–4720	4320+/-50	Marquardt/Watson 2005b
Tennessee River				
Kay's Landing, Tenn.				
	St 5	5301–4966	4470+/-50	W. Fox per.com. 2007
	St 2 sh	4815–3475	4100+/-300	Lewis/Kneberg 1959
	St 1	4807–3367	3630 +/-300	Lewis/Kneberg 1959
	St 5	3975–1978	2800+/-500	Lewis/Kneberg 1959
Eva, Tenn.				
	St IV	8294–7683	7150+/-167	Dye 1996
Perry, Ala.				
	ave. top	5983–487	4764+/-250	Morse 1967:204
Whitesburg Bridge, Ala.				
	290–310cm	5584–5047	4690+/-80	M. Gage per. comm., 2004

(cont.)

Site	Provenience	BPcal 95%	Raw rcy	Reference to Raw
Whitesburg Bridge, Ala. (cont.)				
	F70 L3	4819–4531	4130+/-40	M. Gage per. comm., 2004
	190–210cm	4406–3978	3780+/-70	M. Gage per. comm., 2004
	F70 L5	3886–3691	3510+/-40	M. Gage per. comm., 2004
	F251 hearth	3566–3253	3180+/-40	M. Gage per. comm., 2004
	F32 floor	3469–3337	3170+/-40	M. Gage per. comm., 2004
	F241 sm	3468–3259	3150+/-50	M. Gage per. comm., 2004
	110–130cm	3552–3154	3130+/-80	M. Gage per. comm., 2004
	F70 floor	3442–3251	3120+/-40	M. Gage per. comm., 2004
	F364	3445–3239	3120+/-50	M. Gage per. comm., 2004
	F362	3567–2949	3080+/-140	M. Gage per. comm., 2004
	F315	3478–2956	3070+/-120	M. Gage per. comm., 2004
	StIVL3	3377–3208	3070+/-40	M. Gage per. comm., 2004
	Fea251	3381–3078	3050+/-60	M. Gage per. comm., 2004
	F410	3381–3079	3050+/-60	M. Gage per. comm., 2004
	F92	3365–3081	3040+/-50	M. Gage per. comm., 2004
	F265	3359–3062	3010+/-60	M. Gage per. comm., 2004
	F371	2736–2411	2430+/-70	M. Gage per. comm., 2004
Harpeth River				
Ensworth, Tenn. Shell-free				
	Fea 87	3900–3690	3520+/-40	Deter-Wolf et al. 2004
	Fea 101	3850–3640	3480+/-40	Deter-Wolf et al. 2004
	Fea 19	3700–3480	3370+/-40	Deter-Wolf et al. 2004
	Fea 63	3690–3480	3360+/-40	Deter-Wolf et al. 2004
	Fea 114	1940–1800	1920+/-40	Deter-Wolf et al. 2004
Hart, Tenn.				
	Bu 57 hb	6558–6282	5610+/-75	Parker 1974
Anderson, Tenn.				
	Fea.13c	8292–7583	7180+/-230	Dye 1996
	??	7985–7624	6990+/-120	Dye 1996
	Fea.38	7951–7257	6720+/-220	Dowd 1989
	Fea.13n	7830–7324	6700+/-150	Dye 1996
	Fea.27	7686–6965	6495+/-205	Dye 1996
	Bu73 bu	7244–6290	5680+/-200	Dye 1996

(cont.)

Site	Provenience	BPcal 95%	Raw rcy	Reference to Raw
		Duck River		
Ervin, Tenn.				
	??	8153–7514	7046+/-???	Hall et al. 1985
	base pz	7857–7247	6645+/-185	Hall et al. 1985
	Fea 22 crem	7422–6741	6160+/-175	Hofman 1985
	WS-Sikes	7420–6654	6115+/-205	Hall et al. 1985
	Benton	7162–6301	5765+/-200	Hall et al. 1985
Hayes, Tenn.				
	St.IV1	6995–6546	5970+/-100	Marquardt/Watson 2004
	St.IV2	6967–6317	5870+/-165	Hall et al. 1985
	St.IIIE sm	6698–5920	5525+/-190	Klippel/Morey 1986
	St.IIIE sm	6795–6025	5660+/-190	Marquardt/Watson 2004
	St.III sm	6454–5589	5245+/-230	Hall et al. 1985
	St.IV2	6410–5943	5430+/-120	Marquardt/Watson 2004
	St.IIIA sm	6287–5584	5140+/-185	Marquardt/Watson 2004
	St.IV2	5988–5614	5070+/- 90	Marquardt/Watson 2004
	St.IIIA sm	5475–4697	4390+/-170	Marquardt/Watson 2004
	St.II sf	5317–4579	4270+/-155	Hall et al. 1985
		Ohio River		
Lone Hill, Ky.				
	??	5443–4436	4365+/-185	Maslowski et al. 1995
	??	4794–4146	3935+/-95	Maslowski et al. 1995
Kyang, Ky.				
	??	5914–5599	5010+/-90	Jefferies 1997
Meyer, Ind.				
	??	6209–5917	5280+/-70	Bader 2005
Miles, Ind. Shell-free				
	Fea. 12	4826–4568	4150+/-40	White 2002
	Fea. 37	4823–4568	4140+/-40	White 2002
	Fea. 17	3480–3165	3130+/-70	White 2002
Breeden, Ind.				
	St IV	6674–6399	5750+/-70	Burdin 2008
	St II	6565–6286	5620+/-80	Burdin 2008
	St III	6400–5990	5420+/-100	Burdin 2008

(cont.)

Site	Provenience	BPcal 95%	Raw rcy	Reference to Raw
Breeden, Ind. (cont.)				
	Shell-free	5895–5332	4850+/-110	Burdin 2008
	??	5292–4238	4200+/-200	Bellis 1981
Reid, Ind.				
	??	6628–6287	5644+/-90	Driskell et al. 1979
	Zone 3	6435–6020	5480+/-90	Janzen 1977
	??	5584–5312	4692+/-70	Driskell et al. 1979
	Zone 1	5464–5039	4555+/-70	Janzen 1977
Miller, Ind.				
	6–15"	6492–5733	5377+/-200	Driskell et al. 1979
	6–15"	6381–5606	5220+/-200	Janzen 1977
Hoke, Ind.				
	??	5597–4823	4532+/-185	Driskell et al. 1979
Hornung, Ky.				
	??	6412–5647	5377+/-230	Driskel et al. 1979
	??	6209–5896	5253+/-75	Driskel et al. 1979
	??	6208–5761	5238+/-85	Driskel et al. 1979
	??	6190–5465	5047+/-200	Driskel et al. 1979
	??	5292–4918	4444+/-60	Driskel et al. 1979
	??	5298–4837	4367+/-95	Driskel et al. 1979
Bluegrass, Ind.				
	??	6207–5917	5290+/-70	Bader 2009
	??	5917–5613	5020+/-80	Bader 2009
Old Clarksville/Elrod, Ind.				
	??	5463–4859	4594+/-180	Driskell et al. 1979
	??	5442–4837	4460+/-180	Janzen 1977
	??	5327–4741	4305+/-180	Driskell et al. 1979
Railway Museum, Ky., Shell-free				
	??	5587–5322	4720+/-70	Ross-Stallings 2009
	??	5610–5323	4780+/-80	Ross-Stallings 2009
Habich, Ind., Shell-free				
	Fea. 6	5307–4874	4480+/-80	Bader 2009
	Fea. 81	3977–3488	3480+/-100	Bader 2009
	Fea. 2	2711–2355	2440+/-60	Bader 2009
Panther Rock, Ky.				
	Fea. 2	5747–5586	4920+/-50	Mocas 2009
	Fea. 115	3685–3473	3340+/-40	Mocas 2009
	Fea. 11	2122–1926	2050+/-40	Mocas 2009

(cont.)

Site	Provenience	BPcal 95%	Raw rcy	Reference to Raw
East Steubenville, W. Va.				
	F47 sh	6270–5930	5310+/-60	GAI 2007
	F64 sh	5670–5340	4830+/-70	GAI 2007
	F45 sh	5660–5330	4810+/-70	GAI 2007
	F17 sh	5640–5310	4770+/-80	GAI 2007
	F49 sh	5610–5300	4730+/-80	GAI 2007
	F72 sh	5580–5050	4630+/-80	GAI 2007
	F13b3	4420–4080	3840+/-60	GAI 2007
	F46 hb	4410–4150	3860+/-40	GAI 2007
	F46cL5	4400–3980	3790+/-60	GAI 2007
	F62 hb	4350–4090	3810+/-40	GAI 2007
	F5 hb	4350–4084	3810+/-40	GAI 2007
	F37 hb	4260–4070	3780+/-40	GAI 2007
	F60aL1	4230–3840	3680+/-70	GAI 2007
	F60aL1	4230–3840	3680+/-70	GAI 2007
	F49bL2	3910–3390	3400+/-110	GAI 2007
	sh	1550–1390	1590+/-40	GAI 2007
Globe Hill, W. Va.				
	??	5310–4189	4170+/-220	Hall et al. 1985
Wabash River				
Robeson Hills, Ill.				
	Pit S-14	4240–3383	3490+/-200	Winters 1969
Swan Island, Ill.				
	60"	4060–3453	3450+/-125	Winters 1969
	30–36"	3984–3468	3450+/-120	Winters 1969
Riverton, Ill.				
	36–42"	4232–3220	3460+/-250	Winters 1969
	78–84"	4080–3005	3270+/-250	Winters 1969
	84–123"	3830–3260	3320+/-140	Winters 1969
	60–66"	3811–3062	3200+/-200	Winters 1969
	18–24"	3721–2985	3110+/-200	Winters 1969
Cumberland River				
Robinson, Tenn.				
	Fea43	3612–2956	3230+/-160	Morse 1967
	Bu5 hb	3614–2957	3200+/-160	Morse 1967
	Fea31-32	3394–2794	2970+/-150	Morse 1967
	Fea35	3384–2797	2970+/-150	Morse 1967
	Fea69	3249–2744	2830+/-130	Morse 1967

(cont.)

Site	Provenience	BPcal 95%	Raw rcy	Reference to Raw
Robinson, Tenn. (cont.)				
	Bu56 hb	3000–2432	2630+/-130	Morse 1967
	Fea46	2926–2352	2530+/-150	Morse 1967
	Bu58bone	2949–2304	2410+/-200	Morse 1967
	Fea9	2847–2336	2450+/-140	Morse 1967
Penitentiary Branch, Tenn.				
	??	4270–3359	3600+/-195	Cridlebaugh 1986
	??	3728–2988	3185+/-165	Cridlebaugh 1986
	??	3556–2921	3050+/-140	Cridlebaugh 1986
	??	3445–2849	2975+/-145	Cridlebaugh 1986
	??	3058–2068	2370+/-205	Cridlebaugh 1986

¹sh=shell, hb=human bone, sm=shell midden.

²All dates were calibrated by the author except for one from Panther Rock and from Ward. I used the Bcal on line calibration program from the University of Sheffield (Buck et al. 1999; http://intarch.ac.uk/journal/issue7/buck/). This curve has converted older dates than earlier calibration programs would allow. I used the default parameters: Precision internal calculation 10, MCMC sampling long run size 1000, intervals of 50, minimum sample size 50,000, and convergence check sensitivity level 5. I entered all raw dates as unordered and unconstrained, assumed each was independent of any other, and designated the atmosphere 2004 calibration curve for terrestrial or freshwater samples or the Marine 2004 curve for marine shells. No reservoir number or error was input. The most notable differences in these calibrated dates and those done earlier by other authors are the decreased age of the raws in the 7000s and the increased age of the raws in the 4000s. Generally speaking, for example, the Green River dates previously calibrated by Marquardt and Watson (2005b:64) have, in this calibration, a slightly smaller range at 2sd and terminate at an older date.

Shell accumulations stopped in most of these regions with the close of the Archaic. The shell-free deposits that cap a few of the sites have been dated only at Carlston Annis and Indian Knoll, where shellfishing appears to have ceased about 4800 BP at the former site and a millennium later at the latter site. The latest deposits now known are those on the Tennessee River in the Land Between the Lakes area and upriver in the Wheeler and Guntersville basins, and those on the Cumberland and Wabash rivers, demonstrating that a few groups were still amassing shells as late as 3,400 years ago. Why accumulating freshwater shells fell out of favor is one of the topics of this study.

A review of the Archaic shell-bearing sites found in the Ohio River watershed and comprising the database for this study is appropriate at this point. Much of relevance has been accomplished in the past two decades, such as the new excavations and reports from Haynes (Green River), East Steubenville (upper Ohio River), Hermitage Springs (Cumberland River), Whitesburg Bridge (Tennessee River), and Carlston Annis (Green River), the reassessments of museum collections from Read and Ward (Green River), Eva (Tennessee River), Harris Creek (St. Johns River), and Mulberry Creek (Tennessee River); and new raw dates from the Savannah and St. Johns rivers, Atlantic Coast, East Steubenville, Haynes, Whitesburg Bridge, and Anderson. The greatest strides in understanding the Archaic shell heaps have been made on the Atlantic Coast and in Florida, where a strong argument has been made for ceremonial rings and feasting loci (e.g., Russo 2004), which have greatly influenced my thinking.

Most of the radiocarbon dates available can be found in Table 2.1 by river setting. Table 2.2 specifies the duration of the activities of burying the dead, shellfishing, and the number of years of use when it is possible to calculate these figures. Appendix I offers some information about each of the sites mentioned in this study.

Table 2.2. Duration of Selected Activities (using 2 sd. and the maximum spread between endpoints; number of dates in parentheses)

Site	Years Accumulation	Burials (#Dates)	Shell (#Dates)
Duck River			
Ervin	1852	7422–6741 BP (1)	
Hayes	2416		
Harpeth River			
Anderson	2002	7244–6290 BP (1)	
Hart		6558–6283 BP (1)	
Tennessee River			
Kay's Landing	1934		4815–3475 BP (1)
Whitesburg	3173		
Cypress Creek			
Kirkland	4309	8307–7990 BP (1)	
		7612–7330 BP (1)	
		6607–6298 BP (1)	
		5284–3998 BP (3)	

(cont.)

Site	Years Accumulation	Burials (#Dates)	Shell (#Dates)
Cypress Creek (cont.)			
Ward	4064	8586–8415 BP (1)	
		6636–5326 BP (3)	
		4834–4522 BP (1)	
Pond River			
Barrett	1456	6473–6309 BP (1)	
		5310–5017 BP (1)	
Green River			
Bowles	3718		
Indian Knoll	1946	5467–4983 BP (1) 3962–3639 BP (1)	
Read	670	4048–3378 BP (3)	
Haynes	959		
Carlston Annis	3838		7375+/-500 rcy (1)
			5150+/-300 rcy (1)
DeWeese	880		
Cumberland River			
Robinson	1276	3614–2304 BP (3)	
Penitentiary	2202		
Ohio River			
Carrier Mills	2038		
Lone Hill	1267		
Miles	1661		
Miller	886		
Hornung	1575		
Reid	1589		
Old Clarksville	722		
Bluegrass	594		
Railway Museum	265		
E. Steubenville	952	4410–4070 BP (4)	6270-5930 BP (1)
			5670-5050 BP (5)
Breeden	2436		
Wabash River			
Robeson Hills	975		
Swan Island	607		
Riverton	1247		

A Regional Review of Shell-bearing Archaic Sites

Tennessee River Sites (Figure 2.1)

The lower Tennessee River—now underwater in the Land Between the Lakes park—shows an interesting mix of shell-bearing and non–shell-bearing Archaic and Woodland period sites. Four sites appear to be primarily of Archaic age and are plotted in Figure 2.1—Big Sandy, Cherry (both on a tributary), Kay's Landing, and Eva on the Tennessee River.

Other Archaic aged shell-bearing sites are known in the lower Tennessee River valley. On the Cumberland River in Lexington County, Kentucky, "is a series of shell mounds" (Webb and Funkhouser 1932:240) and there is a possible shell-bearing site in Lyon County. On the Tennessee River in Marshall County, Kentucky, is another series of low shell mounds on the banks of Jonathan Creek. Dates and information are lacking.

Moving upriver into Alabama, shell heaps occur (Figure 2.1) in three reservoirs: Pickwick (Webb and DeJarnette 1942), Wheeler (Webb 1939),

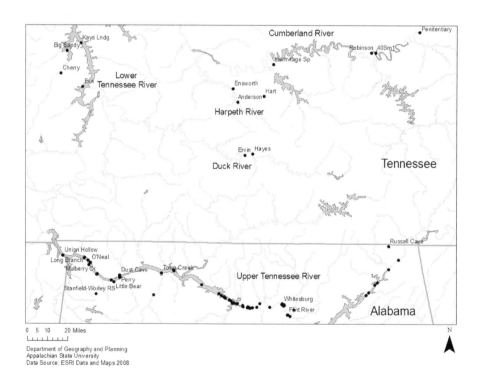

Figure 2.1. Sites on the Tennessee, Duck, Harpeth, and Cumberland Rivers.

and Guntersville (Webb and Wilder 1951, Webb and DeJarnette 1948d). Webb and DeJarnette (1948a:11) estimated that about 340 shell mounds could be found along 200 miles of the Tennessee River in northern Alabama, probably initiated by Morrow Mountain people (Dye 1996, Morse 1967:244). Very few of these shell mounds have been tested and several of them seem too late—Flint River and Widow's Creek—to be of much use in this project. Mussel shells and burials in sites are relatively scarcer in the Guntersville Reservoir than in the lower reservoirs, and this region has the poorest chronological control of any areas surveyed here. Many shell-bearing sites around Seven Mile Island and to the east had few Archaic burials and low densities of shell in them (e.g., 1Ct17). There are several other differences above Pickwick as well. The Wheeler Basin sites have greater quantities of animal bone, greater numbers of clay floors, less-intensive heaping of shell with greater dirt admixture, single rather than multiple strata of shell, a lack of dog burials, and more stone vessels. The rarity of shell heaps above Chattanooga, in spite of the presence of shoals above there, is puzzling (Kneberg 1952:92), particularly when later people did harvest the shoals and incorporate shells in their burial programs. Why were they not collected before?

There are also relevant sites on tributaries west of Guntersville Basin (Curran 1974:164), but these are too poorly known. The Fennel site had "a rather complete trait list, including concentrations of gastropod and mussel shell and flexed burials some with typical Shell Mound associations" (Brock and Clayton 1966). Individuals lacking body parts and with embedded points were among the burials. Farther west are other Archaic tributary sites bearing shells, such as Stanfield-Worley Bluff Shelter (e.g., 1Ct125, 1Fr310, and 1Fr323). Curren (1974:164) asks, "[W]ere there several groups of people occupying both the main river and the tributary sites during the same time period?"

Duck River Sites (Figure 2.1)

Ervin was the first of two excavated gastropod-bearing sites to be founded on this river and is near a dramatic waterfall and Cheek Bend Cave, also with Archaic materials. Ervin's uselife was apparently quite short, relatively speaking. Activities next moved to Hayes, founded farther upriver (Hofman 1986). Several other deeply buried shell-free sites of Early and Middle Archaic age on the Duck are also known (Amick 1985).

Harpeth River Sites (Figure 2.1)

The shell-bearing sites of Hart (Parker 1974) and Anderson (Dowd 1989), and the shell-free site of Ensworth (Deter-Wolf 2004) make a triangle of mortuaries in the Nashville Basin, within which are several other shell-free sites. Curiously, the earliest Morrow Mountain people left a dense stratum of gastropods at the base of Anderson, but subsequent occupations gathered only bivalves. The preservation of infants and children at Anderson was exceptional (Dowd 1989:70). Dye (1996:142) divided the Morrow Mountain occupations of Anderson into Early, Middle, and Late units and gave counts of 25, 22, and 15 burials for each component. The points at Ensworth indicate that the burials are much older than the features and that the radiocarbon dates (Table 2.1) are wrong.

Cumberland River Sites (Figure 2.1)

Robinson and Penitentiary Branch are the best-reported sites but are too late to be of much use in this project. There were 16 other late Archaic sites recorded in the same county as Penitentiary Branch. Robinson (Morse 1967) is 86 river kilometers downstream and seems to have less shell than was found at Penitentiary Branch (Cridlebaugh 1986). Near Robinson was a large site with a badly eroded shell-bearing area in its northwestern section and with Paleoindian and Early Archaic materials on the surface (40Sm1) (Morse 1967). Early Archaic materials were also collected from the surface of another half-acre shell-bearing site. Hermitage Spring is a recently discovered Middle Archaic shell-bearing site that is apparently a contemporary of Anderson, Ervin, Hayes, and Ward (Dan Allen, personal communication, November 2007).

Falls of the Ohio Sites (Figure 2.2)

Late Archaic sites are plentiful in the Falls Area of the Ohio River (nearly 50 in Jefferson County alone) between Owensboro and Carrollton, Kentucky, several of which are large shell heaps on the riverbank and all of which are inadequately published and dated.

The Old Clarksville phase of the Middle Archaic has been placed at 6,000 to 4,000 years ago, based on few 14C dates at Old Clarksville itself and cross dating of side-notched projectile point styles. Old Clarksville-

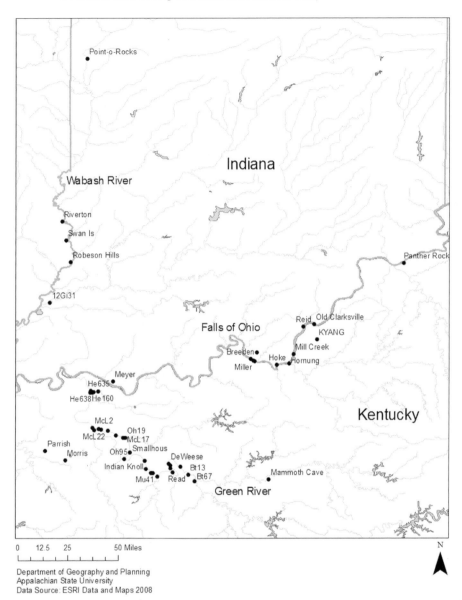

Figure 2.2. Sites on the Green, Ohio, and Wabash Rivers.

phase components have been identified at several additional sites: Hornung, KYANG, Reid, Miller, McNeeley Lake, Durrett Cave, Ferry Landing, Clarks Point, Breeden, and Paddy's West Substation (Angst 1998). Lone Hill Late Archaic components (4950 to 2450 BP) have been ascribed to the sites Lone Hill, KYANG, McNeeley Lake, Minors Lane,

Rosenberger, and several campsites. Lone Hill Phase sites often include a large number of burials, many of which contain exotic material (Bader 2007, 2009). Janzen (1977) believed these accumulations represented permanent residential locations.

A GIS study found that the shell mound sites are clustered and the "spatial association between the sites suggests social-political relationships" (Surface-Evans 2006). The average distance to a tributary stream was 0.6 km, to a karst spring 3.6 km, and to bedrock 4.7 km.

Extensive shell layers have been seen in Breeden, Mill Creek Station, Ferry Landing, Old Clarksville, and Miller sites, and a deep shell deposit was observed at Paddy's West (Bader 2007, 2009). Other sites along the river, such as Hornung, have only limited amounts of shell or none to notice. Late Archaic sites that occur inland from the river in the lowland areas of the Outer Bluegrass, such as Lone Hill, and others on the Salt River, lack shell, fire-cracked rock, and black midden, with the exception of KYANG (Bader 2007, 2009).

Two shell-free sites from this region have been included in this study for comparative purposes. The Meyer Site (6209–5917 BP) is on the Ohio River in Spencer County, Indiana. Curiously, very little fire-cracked rock or debitage was encountered (Anne Bader, personal communication, 2008). Rosenberger is a shell-free mortuary site in Jefferson County, Kentucky, that overlaps in time with some of the activities at Reid and the nearby shell-free camps of Spadie and Villier (Bader 2007). Metrical analysis of the 230 bodies at Rosenberger indicated a distinct population from that of other Archaic cemeteries (Wolf and Brooks 1979), and isotopes indicated a c-3 plant diet and a lower 13C diet for those with grave goods (Collins and Lannie 1979:946). Several other shell-free sites are indicated in Appendix I. Shell-bearing sites with no burials are also present.

Green River Sites (Figure 2.2)

Beginning at the juncture with the Barren River tributary, shell heaps appear in five clusters of shell-bearing sites downstream on the Green River until reaching the Ohio. Works Progress Administration diggers excavated portions of several of these accumulations as well as three non–shell-bearing mortuary sites—Kirkland (Webb and Haag 1947), Parrish (Webb 1951), and Morris (Rolingson and Schwartz 1967), 80 miles to the west—that they thought were essentially of the same culture.

Green River sites can be placed into three groups. One group consists of the tributary sites Parrish, Kirkland, Ward, and Barrett. The first two are shell-free mortuaries while the latter two are shell-bearing mortuaries.

They are located on small tributaries. It is worth noting that the Ward site, a bluff-top site, is the least likely of any of these to have shell present, yet it does. Not only did the shell have to be hauled to the top of the bluff, but this site is on a small stream whose shellfish population must have been miniscule. Were they transporting the mollusks to this location from the Green River? The other three sites were in settings more likely to have molluscan populations, yet two of them are shell-free.

A second group consists of four bluff-top shell-bearing sites: Jimtown Hill, Jackson Bluff, Baker, and Read. The presence of shell in these elevated locations begs for an explanation. Three of them have two shell deposits divided by a central clay zone. Read is remarkable for the number of dog burials, but all of these sites have many dogs.

The third group contains the numerous riverside shell-bearing sites, all of which appear to have had a mortuary function and shell discard. They have unusual quantities of marine shell items and of individuals who met violent deaths.

At least eight of these sites had Paleoindian items. Because only two shells in the Green River valley have been dated and only 21 of the bodies have been dated, we have a very poor temporal understanding of the two most conspicuous activities in this region, shellfishing and burial (Table 2.2). Either activity could have started much earlier than we now realize.

A shell-free midden stratum caps 21 Green River sites (Marquardt and Watson 2005c:116), including Carlston Annis (Webb 1950a), Indian Knoll (Webb 1974), DeWeese (Marquardt and Watson 2005c), Read (Webb 1950b), and Chiggerville (Webb and Haag 1939). There is not much use of these shell-bearing sites after the Archaic (Morey et al. 2002:539). The quantity of Woodland- and Mississippian-era ceramics recovered never suggests more than very short visitations to these locations.

The Green River landscape includes not only the shell heaps located along the river and on bluff tops but also shell-free mortuaries, midden mounds containing fire-cracked rock, rock shelters, sinks, lithic scatters, campsites, and extraction loci. There is a non–shell-bearing Middle Archaic site (15Bt92) on the opposite side of the river from the big shell sites in the Big Bend (Hensley 1994) that might be older than Carlston Annis.

Wabash River Sites (Figure 2.2)

The Riverton culture consists of three late, Late Archaic shell-bearing sites—Robeson Hills, Swan Island, Riverton—10 miles apart on the

Wabash, and at least two bluff-top sites on the White River, 12Gi31 and Bono (Bader 2009). There are many more small shell-free camps and shell deposits spanning a distance of 40 miles along the Indiana side of the Wabash River above its confluence with the Embarrass River (Winters 1969). A few shell-free sites were found on the T-1 terrace. The most northerly of these sites is the shell midden Point of Rocks (12Fo13), 80 miles north of Riverton (Anslinger 1986:33). Robeson Hills and Swan Island were contemporaneous with East Steubenville, Bowles and Read on the Green River, Whitesburg Bridge and Penitentiary Branch, and several shell-ring sites on the coast of South Carolina and Georgia.

There are very few exotic items in these sites, and very little use of marine shell. There were marked differences in artifacts and features between the three published Wabash sites, interpreted by others as seasonal/functional differences. Only 35 percent of the 80 traits outlined by Winters were common to all three of the shell heaps, partially the result of their differences in age, no doubt. Robeson Hills had numerous house patterns (or pits), rare or lacking at the other two sites. Riverton had considerably more ceremonial objects. No site had atlatl parts and the incidence of groundstone axes and celts was low (Anslinger 1986).

Riverton culture as formulated by Winters was thought to be unique because of the exclusive appearance of antler spoons, Riverton flutes, antler projectile points with notched sides, and the artifact combination of a micro-tool industry, grooved sinkers, chipped limonite axes, cloud blower pipes, and Robeson gouges (Anslinger 1986). The micro-tool industry was touted by Anslinger as one of the most important distinctions of Riverton culture.

Winters thought that Riverton culture sites were more like those on the Tennessee River than those on the Green. However, the small number of burials, the lack of dog burials, and the apparent lack of burial concentrations within any of the shell heaps are characteristics far more like the bluff-top sites of the Green River. Nevertheless, ritual behavior is quite different in these Wabash sites from those to the south and southwest. The extensive use of red ocher, the absence of any kind of beads, and the near lack of headless or dismembered bodies among the Wabash burials are distinctive. Today it is known that most Riverton sites are shell-free, in fact, and had at most a few burials (Anslinger 1986:31). There are a few older Archaic sites in Indiana that are shell-bearing, particularly in the White and lower Wabash valleys, about which little is known (Anslinger 1986:40, Morse 1967:157).

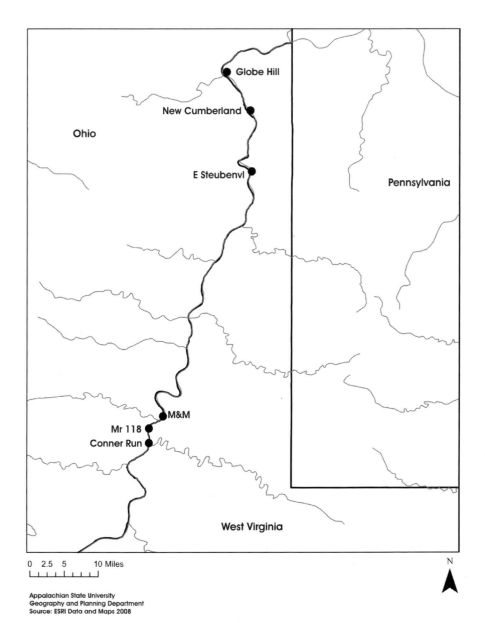

Ohio

● Globe Hill

New Cumberland ●

E Steubenvl ●

Pennsylvania

●M&M
Mr 118 ●
Conner Run ●

West Virginia

0   2.5   5   10 Miles

N

Appalachian State University
Geography and Planning Department
Source: ESRI Data and Maps 2008

Figure 2.3. Some West Virginia Sites on the Ohio River.

Upper Ohio River Sites (Figure 2.3)

The shell-bearing sites in the panhandle of West Virginia are several but underreported, with the notable exception of East Steubenville (GAI 2007). These shell-bearing sites are primarily found on bluff tops but with few human burials, like the situation in other bluff-top sites. In addition to the bluff-top East Steubenville site, there are other bluff-top sites like New Cumberland (310 feet or 94.5 meters above the river) and Globe Hill (Mayer-Oakes 1955a), several riverside shell sites, and riverside shell-free sites (Half Moon).

Although I have argued in the past that the freshwater shell heaps and mounds of the St. Johns and Savannah rivers are a similar phenomenon to those annotated above, I have elected to focus this study on the sites found in the southern Ohio Valley, where the case for Archaic ceremonialism with freshwater shells has yet to be made. The reader looking for information on the Florida sites should consult Aten (1999), Russo (2004), Sassaman (2006), and R. Saunders (2004). These authors have compiled impressive numbers of radiocarbon dates, performed careful excavation, and used sophisticated methodologies and theories over the last decade to argue that shell accumulations are far more significant as ritual places than had been realized.

The Shell Accumulation Phenomenon

All of the concerns about hunter-gatherer complexity mentioned in Chapter 1, as well as other concerns, are intimately linked to an understanding of what caused the shell accumulation phenomenon of the Middle and Late Archaic in the southern Ohio Valley. Why, when shellfish were an easily acquired and rapidly replenishing resource, did their harvest quantities reach such great proportions in this region and in that of the Florida area, and then on just a few rivers in each region but nowhere else?

The basic motivation for shellfishing, as for all edibles, is believed to have been for food. Because shells represent food, their locations on land are understood by most archaeologists to be indicative either of extraction camps (low artifact quantity and variety) or villages (high artifact numbers and variability and other fauna). Ethnographic records indicate that shellfish for family meals were collected by women (Claassen 1996, 1998), which sets up the following logic: women focused their activities around villages or encampments; therefore, shells were discarded at villages or encampments as food garbage. Other functions for shell or shellfish, such as for construction material or as bait, or as symbols of rejuvenation/fertility, are rarely considered.

As has already been indicated, the most frequently cited explanation for the appearance and disappearance of shell heaps is climate change. The specific climatic stimulant is the Hypsithermal drying period. For some authors, the decreased river levels allowed humans to discover shellfish and their edibility, while for others shallower rivers permitted shellfishing. I will devote Chapter 5 to an in-depth exploration of the Hypsithermal and its correspondence to shell heaping, and will set it aside for now.

Cultural practices have also been cited for the phenomenon of shellfishing. William Ritchie (1965) toyed with food taboos or a rejection of molluscan flesh as inferior food to explain the paucity of shell in Archaic-age Lamoka culture (New York) sites but dismissed these ideas in favor of simple ignorance of edibleness. Winters (1969:2), seeing shellfishing beginning abruptly in riverside settings, rejected taboos and distaste (and presumably ignorance) as deterrents because of the use of molluscan flesh for several thousand years at Modoc Rock Shelter. For him cultural preferences were relevant because Eva people used shellfish as early as 5000 BC, but Green River people waited until later.

Winters (1969:4) thought cultural practices were equally relevant to the end of shellfishing in the mid-South, highlighting the adoption of horticulture. Where the earlier shell collecting had occurred in broad valley settings suitable for planting, shell collecting continued simultaneously with horticulture. Where shell collecting had occurred in narrow valleys, those sites (Riverton) and valleys were abandoned.

The notion that domesticates (or even intensified nut harvesting) would obviate the need for shellfish or prevent shellfishing because of scheduling conflicts was addressed in an earlier publication (Claassen 1996). To that information I can add that there is still no evidence that horticulture had taken hold of the populace by 4,000 years ago, and Marquardt and Watson (2005a) have specifically rejected this hypothesis for the Green River case. In late prehistoric Atlantic coastal communities, people not only grew maize, but they also shellfished (Hariot 1951).

By 1974, however, Winters (1974) was attributing the cause for the abandonment of these places to overexploitation, debunking the ideas of environmental change and natural catastrophe. The overexploitation argument is relevant if one believes that shellfish occurred in only extremely limited localities and that their numbers were few. Because overexploitation of mollusks is the premier explanation in our profession for changes in molluscan sizes, species proportions, and the cessation of shellfishing in many settings worldwide, I will devote a chapter to this topic. For now, suffice it to say that this hypothesis is untenable.

In a previous publication (Claassen 1991), I presented the possibility that the flesh of these mollusks was used as fish (or turtle, bird) bait until nonbaited techniques superseded them. Where fine screening has been done, the fish remains (and turtle and bird) are still inadequate to account for all of the bait represented by the tons of shells. The species that would take a hook are not clearly superseded by those that would not, and fishhook debris is surprisingly scarce.

I do think that it is in human choices that we will find our answers for the rise and fall of these types of sites and our explanation for their function in Archaic social life. But those ideas are the subject of this study.

My own questions about these explanations begin to form when I traveled to the DeWeese site on the Green River in 1982 to remove a column sample for seasonality analysis (Claassen 2005). On site, in a 4-foot-deep looter's pit, my eyes only inches from the profile (Marquardt and Watson 2005b:52–54), I comprehended for the first time the impressive size, depth, and height of these sites, as well as their precipitous riverside locations. Furthermore, as the team removed the three-meter-long column from DeWeese, the high proportion of valves still paired further impressed me. What was going on in these sites where the valves were still paired and access to the river was not easy, yet there were tons of shells hauled up the bluff face?

Simultaneous with my work on a dissertation about shell seasonality on the coast of North Carolina and work on the DeWeese column sample, I discovered the historic freshwater shell button industry and pursued this topic as a hobby through the decade of the 1980s. As I uncovered records of shell sales and the hundreds of rivers tapped, the prehistoric activity became more and more of an enigma for me. The potential for shellfishing in the Archaic surely had been far greater than was evident in the archaeological record. The concept that the prehistoric population would have exploited the resource to extinction when the intensive, often tool-aided historic harvesting and 150 years of impoundment and pollution had not, was untenable. Yet this explanation appeared again and again in the archaeological literature.

It is also relevant to the development of my ideas that from 1986 until 1992 I directed excavations at the oldest marine shell heap on the Atlantic Coast, that of Dogan Point, in Westchester County, New York. The Dogan Point oyster heap is but one of many Archaic sites clustered in the lower Hudson River lacking evidence of intensive occupation, burials, or later use. All are positioned some 40 feet above the Hudson and at a distance from its banks when used during the Middle Archaic (Claassen 1995).

The fact that Archaic shell-bearing sites show up on so few rivers suggests that neither environmental change, population pressure, optimal foraging strategies, nor overexploitation account for either the beginning or end of the phenomenon under study. A few archaeologists have likewise noted the incongruous distribution of these shellfishing camps/ villages with historic river records (Dye 1980:174, Kneberg 1952:92, Nance 1986, Rolingson 1967). Why are they located where they are and not elsewhere? Why did shellfishing never again occur in prehistory on the Green, the Ohio, the Harpeth, the Duck, and the Cumberland rivers? Why would a resource that all members of a community could collect, that was plentiful, and that could be dried for later consumption, be eliminated from the diet on the Green River at the same time (archaeologists were rushing to demonstrate) that population pressure was mounting in the interior United States and diets were expanding? Why did people need to import marine shell when freshwater shells were abundant?

There is much work to be done. To reexamine these hypotheses and to explore further the shellfishing activities and the social context of the Middle and Late Archaic, I will, in Chapter 3, examine the locations of these sites with respect to their topographic situation, distribution along the rivers, and distribution across the midcontinental United States. I propose that their locations were not randomly chosen. Shoals were not the only landscape feature of interest in this regard.

The succeeding three chapters examine one or more hypotheses that could explain the apparent sudden end to shellfishing in the Ohio River valley. In Chapter 4 I establish the parameters of truly intensive shellfishing and then show that such a scenario for the Archaic is unreasonable (or for any other prehistoric period). Chapter 5 looks at the environmental impact of the Hypsithermal and subsequent Medithermal on the shellfish and the rivers. I will show in detail how this climatic episode fails to explain the facts, and even provides counterintuitive expectations.

Chapter 6 examines in detail the village function of these heaps. It examines the size of these heaps, the artifact types and ratios, the grave goods, and several aspects of the burial program heretofore unexamined to unmask the ritualized, rather than routinized, nature of these deposits. I find much to suggest that the mortuaries were founded with consecration rites, and that their burial populations consisted of the bodies of numerous victims of violence. Chapter 7 specifies the activities and the different site types I perceive among the shell-bearing and mortuary sites: the public feasting with shell ceremonial centers, the hilltop renewal camps, and the shell-free private mortuaries. I present the feasting and ceremonial evidence and the biological and artifactual evidence suggesting which people interacted positively with each other and who were enemies. The rituals that were conducted at the ceremonial centers and on hilltops are explored in Chapter 8, as are the feasts that attended them. The final chapter summarizes the preceding information and situates these ritual/mortuary sites in the broader discussion of various archaeological theories, hunter-gatherer complexity, and the concept of a sacred landscape.

Conclusion

In this chapter I have reviewed the Archaic-aged shell-bearing sites of relevance to this project. We are learning more each year, and other sites are being identified and excavated, such as those along the Ohio and Harpeth rivers. The fact remains, however, that though naiads could have been harvested from any river in the eastern United States (and probably were), they accumulated at only a few locations, and along only a few rivers. There are sites with many burials and shells, sites with many burials and no shells, sites with shells and few burials, sites on bluffs with more dog burials than human burials, and sites with barely enough shell to be called "shell-bearing."

All of the dates used in this study have been calibrated and can be found in Tables 2.1 and 2.2. The most notable change in these calibrated dates and the earlier published calibrations is that those uncalibrated dates in the 4,000s are now considerably older. Not surprisingly, the more dates available, the longer the apparent utilization of a locus. Shell accumulation began as early as 8586 BP and as late as 2866 BP and ended as early as 5765 BP and as late as 1315 BP. The first signs of the so-called Shell Mound Archaic appeared on tributary sites to the Green and the Tennessee, or on the Tennessee River proper.

Ignoring their geographical specificity, ignoring the often unusual locations, ignoring the quantity and density of burials, ignoring the unusual grave goods, ignoring the progressive end of shell heaping and its progressive diffusion through the Ohio Valley, and failing to date the most visible activities in any serious fashion, researchers have made short work of explaining the beginning and the end of this behavior: what nature first provided, nature took away—the shellfish and the shoals. By the end of this study, however, the reader will be dislodged from thinking of the shell heap as mundane village and be more attuned to the ritual lives and living landscape of these Archaic actors. May all of our thoughts about this historical phenomenon continue to evolve.

CHAPTER 3
LOCATIONS OF SHELL-BEARING SITES

To read the pre-1975 literature, one would think that Archaic shell heaps could be found on many rivers in the eastern United States. "[L]argely through the studies of Fairbanks (1942) and Haag (1942) Archaic came to be a near synonym for shell midden cultures found all over the East" (Jennings 1974:128). Rather than being ubiquitous, however, these shell-bearing sites are clustered on few rivers (Figure 3.1). I am convinced that the geographical distribution in the eastern United States of shell heaps

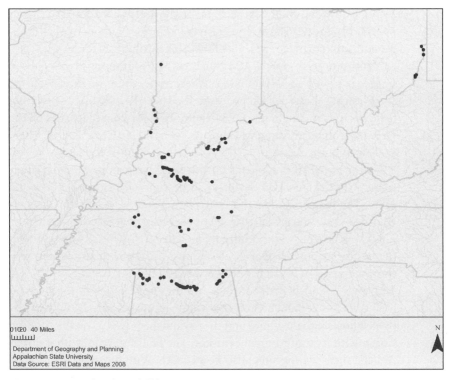

01020 40 Miles

Department of Geography and Planning
Appalachian State University
Data Source: ESRI Data and Maps 2008

N

Figure 3.1. Map of Archaic Shell-bearing Sites.

indicates great selectivity of place. Just what these locational rules might be is explored in this chapter.

Characteristics of Place and Space

Let us begin with some basic geographical facts. 1) All of the rivers with Archaic shell sites west of the Appalachians are tributaries of the Ohio River. 2) Most of the sites are found in clusters. 3) Most of the clusters are situated midway up a river, in center locations. 4) No sites are found on east-flowing rivers or segments of rivers.

The Tennessee, Green, and Cumberland rivers are remarkably similar in their courses—they start in the Appalachians, run west or northwest for the majority of their courses, and then turn abruptly northward to flow into the Ohio River. The Harpeth flows northwestward to join the Cumberland. The Duck, with just two early sites, runs westward and empties into the Tennessee as it flows northward. The tributaries of the Tennessee chosen for shell-bearing mortuaries also all flow northward—Flint River, Little Bear Creek, Mulberry Creek, and Big Sandy Creek—even though there are south-flowing tributaries of the Tennessee. In keeping with the north theme, 75 percent of the Pickwick-basin sites recorded in Webb and DeJarnette are on the north shore of the river (but not on tributaries). The St. Johns River in Florida, with many shell-heap mound and mortuary sites, also flows due north.

Not only were north- and northwestward-draining rivers chosen most often, but small sections of these rivers were often chosen for shell-bearing sites, such as the lower Tennessee River cluster of Eva/Big Sandy/Kay's Landing (Figure 2.1). Four of the five clusters of sites on the Green are on north-running segments of that river. Curiously, the three shell sites in the western portion of the Big Bend of the Green are on a south-flowing section of this northwest-flowing river, a unique situation for this and most other rivers except for two clusters of sites on the Ohio. The long stretch of the Green River that flows eastward has no recorded shell-bearing sites. It seems that this preference for north- or northwest-flowing water could explain why no shell heaps were founded on the Green above the Barren River junction, where there are only very short segments of north- or northwestward-flowing water.

Newly founded shell-bearing sites that appear late in the Archaic (Table 2.1) are often sited on south-flowing rivers such as the Wabash (which flows into the Ohio) and the Savannah, as well as on the Atlantic Coast, with its south-moving current. The Hudson River, with a dozen Archaic shell-bearing sites, also flows south. With the one exception of

Stallings Island, however, shell-bearing sites founded on south-flowing rivers or the Atlantic Coast lack burials or have very few burials, including the Hudson River sites.

DeBoer (2005:67) points out that north and west are conceptually conflated twice as often as are south+east or north+east among societies in North America. North and west are also conflated conceptually with female, earth, left, moist, and down. West is commonly associated with death and the land of the dead, as the direction of the setting sun. Perhaps, then, the preference for locating mortuaries on north- and west-flowing rivers was a considered one.

The animal and plant resources vary little between these rivers or within these rivers. All had shellfish, as did hundreds of other rivers (see Chapter 4), and all had fish and waterfowl, as did all other rivers. The aquatic resources, then, were not a basis for discrimination between rivers. In fact, several investigators have commented on the striking *lack* of aquatic resources, other than shells, present in these sites. There are few water birds, few fish, and but small numbers of fishing items in most sites. Glore (2005), considering the fauna in recent samples taken at Carlston Annis on the Green River, opines that aquatic resources could not have been the motivation behind the selection of its location.

Instead of unusual food resources, the large region circumscribed by the Ohio, Green, and Tennessee rivers is typified by black-colored coal, black asphalt/oil-oozing rocks (Watson 2005:623), the most diverse molluscan fauna found anywhere in the world (Stansbery 1970:9), sporting a rainbow of nacre colors and colored pearls, and by karst. Caves, rock shelters, sinkholes, sinking rivers, waterfalls, and springs abound in central Kentucky, central Tennessee, and northern Alabama, many of which attracted human interest.

Once a north- or northwesterly flowing river had been selected, there appear to have been several criteria employed in choosing the precise location for an eventual shell heap, criteria of place and distance. Favored river segments seem to include dramatic meanders, islands, major shoals, river mouths, and bluff or knoll tops.

Characteristics of Place

Shell heaps situated on islands are found on the Savannah, St. Johns, and Tennessee rivers and include several famous Archaic sites: Stallings Island, Harris Creek (née Tick Island), and Perry. When the Green River flooded, Indian Knoll was isolated as an island, as well. Several Tennessee River sites are located on the north bank opposite islands: Bluff Creek,

O'Neal, Long Branch, and on the south bank, Little Bear Creek (Webb and DeJarnette 1948b). Farther up the Tennessee River in Late Woodland times, burials were made on islands such as Hiwassee Island, and were marked by naiad shells (Lewis and Kneberg 1970).

Islands, surrounded by water, are spiritually charged places, many of which are still revered as sacred (Milne 1995). Several islands in the eastern United States were/are places where gods dwelled. Among these are Manitoulin, an island sacred to the Ojibway, Odawa, and Potawatami, and a tiny island in a lake on Manitoulin, where Gitchi Manitou dwells (Milne 1995). Several archaeologists have referred to the Stallings Island shell mound as the Island of the Dead (Sassaman 2006). Perhaps the Perry mortuary was similarly referred to in Archaic times.

In several cases, the largest shoal on a river, also the fall line, was the location of a shell heap: Perry at Muscle Shoals on the Tennessee River, 40Sm1 on the Cumberland River, Old Clarksville at the Falls of the Ohio, and Stallings Island on the Savannah River. Shoals and falls were spiritually charged locations for historic groups in the eastern United States, as well (Milne 1995).

There are numerous shell heaps on bluffs and knolls of the Ohio, Wabash, White, and Green rivers. Other sites are located not on top of bluffs but at the base of bluffs on the Cumberland River. A bluff abuts Penitentiary Branch where limestone, black shale, Fort Payne chert, and crinoids are available. Robinson is also against a bluff on the Cumberland. The spiritual significance of bluffs as homes to various deities is featured in Irwin (1994) and in Milne (1995).

River confluences were chosen for other sites: Little Bear Creek, Flint River, Mulberry Creek. On the Green River there is usually a shell heap at a confluence, but on the opposite bank from the junction (Barren River, Mud River, Rough River).

As several people have pointed out, shells could have been aggregated along thousands of miles of riverbank in this and other regions, but were not. We will not know why the southern Ohio Valley was chosen over the northern Ohio Valley or Missouri River, for instance. Perhaps similar events and ritual expression in Florida created a southeastwardly "pull." Perhaps Mammoth Cave, some 50 miles upriver from the Green River shell sites, or Russell Cave, or a particular set of landscape features attracted the accumulation of these underworld dwellers. The Green River is conceptually the source of the water in Mammoth Cave, which is enhanced with speleothems, waterfalls, lakes, and rivers found inside this cave. It carries the same water that formed the cave and the shells of the mollusks found farther downriver.

Characteristics of Spacing

In addition to physical features that may have governed the siting of riverside mortuaries, there were social factors as well.

CLUSTERING

Sites occur in clusters on all of the rivers. There are obvious clusters visible on Figures 2.1 and 2.2 south of Nashville on the Harpeth and Duck, west and south of Louisville on the Ohio, and in the West Virginia panhandle on the Ohio. Clusters on the Green River and the central Tennessee River are the most marked and occur as groups of sites that occupy alternate banks.

There are 46 sites on the banks of the Green in a 135-mile stretch of river. The site the farthest downstream is 15He160, and the farthest upstream is 15Bt67, near the confluence of the Green and Barren rivers (Hockensmith et al. 1983). Rolingson (1967:37) pointed out that the shell heaps on the Green make three clusters: one in Butler County where eight sites are found in 13 river miles, then, 20 river miles or so downstream, a second cluster in Ohio County where seven sites are found in 15 miles, and the third cluster, approximately 98 miles farther downstream in McLean County, from the Rough River to the Pond River, of 11 sites in 15 miles. I annotate these clusters and three others below. Clustering suggests that social considerations about location were at work.

Cluster 1 is comprised of the four Henderson County sites on the left, or south, bank of the river (Figure 3.2a) and two oppositional heaps on the north bank. Only one of these heaps has been excavated (Moore 1916), 15He160, and no radiocarbon dates are available. Their proximity to the Ohio River and their distance from Cluster 2 make them intriguing.

Cluster 2 begins at the Pond River junction and continues upriver to the Rough River junction, with sites on the left or south side of the river (Figure 3.2b) in McLean County. This cluster overlaps two sites upstream and one downstream. Butterfield (15Mc7), which is a linear spread of shell, and Austin (15Mc15) were tested by the WPA. No radiocarbon dates are available for any of these sites.

Cluster 3 (Figure 3.2b) is comprised of those eight sites on the east or north bank of the river as it flows northward once again. Moving upriver starting at the confluence with the Rough River, it consists of bluff-top Jimtown Hill (15Oh19), riverside mounds 15Oh97, and Smallhous, bluff-top Jackson Bluff, and riverside mounds Indian Knoll, Chiggerville, and Bowles (15Oh 13), ending there at the confluence with the Mud River. On the opposite bank, also at the confluence with the Mud River, are shell sites 15Mu41 and bluff-top Baker (15Mu12).

Three of the five known bluff-top heaps are found in this north-flowing section of the Green River, and a fourth, Read, is the next site upstream. The positioning of these bluff-top sites—bluff-top followed by two to three floodplain sites upstream—would seem to indicate a particular function for them distinct from what was occurring at the riverside, such as sentinel locations or even mortuary camps for the preparation of the bodies to be buried in the riverside heaps. Baker may have been contemporaneous with 15Mu41 and Bowles, and Jackson Bluff may be part of the activities at Indian Knoll. Jimtown Hill would be the bluff-top site associated with 15Oh97, Smallhous, and 15Oh95. Jimtown Hill could also be related to activities at 15McL109 on the opposite bank and to people traveling on the Rough River. Dates from Read, the only bluff-top site on the Green River for which we have dates, indicate late activities, and the other dated loci in this cluster (Read, Bowles, Indian Knoll) began later than those upriver in the Big Bend (Table 2.1). However, those two clusters overlap in use from 5585 to 4720 BP.

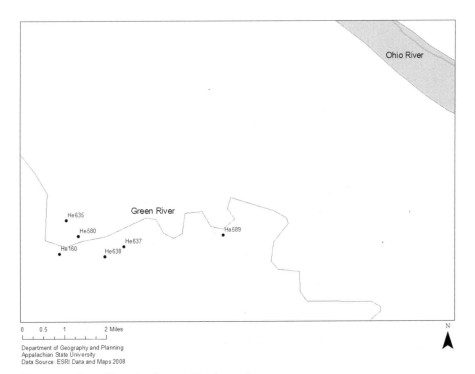

Figure 3.2a. Green River site cluster 1, Henderson County.

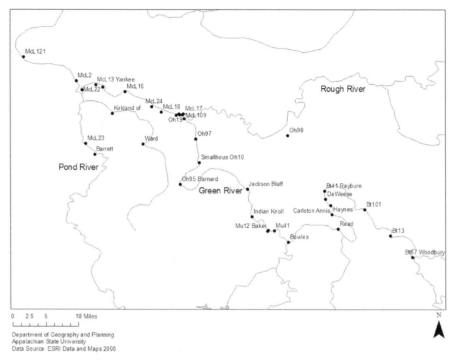

Figure 3.2b. Green River site clusters 2, 3, 4, 5, and 6.

Cluster 4 is found inside the Big Bend on the western side of the meander and includes 15Bt 5, 6, 11, and 41 (Figure 3.2b). Excavation occurred at 15Bt5 (Carlston Annis), 15Bt6 (DeWeese), and 15Bt11 (Haynes). The Rayburn site, 15Bt41, is a small "shell mound" that has only been cored (Marquardt and Watson 2005c:60). Calibrated radiocarbon dates range from 6276 to 2438 BP, indicating simultaneous use of all three large sites from 5600 to 4983 BP (Table 2.1). Carlston Annis and Haynes overlap in usage from 5942 to 4983 BP. This cluster is the best dated of any in the southern Ohio Valley. Carlston Annis seems to have been one of the earliest sites, if not the earliest started on the Green proper, and it and DeWeese are quite large. This is the only place on the Green River where shell-bearing sites are found on a southward-flowing section of a river.

The Read site might be part of this cluster, but there are several reasons to leave it out. It is on the opposite bank, is on top of a knoll, is on a north-flowing river section, was founded some 700 years after two of the Big Bend heaps ended, and has the largest collection of Archaic dogs in the United States.

Cluster 5 is comprised of three sites on the eastern outside bank of the Big Bend—15Bt13, 15Bt67, and 15Bt101 (Figure 3.2b). They have been surface collected only (Hockensmith et al. 1983). There is one meander pair and one confluence site. They are the sites located closest to Mammoth Cave.

Cluster 6 (Figure 3.2b) is composed of those four sites not on the Green but to the west in McLean and Hopkins Counties. Largely shell-free mortuaries, they are Kirkland and Ward on Cypress Creek, then farther west, Barrett and 15McL23 on Pond River. Ward is curious in this cluster as it is a bluff-top site with shell, many burials, and a fair number of dogs. In many respects it is like Read. Perhaps Parrish and Morris, farther west still, should be included, yet they seem to lie in between the Falls and Green districts.

Two other shell heaps appear to be quite isolated, 15McL121 between Clusters 1 and 2 and 15Oh98 on a tributary of the Rough River. Neither is included in a cluster, although 15Oh98 is visually part of cluster 3 and 15McL121 is on the eastern side of the river as well.

The average distance between sites on the Green, within the clusters, is 2.67 miles (4.2 km) (Rolingson 1967). This spacing suggests that social considerations were at work. Furthermore, as one moves upriver, the site clusters are found first on the west bank of the Green and then on the east, or right, bank. The flipping of clusters from one side of the river to the other suggests social considerations as well.

Wondering what the orientation of these mounded places would have been, I turned to the dog burials for a possible answer. Water is seen by dozens of cultures as the boundary between this world and the Underworld. In many U.S. cultures, dogs lead the dead, and in several Mexican myths, dogs lead the dead across a river into the Underworld (Miller and Taube 1993:80). If dogs also led the dead across a river to the Underworld during Archaic times, then the bodies may have been brought to the mortuary facilities over land, with the river beyond the burial place. Bodies would not have been carried across the river or on the river by boat, for to do so was for the living to enter the Underworld symbolically, an extremely risky enterprise. The Green River, the Tennessee River, and the other rivers were possibly symbolic boundaries, not between groups but between this world and the Underworld.

Perhaps the clusters of sites on opposite sides of the river are indicative of multiple subgroups, tribal segments such as clans, from within one population, each with habitually used mortuary areas. Perhaps the hosts roamed the same side of the river as the shell sites and the guests came from elsewhere. Under this assumption, the eastern population in the Green River valley would have frequently hosted feasts in Cluster 3 and the western population in Clusters 1, 2, 4, and 5. The shell-free mortuaries in Cluster 6 also lie to the west of the Green.

Occasionally sites were placed to form a pair across a river, such as Mulberry Creek and Smithsonia Landing on the Tennessee River, or Chiggerville and Baker on the Green River (Rolingson 1967:37). Pairs were also created by positioning heaps at each end of a meander on the same side of the river. The marking of meanders with shell-bearing mortuary sites is clearly seen in Cluster 2 (Figure 3.2b). Yankee and Austin mark off one small meander and half of a larger one. 15McL22 and Yankee mark that larger meander. Austin and 15McL16 mark another meander. Bowles and Read are so paired. The placement of Ward and Kirkland are striking in this regard as well. On the Ohio River, Reid and Old Clarksville form such a pair. These pairings might have served many purposes.

The site distribution on the Tennessee River in Alabama (Figure 3.3) shows similarities to that on the Green River. Sites appear to cluster once again in six groups and have some of the flipping of banks seen on the Green. Again, one could argue that there were groups from the north and from the south meeting at the Tennessee River.

Site surveys on the upper Green, Rough, Nolen and Barren rivers, all tributaries of the Green, found only small, thin, shell-free sites (Herrmann 2004:17, Rolingson 1967:42–45). The same situation was found in those counties contiguous to the Wabash River sites, and in the Land Between the Lakes area (Anslinger 1986, Nance 1986). That these heaps are found on so few rivers, and even then only on certain sections of those rivers, is indicative of social/cultural concerns, not limited shellfish. Several voices have now highlighted the sociality of the shell accumulators. The spacing and clustering of sites are the primary clues to this sociality and has been remarked upon by Rolingson (1967) for the Green River sites, Surface-Evans (2006) for the Falls sites, and Homsey (1999) for the St. Johns sites. The shell-bearing sites are found in districts within which there are clusters of fairly uniformly spaced mortuaries.

A Review of the Historical Development of the Social Landscape

The calibrated dates with two sigma ranges provided in Table 2.1 indicate that the act of shell accumulation was a prolonged process that

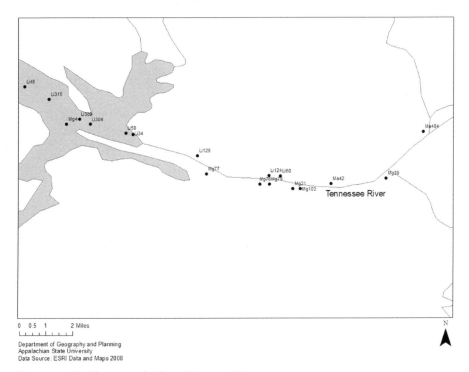

0   0.5   1   2 Miles

Department of Geography and Planning
Appalachian State University
Data Source: ESRI Data and Maps 2008

N

Figure 3.3. Site Clusters on the Upper Tennessee River.

was employed by very few groups for quite some time, but then spread noticeably between 6,500 and 4,000 years ago. The earliest sites with dates before 7,500 years ago are mapped in Figure 3.4.

The main locational characteristics at this early phase of shell accumulation appear to have been midriver location and proximity to another shell-bearing site. There are six sites on six rivers suggesting six possible social groups. There is one site grouping consisting of Ervin, Anderson, and Hermitage Springs, seemingly in the center, and three isolated shell sites, Ward to the north, Eva to the west, and Mulberry to the south. Ervin and Anderson began as aquatic gastropod accumulations, unique in the universe of southern Ohio Valley shell sites. Perhaps it is significant that historic Indian groups tell us that in the beginning, a conceptual center, the world was spiraling, spinning (Bassie-Sweat 1996, Schaefer 2002); the spiraling gastropod is a symbol of that condition. Hermitage Springs, at a spring, and Ward, on a bluff, are both at spiritually important kinds of places.

Like the failure of any shell-bearing site to be founded on an eastward-flowing river or river segment, this distribution of sites lacks only an eastern location in the cardinal points. Near Ward are three shell-free mortuaries, Kirkland to the north and Parrish and Morris to the west, and near Anderson is a shell-free mortuary, Ensworth, also to the west. Perhaps the earliest mortuaries in this district were shell free. Shell-free mortuaries were more common in the Green River district than were

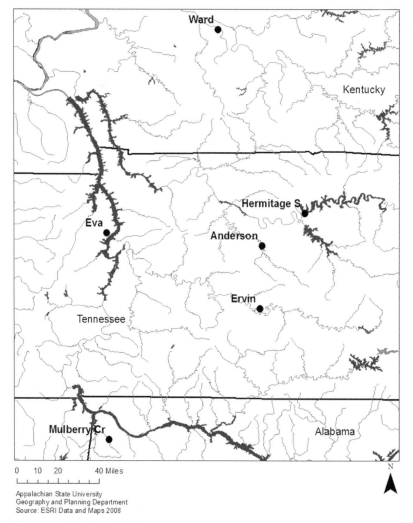

0   10   20   40 Miles

Appalachian State University
Geography and Planning Department
Source: ESRI Data and Maps 2008

N

Figure 3.4. Sites Founded Before 7,500 years ago.

shell-bearing mortuaries in the first thousand years of shell accumulation, while the opposite is true for this district and others at the end of shell accumulation.

Although shellfish surely were available to the users of Ensworth, shells were not accumulated there. Bivalves were certainly available in the Duck River and in the Harpeth at Ervin and Anderson, yet the people *chose* to harvest only gastropods. Mollusks were certainly available on the Green River proper, yet they seem not to have been used. Shell collecting began in Kentucky at Ward on a bluff midway up and overlooking the small tributary of Cypress Creek. This creek was highly unlikely to yield an abundance of mollusks, suggesting that the collectors hiked to the Green and back with shellfish. The shells then had to be carried to the top of the bluff. If riverine resources were the target of exploitation, why was Ward—the oldest shell-bearing site in the Green River district—not founded on the Green? If shellfish were scarce and in need of claiming, why was Ward founded on a tiny tributary, away from those shoals and on top of bluff? If Ward began as a village, why was it put on a bluff top overlooking a creek instead of on the riverbank? If Ervin and Anderson were founded as villages, why were only gastropods pulled from those rivers? Were these places founded as mortuaries and intentionally put in places with low visibility?

Then, 6500 until 6000 BP, multiple shell accumulations began at the falls on the Ohio (Miller, Hornung and Reid), suggesting that another social group had taken up the practice of aggregating their shell debris. Another tributary mortuary began in the Green River drainage (Barrett), and the first shell-bearing site on the Green River proper appears, Carlston Annis, possibly at a shoal (Morey et al. 1999). At this point, there are still but a few shell-bearing sites on any one river. Shoal and cave associations are the most evident locational features in this set of new sites.

In the period from 5,999 to 5,500 years ago three shell accumulations begin on a south-flowing segment of the Green River known as the Big Bend, joining the older Carlston Annis site to make four mortuaries in total. Perhaps one or more of these places began as villages but were eventually transformed into mortuaries. This density of sites in the Big Bend is curious given the practice until now of much greater spacing between sites. All accumulations appear to have been utilized simultaneously and are within sight of one another. The bluff-top Ward site to the west of the Green, at the opposite end of the shell-heap distribution from the Big Bend, was also being used, as was the neighboring shell-free Kirkland site. Midway between the two groups, Indian Knoll was in use. Elsewhere, Perry and Whitesburg Bridge heaps were accumulating on the Tennessee. The Harpeth River social group appears to have dissolved during this interval.

Shell-bearing sites proliferated in the period from 5499 to 5000 BP, particularly in close vicinity to older sites. Clusters of sites formed during this interval. The phenomenon also spread eastward to the Atlantic. Many of the older sites continued in use. The florescence was short-lived, however. A notable decline in shell accumulation occurred from 4499 to 4000 BP. Nevertheless, shell-bearing sites appeared for the first time on the Wabash (Robeson Hills, Riverton) and the upper Cumberland (Penitentiary). A second bluff-top site was founded on the upper Ohio, East Steubenville, a neighbor to and contemporary of Globe Hill. Still active on the Green River were at least Carlston Annis, Bowles, and Indian Knoll. Other active sites were Stallings Island on the Savannah River and Kay's Landing on the lower Tennessee.

Our understanding of the sites in use between 3999 and 3500 is hampered by several presumably bad late dates. These come from Carlston Annis, Bowles, and Ensworth. Activities continued at Carlston Annis, Indian Knoll, Whitesburg Bridge, Kay's Landing, East Steubenville, Penitentiary Branch, Robeson Hills, and Riverton. Robinson on the Cumberland, Swan Island on the Wabash, and Read on the Green were the newly founded sites among the dated set. Even though pottery was present at other non-shell sites during this time, it was rare in these assemblages. Domesticated native plants are more in evidence than is pottery but are infrequent enough to indicate conservatism.

The close of the era around 3,500 years ago saw but a few heaps still in use. The large shell heaps on the Ohio River around Louisville may have been abandoned, as were those on Cypress Creek and Pond River. Robinson and Penitentiary Branch continued to attract attention on the Cumberland, as did Robeson, on a bluff, and Riverton. Carlston Annis, Bowles (the late dates from both are suspect), and Read in Clusters 2 and 3 on the Green remained viable mortuaries. Activities continued at Kay's Landing, but these would soon cease, while at Whitesburg Bridge and Widow's Creek, shell-bearing sites upriver in northern Alabama, burial programs continued into the Woodland period. Shell-ring building and feasting on the coast was in full swing at this time but no burial program was practiced at shell rings.

Conclusion

Though shell mounds are prolific on the Green and Tennessee rivers, they are quite uncommon elsewhere. The idea that shellfish were only available in five rivers of the Ohio Valley 7,500 years ago is untenable. The idea that only these people would have sought out the aquatic resources is untenable, and the disappointing record of aquatic resources at them (except for turtles) makes any resource availability explanation untenable as well. The spacing between the earliest shell-bearing sites suggests four to six different social groups, and some attention to obscuring their location. The location of Ward on a bluff top, away from shellfish resources, suggests that it was founded as something other than a village.

Burial sites like these could be an expression of corporate group ownership (e.g., Byers 1998, Charles and Buikstra 1983). I think not and will explore this idea and others related to evolving social complexity during the Archaic in Chapter 9. There is clear evidence of sociality in site clustering and, I believe, clear evidence of ritual practice. It seems necessary in the future to proceed with investigating these sites as cluster members, and investigating differences between clusters. There is reason to suspect that many of the mounds within a cluster were used simultaneously, given that situation in the Big Bend.

There are then several reasons, based on the locations of these sites, to conclude that the presence of shellfish was not the primary determinant of their locations. These accumulations appeared on few rivers, when hundreds of rivers with shellfish populations were available. They appeared earliest on water bodies where shellfish populations would have been much smaller than in the nearby rivers. They appeared mostly on rivers that flow northward or on sections of rivers that flow northward. They did not appear on eastward-flowing segments of rivers. A random choice of rivers would have these heaps appearing throughout the Mississippi watershed wherever there were shellfish beds. They tend to have been sited at physical features known to have ritual import in later cultures. They appeared in clusters with hints of regularity in spacing. Occasionally they are paired across a river, which would encourage competition for shellfish, not conservation. Finally, the density of sites on the Green River—particularly in the Big Bend where three sites were used simultaneously—does not support the idea that overharvesting of shellfish was a problem or a concern.

In later chapters I will present the idea that these shell-bearing sites with burials were destinations for ritual practices rather than year-round villages. Different social groups may have met at these heaps to share mortuary rituals. I do not believe that these large mortuaries would have been situated at contested social frontiers, where they would have been susceptible to violation. The founding of so many of them midriver or on tributaries suggests that they were situated in "interior space," not at borders.

Having explored the individual site records in Chapter 2 and their locations in this chapter, it is time to address the two major hypotheses for why this site type began and ended in so many places before the Woodland period. In Chapter 4 I consider the overharvesting explanation by examining the molluscan resource of the Mississippi watershed.

CHAPTER 4
OVEREXPLOITATION OF MOLLUSKS

As rich as the riverine life appeared to have been at the shell-bearing sites, shellfishing declined and then stopped at most of the locations annotated in Chapter 2. One explanation given for the apparent abandonment of this activity and foodstuff is human overexploitation of this resource. The purpose of this chapter is to examine the hypothesized extirpation of the molluscan resource at the hand of humans after 5000 BP, and the hypothesis that shellfish were a restricted resource that attracted Archaic peoples to these (few) locations 8,000 to 5,000 years ago. I will establish the parameters of truly intensive shellfishing and develop the picture of how big and how productive the beds were, how long the beds could sustain harvesting pressures, how quickly they regenerate, and how many shells one person can harvest with different extraction methods. To do so, I will draw on information from historic pearl rushes, the U.S. freshwater shell button industry, and modern musseling for the Japanese cultured pearl industry. It is my goal to convince the reader that this resource was neither limited in occurrence nor in fecundity during either the terminal Archaic or the subsequent centuries and that the human populations of the pre-Columbian Ohio Valley were never so large or so intent on shellfishing that they would have denuded rivers of shellfish.

The Mississippi and St. Lawrence River systems have the richest freshwater molluscan fauna in the world. Eastern North American is home to roughly one-half of all the world's species of freshwater bivalves (Stansbery 1970:9). Their abundance was so great and shellfish so prolific across the Mississippi watershed that thousands of tons of shellfish were wrested from rivers such as the Wabash, Wisconsin, Mississippi, Black, White, and Pearl from 1857 until 1913 by individuals and families both casually and intently searching for pearls. Natural pearls, in numerous colors, were and are common in bivalves of eastern North America. In fact, an assessment of the harvest of these pearls during Archaic times is a major missing element in this study—what became of the thousands of pearls that were found in the open shells piled around the Ohio Valley? In the period from 1850 to 1940, those pearls earned their finders and buyers hundreds of thousands of dollars. It is fair to say that those rivers that by 1912 would become the focus of intensive mussel harvesting for the pearl button industry had already sustained years of hand and rake harvesting by pearl hunters. (See Claassen 1994 for a survey of U.S. pearl rushes.)

The United States freshwater shell button industry began in 1891. From 1891 until World War II, the domestic freshwater button industry employed hundreds of thousands of workers, either at the river, in cutting shops, in factories, or as sales representatives. About 20 million gross of U.S.-made shell buttons were sold in the United States in 1909, 26 million gross in 1912, and 40 million gross in 1916. That year the industry claimed 9,500 workers in factories, 9,746 musselers, 585 shoremen and boatmen, and shells bought worth $1.2 million. The value of exported freshwater shell buttons reached $2.1 million in 1918 (Claassen 1994).

After World War I the industry steadily declined in revenue for various reasons, including zippers, labor costs, buttons of cheaper materials like casein and composition, and the washing machine, which discolored and broke shell buttons. In spite of intensive harvesting for more than 50 years, the shell supply was not a factor in the button industry's decline. While the U.S. freshwater shell button industry became a mere shadow of its former self by 1945, musselers quickly found a market for the same shells gathered in the same way in the cultured pearl industry of Japan.

The various saltwater pearl oysters and freshwater bivalves (naiads) will deposit nacre around any irritant, but research and experience proved that a calcareous nucleus (a piece of nacreous shell) was optimum for pearl formation. The layers of nacre adhere best to other nacre (which most marine shells lack but naiads have) and are therefore less likely to fracture when they are drilled for stringing (Claassen 1994).

To form the nucleus or bead, a naiad shell is cut into strips, the strips cubed, the cubes tumbled into an oval shape, and then pressure ground into round beads. Japan lacks naiad populations in quantity sufficient to supply beads to the pearl farmers, and experimentation with U.S. shells may have begun as early as the 1910s (Claassen 1994). During World War II, United States soldiers bought thousands of dollars worth of pearls, creating a postwar demand that soon put the Japanese cultured pearl industry on its feet and the American shell exporters into business. American military officers, many of whom were musselers as boys, arranged to obtain shells from the Mississippi watershed and ship them to Japanese pearl farms (Sebring 1985).

The cultured pearl–driven revival of musseling in the eastern United States, which began in the late 1940s, centered first on the Tennessee River. In 1954, the United States exported 1,000 tons of shells to Japan (Sebring 1985) and by the late 1950s virtually the sole source of Japan's pearl slugs were shells from the Tennessee River (Stansbery 1971). Three and one-half million tons of Tennessee River shells were exported to Japan in 1959 and 1960. In 1985, 6,000 short tons of shell worth about $10 million were exported (Claassen 1994). In the paragraphs that follow, I will present evidence on each element that I believe to be crucial to demonstrating the ubiquity, supply, and human effort of relevance to the Archaic shellfishing endeavor.

The Molluscan Resource

Approximately 40 different bivalve shellfish species had commercial value to the button industry, a subset of the species available. Some commercially important species dominate their molluscan communities, most significantly the ebony shell, the mucket, and the pig-toe, and are fairly easy to harvest. The ebony shell quickly became the principal button shell (Coker 1919:16) because of its smooth exterior surface, clear luster, size of iridescent portion, uniform quality, thickness, and abundance in large rivers. Its major drawback was its very thick umbo (hinge/beak area) that was unusable and represented a high percentage of wasted shell weight. Above Keokuk, Iowa, the Mississippi was an ebony shell river. The Pearl River of Louisiana and Mississippi was reportedly 99 percent ebony shells. Ebonies in the St. Francis River (Arkansas) were of exceptional quality (Coker 1919).

Several other species were of great importance to the button industry as well (Figure 4.1). As the favored mussel resources decreased below economical levels for button factories, and as the demand for U.S.-produced shell buttons increased, less attractive but still easy to procure shells with rough surfaces came into use: washboards, three-ridges, blue points, and others. The Spoon River was inhabited by 95 percent washboards and blue points; the Illinois River 50–60 percent blue points, 23–50 percent washboards, and up to 31 percent warty backs. Washboards and three-ridges were quite abundant in smaller streams. Today they are the principal shells for export to Japan (Figure 4.1). Harvest

Figure 4.1. Various Freshwater Mollusks. Photo by author.

records apply to a select few species, not the entire community of 20 to 40 species that would have been available to Archaic Indians gleaning any one bed or river.

The Rivers

In 1912, 57 rivers in 18 states were contributing shells to the button industry (Table 4.1). By 1950, at least 108 rivers had been harvested for shell button needs, from Texas to Iowa to New York to Alabama (see also Tables 4.2, 4.3). This activity meant that these rivers had shells in quantities sufficient for commercial interest, and the primary harvest locales were close enough to transportation facilities to get them to market. No doubt dozens more rivers had suitable quantities of shells of the preferred species but failed the latter criterion for commercial interest. I suspect that transportation costs were one of the primary reasons why rivers located east of the Appalachian divide were not exploited by either industry, although some were the scene of pearl rushes. The Kentucky River situation is instructive when trying to understand why some rivers were not used in historic times. Twenty-two species of commercially useful shells could be found in the Kentucky River, but the two prime button shells, the ebony shell and the Ohio River pig-toe,

Table 4.1 Mussel Fishery Statistics for 1912–1914 (Coker 1919, Claassen 1994)

River	Tonnage	Proceeds	Cost/Ton	Year
Alabama				
Tombigbee	55			
Arkansas				
Black	1996	$24,054	$17.19	1912
Little Red	15			
Little St. Francis	256			
Ouachita	187			
St. Francis	1210	$24,708	$20.39	1912
Saline	67			
White	3709	$76,103	$20.44	1912
Illinois				
Embarrass	78			
Fox	353	$7,762	$22.09	1913
Illinois	5890	$88,797	$14.95	1913
Iroquois	100			
Kankakee	202			
Kaskaskia	12			
Okaw		$17,977	$14.70	1913
Rock	7420	$119,049	$16.01	1913
Saline	209			1913
Sangamon	144			1913
Indiana				
Eel	91			1913
Mississinewa	141			1913
White	120			1913
White, east	2054	$36,514		1913
White, west	41			1913
Wabash	2653	$44,194	$16.51	1913

Table 4.1 (cont.)

River	Tonnage	Proceeds	Cost/Ton	Year
Iowa				
Buffalo	132			
Cedar	485			
Des Moines	336			
Iowa	93			
Shell Rock	32			
Kansas				
Cottonwood	55			
Osage	204			
Vermillion	55			
Kentucky				
Cumberland	1267	$22,136	$11.73	1912
Green	100			1912
Kentucky	30			1912
Michigan				
Grand	380			1913
Huron	56			1913
Kalamazoo	224			1913
Maple	74			1913
Muskegon	55			1913
St. Joseph	267			1913
Minnesota				
Minnesota	11			
Red River	40			1910
St. Croix	753	$13,701	$18.87	1913
Mississippi				
Big Sunflower	160			1912
Pearl	212			1912
Missouri				
Meramec	100			
Ohio				
Maumee	101			1913
Muskingum	668	$12,276	$20.00	1913
Scioto	25			1913

(cont.)

River	Tonnage	Proceeds	Cost/Ton	Year
Oklahoma				
Neosho (Grand)	1000			1912
Pennsylvania				
French	6			1913
South Dakota				
James	260			1914
Tennessee				
Clinch	50			1912
Holston	98			1912
Tennessee	908	$10,176	$11.18	1912
Wisconsin				
Pectonica	617	$10,660	$17.31	1913
Mississippi River	6626	$125,322	$19.47	1914
Ohio River	8287	$107,001	$12.88	1912

were absent. Nevertheless, by 1920 this river was supplying other species of shells to button factories. In 1920, the commercial harvest from the Kentucky River would have been much higher if rain, high water, and a general shortage of help had not been a hindrance. Finally, neither barge nor railroad transportation was adequate on the Middle Fork and was lacking on the South Fork, impeding full use of the river's resources (Danglade 1922).

In 1912–1913 the most important rivers from the perspective of poundage were the Ohio (8200 tons), the Rock of Illinois (7400 tons), the Mississippi above Louisiana, Missouri (6600 tons), the Illinois of Illinois (5900 tons), and the White of Arkansas (3700 tons). In 1966 the most important rivers were the Tennessee, Illinois (1100 tons), and Wabash (1200 tons). In the period 1985–1987 it was shell from the Mississippi River between St. Louis and Muscatine, Iowa; Kentucky Lake in Tennessee/Kentucky; and the Tennessee River in Alabama that formed the pearls of Japan.

Shells were abundant in other rivers, as well. There were an estimated 10,000 tons of shells between Ellis Dam and Marietta (1967–1970) on the Muskingum River (Clark 1971:30–31). A 1969 report on the shell resources of the Ohio River and the Green River of Kentucky found the supply of commercial shells plentiful and 77 percent of legal size (Williams 1969).

What I find particularly striking about the yields from the various rivers is not the quantities, surprising as they are, but the rivers that yielded shells. Dozens of rivers—in Iowa, Illinois, Wisconsin, Ohio, Arkansas, and Mississippi, far beyond the shell mound heartland, were prolific producers, as were rivers in the heartland itself—particularly the Tennessee, Wabash, Cumberland, and Ohio. Twenty-six Ohio streams were gleaned, as were seven in Michigan, six in Minnesota, and ten rivers in Missouri. Why was there not a greater Archaic human interest in these rivers in the era of primary forest efficiency? Instead, dozens of rivers where Archaic people never seemed to have noticed the mollusks were the backbone of the button industry and of commerce in their valleys, including the Mississippi River itself. The incongruity between the importance of the Cumberland River for these historic musseling industries and its unanimity in early Late Archaic times was a major concern of the archaeological project conducted by Jack Nance (1986). At various times the Grand River of Michigan, the Grand River of Missouri, the St. Francis River (Arkansas), the Iowa River (Iowa), the St. Croix River (Minnesota), the Pearl River (Mississippi), the Neosho River (Oklahoma), and the James River (South Dakota) were the principal mussel-producing rivers in their respective state (Claassen 1994), and in some cases a leading river for the entire button industry (e.g., Neosho, St. Francis, Pearl). None of these rivers attracted Archaic collectors.

Shell Bed Sizes and Quantities Gleaned

Naiads live in communities that are typically called "beds" that vary in size. I have rarely seen a report that offered information on the size of the bed in the vicinity of a site or even mentioned the size of beds in the relevant river at any point in its history. Warren (1975:163), however, estimated the prehistoric standing crop of mussels within a half-mile of the Widow's Creek mound on the Tennessee River to be anywhere from 147,000 to 74.2 million individuals, with a mean of 11 million (at 7.46 individuals per square foot). It should come as no surprise, then, that shellfishing could begin at Widow's Creek in Middle Archaic times and continue well into Woodland times.

Data from particular beds are rare. There are accounts of a bed at Muscatine, Iowa, that was two miles long and one-quarter of a mile wide.

In three years' time, 7,642 tons of live animals were pulled out. This same bed was productive in the mid-1980s as well. At New Boston, Illinois, a large Mississippi River mussel bed was discovered in 1896, offering principally ebony shells and muckets. A bed at LeClaire, Wisconsin, one mile long and 100 yards wide, yielded more than 500 tons in the first three months of work in 1897 (Smith 1898). Work continued there over the next 14 years. From the rapids above Keokuk, 1,600 tons of shells were marketed in 1910. A little more than 400 tons were taken from the same area two years later (Coker 1919:40). Commercial shelling occurred on the Des Moines River from at least 1912 into the 1960s, primarily from three beds at Douds, Pittsburg, and Eldon (Coker 1919:40).

During the current musseling activity for the cultured pearl industry, musselers are again working the beds of the Mississippi from the Iowa to Prairie du Chien. Buyer Butch Ballinger said:

> I bought 880 tons off of this one bed here, [at Moline], 17 mi. long, diving 8–20 ft. This year [1987] there are seven companies buying here. There were 40 boats in this Moline pool three weeks ago. This bed [Moline] has been worked for eleven years. Six years ago they dredged the bed, ignored it the next year, worked it clean the next, and it is still producing. I am buying dead washboards from a die-off in the early 1980s as well as live washboards, three-ridges, pig toes. Today I'll buy about 17 tons. There are other active beds at Prairie du Chien and Princeton. I am also working three other beds in East Hannibal and Bellview (author's interview with Butch Ballinger, 1987).

The prime section of the Cumberland River for button shell was that between Nashville and Dover. At the foot of Gowers Island in 1912 was an 88-ton pile of shells. The bed at Owl Hollow Bar had been worked for 10 years by three to six boats every season. Meeks Spring bar had been worked for 10 years, yielding an estimated 600 tons of shells (Coker 1919).

The quantity of shells taken from any one river, in any one year, is at best underestimated. Most of the reported numbers refer to shells sold. Far more shellfish were removed from a bed than were sold. The river inventories in Tables 4.1, 4.2, and 4.3 provide much information on the quantity of shells sold at various times and places for the button industry. Tonnage since 1963 is provided in Table 4.3, although it is quite incomplete.

In many cases, the shell resource has been so great that musseling activity has gone on for more than 50 years, in some cases with only

Table 4.2 Mussel Poundage Taken from Iowa's Rivers, 1920–1942 (Claassen 1994)

Year	Mississippi	Cedar	Iowa	Des Moines	Wapsipinicon	Skunk
1920	1,866,580	696,257	8,600	145,100	67,210	31,430
1921	1,430,894	89,500	15,660	149,005	157,210	6,000
1922	1,200,355	70,150	32,940	466,400	83,705	27,540
1923	1,424,933	9,410	36,369	553,786	155,641	43,297
1924	1,165,667	9,100		193,390	29,340	
1925	1,144,687	100,366	26,000	231,271	100,040	57,149
1926	2,058,626	1,225,456		228,633	1,205,692	24,252
1927	888,982	663,848		205,663	322,603	14,490
1928	2,422,897	669,128		64,665	236,384	136,861
1929	1,020,484	NR	79,705		172,015	24,860
1930	1,482,679	76,281	81,181	43,293	41,362	7,700
1931	858,334	386,947	10,130	856,906	61,173	17,500
1932	299,181	87,277	91,652		1,890	2,010
1933	NR	NR	NR	NR	NR	NR
1934	435,269	186,227	4,150	87,257	2,830	7,240
1935	324,344	130,296	20,917	46,316	7,385	12,704
1936	128,499	24,240	2,000		7,999	300
1937	192,438	94,117	1,468	390,062		
1938	266,449	8,310		1,906	226,118	
1939	148,665	7,590		7,298	7,800	
1940	296,735	6,300		180	21,183	
1941	225,960	6,600			39,830	
1942	365,852					

NR=no record

short (3–5 year) interruptions. The Black River of Arkansas produced enough shells to sustain button blank cutting shops on its shores from 1910 until 1954. Sometime in the 1950s shells from the Black started shipping to Japan and were still going there in 1980. The Pearl River in Mississippi was productive from 1908 until at least 1962. The beds near Moline, Muscatine, and Prairie du Chien have been remarkably dependable for more than a century of mussel harvesting (Claassen 1994).

The quantities of shellfish are simply tremendous and abundant in all the rivers of the Mississippi, Ohio, and Tennessee watersheds. They are only slightly less abundant in the rivers of the Gulf of Mexico coastal plain. Minimal commercially viable population sizes are at least an order of magnitude greater than the minimal molluscan population sizes that would have been attractive to Archaic human collectors.

Predation Pressure and Regeneration of Populations

Where human predation presumably caused a decline in shellfish, their numbers did recover and recover rapidly. Naiad species reproduce by

Table 4.3 Shell Tonnage by River, 1965–1987 (Claassen 1994)

Year	Tennessee	Wabash	Illinois	Mississippi	Virdigris
1965	2,418.0	191.0	1,159.0	181.0	
1966	2,734.0	1,194.6	1,118.4		750.0
1967	2,361.0	317.2	388.5	74.3	0
1968			93.0		0
1969		32.7	331.7	272.8	205.7
1970		58.8	358.9	0	81.0
1971		12.0	0	0	0
1972		31.3	0	175.0	0
1973					
1974			80.0	213.8	0
1975			220.0	149.8	53.5
1976		35.0	80.2	736.3	814.0
1977		59.0	288.0	891.0	1,027.0
1978		40.0	110.1	817.8	987.0
1979		37.0	12.4	263.0	667.0
1980		28.4	83.6	849.5	408.0
1981		19.4	132.8	1968.7	
1982		16.0	240.7	519.7	476.0
1983		28.5	333.2	830.3	352.0
1984		0	662.7	1,065.6	111.0
1985		0	731.1	2,153.3	167.0
1986		12.2	204.5	2,915.7	
1987				1,016.0	

spewing glocidia into the water current that are immediately carried downstream from the spawning parent. These glocidia (for most species of naiads) then attach themselves to the gills of fish, where they pass through a parasitic stage growing a tiny shell, before detaching and settling to the bottom. Therefore, the propagation of molluscan communities is most dependent on the host fish population. If runoff is too little to allow fish to swim through an area, or if the fish host population is extirpated in a section of river or in an entire river, new shellfish will not be able to settle there. If the river bottom or water conditions change drastically for the worse, shellfish will not be able to live there. Otherwise, given fish and sexually mature shellfish somewhere upstream, new shellfish will establish in beds downstream the following season. Population recovery is very fast.

Even when a bed or entire river was abandoned in historic times, often a period of three to five years was sufficient to entice commercial musselers again. Consider the case of the Ohio rivers closed by the state in 1930 and reopened in 1934 to huge hauls, or Lake Pepin, where a moratorium on shelling was enforced for five years. The year it reopened to musselers, 840 tons of shells were sold off the upper lake and 1160 tons from the lower lake (Carlander 1954:46–47). From 1924 to 1932 the Wabash River was legally closed to musselers to allow the supply to increase, but shellfish were apparently harvested anyway. In a river where the supply of shellfish was determined to be low by state officials, two buyers were working the Wabash, implying numerous musselers still at work (Claassen 1994).

Human Effort

What do the records of these two industries tell us about the Archaic human potential to harvest these vast quantities of mollusks? In the prior paragraphs I have laid out the extent of the resource. In the paragraphs that follow I will present information on the different yields with different harvest techniques.

Harvesting Techniques

Commercial musselers have used hands and feet, or innovations such as rakes, rakes modified into giant scissors and tongs, dredges, and the crowbar to harvest shellfish. The crowbar, still in use in Kentucky, consists of hooks with four pronged knobs strung two to seven hooks per chain. Chains of hooks were placed four to five inches apart on a 16- or

20-foot bar, called a braile, and dragged from the back of a johnboat (Claassen 1994). Many modern musselers also use homemade diving equipment to harvest by hand at depths greater than 20 feet.

Coker reported that before 1912 about 500 tons of shells a year were taken by hand from the rivers in Tables 4.1 (Coker 1919). A state-commissioned study of diving efficiency in Ft. Gibson Lake, Oklahoma, determined hand harvest by diving to be 10 to 20 percent efficient (Donovan 1979). By this estimate, then, hand gathering by Indians would have been quite inefficient, missing some 80 to 90 percent of the mussels.

The estimate of 300 to 1000 pounds a day per person harvested for the button industry are figures generated using the braile bar behind a drifting or gasoline motor-powered boat. Guessing that brailing is 75 percent efficient would mean that the musseler passed over a potential 400 to 1350 pounds of shells. Of the 51,571 tons of shells taken in selected portions of the country from 1912 through 1914, crowfoot hooks on braile bars captured 70 percent of them, forks 10.5 percent, tongs 7.8 percent, hands 5.3 percent, dip nets 3.3 percent, dredges 1.2 percent, and rakes 1.2 percent (Coker 1919). Consequently, very little of the harvest recorded in Tables 4.1–4.3 was generated by hand collecting.

Not all species are equally capturable by all techniques. Brailing, raking, tonging, and wading "secured an unduly large number of some species and an unduly small number of other species" (Wilson and Clark 1914:20). For instance, some species colonize the edges of beds, where a braile was least likely to drag. It is also true that when the water is low the musseler gets a very different proportion of species, and even different species than when working in high water (Wilson and Clark 1914:20). Cold water, such as occurs seasonally in streams or a flush of water from snowmelt, will cause the mollusk to close up and be inaccessible to brailing. When the water is very warm they also close up. Lund's informants told him that from mid-July to early September the mussels close up and are impossible to catch with crowfoot hooks, except before 8:00 A.M. (Lund 1983:641).

The crowfoot hooks failed to bring up every shell they came in contact with and wounded most creatures, so that those creatures that fell back to the bottom or were discarded onboard as too small or of the wrong species surely died of their wounds. Gravid (pregnant) individuals often aborted. Brailing could destroy a bed as well, by plowing it. This information means that bed utility and longevity and the capture figures in the tables indicate a minimal estimate of the quantities of mollusks available.

One of the hypotheses for the demise of shell mound use at the close of the Archaic on the Green, Ohio, Savannah, and western Tennessee rivers is that the rivers became too deep for humans to harvest shellfish as the climate grew increasingly wetter. The historic and modern musseling activities can provide information on this notion. Modern musselers have used 30-foot-long rakes, tongs, and dredges to remove shells from beds 10–20 feet deep in colder rivers and lakes. Branch dragging from a canoe or log raft would probably work for beds as deep as 6 feet. Toe digging and free diving allow motivated individuals to get shells from five to 40 feet deep.

Harvesters

Being largely nomadic, the numbers of historic musselers may actually be more than are reported. Women as well as men brailed, gleaned, and dove. The prehistoric communities of shellfishers envisioned had 50 to 100 individuals to deploy and, in some older scenarios, were thought to harvest continually, for hours a day, not unlike the modern musseler.

As many as 500 women, children, and men were seen on one sandbar one day in 1897 hand-gathering on the Black River in Arkansas (Stockard 1904:166–171). The upper Cumberland River was the scene of active pearling. One hundred men were often pearling near Rowena on a single bed. There were as many as 50 pearl hunters on Clouds Island and as many as 150 people at Goodall Island daily (Coker 1919:25, 40).

"During the 1920s and 1930s, 100 to 150 men worked the lower Tennessee River from approximately mile 31 to the mouth. Each boat collected from 300 to 600 pounds of shells per day" (Williams 1969:2), or 30,000 pounds a day for an unknown number of days over *20 years*. Often a crew as large as 100 or 150 people camped on the Clinch River (eastern Tennessee) bank, musseled all day, cooked out, and sold the shells and pearls.

Turning to the Mississippi River, during the winter of 1898–1899 at LeClaire, Wisconsin, Smith (1898) observed 142 musselers "ice fishing" using rakes. Between Burlington and Clinton, Iowa, Smith reported 300 musselers, and 1,000 musselers between Ft. Madison and Sabula in 1898. Fifty musselers around Muscatine were estimated on one bed ice fishing in 1897–1898 and 100 in the summer of 1898. In the period 1912 to 1914, 9,746 shellers worked the Mississippi River between Minnesota and the town of Louisiana, Missouri (Scarpino 1985:99). Hiller (1939:38) reported that colonies of 30-40, or even of 75, families were sent to the mussel beds on the Ohio and Mississippi rivers, where they remained until the season was closed or the mussel beds were worked over.

The peak year for button shell collecting on the Illinois River was 1909, when there were more than 2,600 boats afloat daily from Peru to Grafton. Eldridge (1914) estimated that there were 100 individuals on the Fox in midsummer 1911 and 70 during September 1911.

Modern Yields per Person

During the days of the button industry, the various types of equipment used had much to do with the yield per person. At the Le Clair bed, one person could rake up to 800 pounds daily. Rewards for brailing could be as high as 2000 pounds/day at the beginning of a season and sink to 1000 pounds/day at the end of the season. Other figures found in the reports (see Claassen 1994) were 500–700 pounds/day, 300–800 pounds/ day, and 400 pounds/day. Seasonal figures were 12.5 tons, 15–20 tons, 12–14 tons, seven tons, and four tons per sheller.

"I buy seven days a week from about 130–140 divers. Have 13 men at the home base. Monday I bought 23 tons, Tuesday 20 tons, Wednesday 17.5 tons—it lessens each day of the week as people get tired" (author's interview with Butch Ballinger 1987). Ballinger's figures mean that each diver was bringing up 353 pounds on Monday, declining to 269 pounds on Friday.

It would appear from these reports that a yield below 300 pounds daily or four tons annually during the button industry days would cause the musseler to lose interest and a stream to be declared "unproductive" by industry buyers. Today's buyers pay well enough that a daily win of 269 pounds proves profitable.

This intensive harvesting by modern musselers did have its impact on the populations of species being exploited. Musselers knew that they simply could move to a different section of river or to a different river to continue to harvest shells when their income fell below their own standard. However, the standards for the button businesses often changed, thus changing the definition of a marketable shell. In the initial years only four or five species were considered usable for button production. As the supply of these shells dwindled at the favored beds (closest to the factories), companies experimented with other species and, upon finding them suitable, enlarged the list of shell species they were willing to buy. In some cases this redefinition of a usable shell made it possible to return to rivers earlier pronounced "exhausted." An unusual export demand would cause high prices for the best shells, forcing the companies to use lower-quality shells for domestic button production. Rivers where the shells had been pronounced inferior subsequently could support a mussel fishery. These changes in the national and international markets produced a rather complex mosaic of musseling history and economics in a region. However, the role of commercial stimulation in these harvest records and in the river-use records far outstrips the motivation that could be expected in the Indian communities. They also emphasize again the size and extent of the resource that was ignored by the Indians.

Conclusion and Discussion

Shellfish populations have sustained two industries in the past 120 years and they still manage to colonize impoundments and filthy rivers and to support the Japanese cultured pearl industry, as well as now a domestic pearl industry. These industries have gleaned millions of tons of shellfish, employed thousands of people, and scoured more than a hundred rivers, some producing for a century. Whereas a yield below 300 pounds daily or four tons annually of one to four target species would cause the musseler to lose interest and a stream to be declared unproductive by industry buyers, quantities below these figures would surely have sustained Indian interest. The activities of Indians never equaled these records of yields and individual effort and did not target specific species, except for the *Leptoxis* gastropod destined for beads. Furthermore, the quantities of shells in the beds as I have recorded them are modern figures and are quite probably reduced in number from prehistoric times. Conditions for shellfish reproduction and settling have steadily deteriorated during the last century. Dozens of species are now extinct or endangered.

Having reviewed these two historic musseling industries, it is time to turn our attention once again to the heaps of shells made during the Middle and Late Archaic period on the Green, Tennessee, Duck, Harpeth, Wabash, Cumberland, Ohio, Savannah, and St. Johns rivers. This list of rivers seems puzzling. It should be clear to the reader from the records reviewed here that the freshwater nacreous molluscan populations from 10,000 years ago until today were ubiquitous, quite prolific, and easily replenished. If the initial attraction to shellfish for Archaic peoples of the mid-South was purely the result of environmental availability, then why were not shellfish collected in noticeable quantities throughout the region and beyond? If shellfish were added to the diet because of shrinking territories, then why were they harvested so prodigiously in only a few territories? Most of the extremely productive rivers for the historic industries—the Black, White, St. Francis, Neosho, Des Moines, Illinois, Fox, Mississippi, Muskingum, Clinch—lack Archaic sites with freshwater shell.

Only in Alabama, on the Tennessee River, does the prehistoric level of exploitation foreshadow the historic level of shellfishing; I am not the first to make this observation. "The concentration of Archaic shell midden sites in the Green River drainage is most remarkable, given the fact that mussel beds were common in streams throughout Kentucky" (Hockensmith et al. 1983). Ortmann (1927) collected specimens of 66 varieties from nine loci on the upper Green River, above Mammoth Cave, but there are no shell-bearing sites there. Kneberg (1952:92) observed that shell mounds were not found upriver from Chattanooga on the Tennessee, even though "shoals where clams might be secured are present." The same can be said of the streams throughout the East.

Our prehistoric actors would have gathered by hand or foot or swept beds from slow-moving canoes with branches (the forerunner of braile bars), like the Canadian loggers were seen doing (Rankin 1982). Increasing the brailing haul of 300 to 100 pounds/day by 25 percent to accommodate brailing inefficiencies, a 20 percent harvest by hand of the estimated 400 to 1350 pounds of shellfish harvestable would mean 80 to 270 pounds of shellfish per day per Indian. That larger figure is in keeping with the poundage brought up late in the week by divers on the Moline bed in 1987, achieved by individuals who work eight- to 12-hour days using wenches and motors to lift and move the load, and are motivated to do so by a capitalistic system. It would take one such motivated Indian harvester seven to 25 days working eight to 12 hours per day to remove one ton of shells from a bed. A more modern impression is that native women would spend no more than five to eight hours per week in such a pursuit—unless large numbers were needed for a feast.

The seasonal molluscan meat and shell demand for Indian families for food, bait, and raw material surely could have been satisfied with fewer pounds than that needed by the button industry each year. It is unreasonable to think that a riverside community of collectors could have depleted the molluscan resource at hand, even if this foodstuff was used periodically for feasts. Remembering that tons of shells could come from a single bed, that the food value of shellfish meat is but supplemental, that the human community sizes were that of tribes or smaller, that occupation was seasonal, that collection was via hand or branch, and that molluscan populations recover quickly, does it make sense to attribute the end of this phenomenon to overharvesting? No.

If the shellfish resource was the driving factor behind the site location, why did the people not move to other rivers if the local beds proved unproductive? Perhaps the numerous sites on the Tennessee, the Green, and the St. Johns do represent relocations, but the peoples' failure to expand to other rivers suggests something more was at work in the criteria for location and use.

We are, it seems, seeing an expression of a social phenomenon, not a natural one. Suffice it to say that the idea of overharvesting the molluscan resources of the Green, the Ohio, the Duck, or the Harpeth simply has no validity in light of these historic activities. I will offer an exploration of the social aspects of these sites in later chapters. In the next chapter I address a rival and even more popular idea that a climatic change known as the Hypsithermal can account for both the beginning and the end of shellfishing in the Ohio River Valley.

CHAPTER 5
THE DEMISE OF THE HYPSITHERMAL

Numerous authors have assigned the beginning and end of intensive shellfishing in the Archaic period to the Hypsithermal climatic episode (e.g., Klippel et al. 1978, Marquardt and Watson 2005a). A compendium of the various arguments goes like this: Prior to the onset of intensive shellfishing in the Archaic, humans, who did not live by rivers, either did not know mussels existed or could not get to the shellfish because of deep water year-round. Drier conditions were brought about by decreased rainfall and greater evaporation of water because of warmer air temperatures early in the Archaic. The rivers received less water and lost more to evaporation, becoming shallower. Humans were pulled out of the drying uplands to the moister river valleys, where they could access shellfish. This period of riverine-focused gathering lasted for the duration of this drier period known as the Hypsithermal. About 7,000 years ago, these favorable hydrologic conditions peaked. Subsequently, air temperatures began to cool and rainfall increased, so that by the end of the Late Archaic, the rivers were deeper, taking naiads out of the reach of humans once again.

In Chapter 4 I showed that the resource occurred on hundreds of rivers, but that shells were mounded in a far more restricted manner. In this chapter I will show that the Hypsithermal did not control the temporal expression of shell mounding, either. Once the environmental explanations are eliminated, the way is paved for a cultural explanation of shell mounding and its cessation in the southern Ohio Valley.

The Hypsithermal Climatic Event

It is hard to find a consensus among students of the Hypsithermal (also known as the Altithermal, Holocene Climatic Optimum warm event, Holocene Thermal Maximum, and Holocene Megathermal) about the period of time in the eastern United States that is implicated. Some start the drying 10,000 years ago, or 9,450 years ago (McNutt 2008), others at 8,500 years ago (Wendland 1978), and even 8,000 years ago (Delcourt and Delcourt 1980), with river stabilization by 6,000 years ago (Fagan 2000:371). Some give a peak in dryness around 7000 BP (e.g., Delcourt and Delcourt 1980:150). Some scientists end the era at 6,000 years ago (museum.state.il.us/exhibits/midewin/coreact 01.html), 5,000 years ago (e.g., Wendland 1978), 4,000 years ago (e.g., Delcourt and Delcourt 1980) and even 3,000 years ago (Lubsen 2004). Other scientists go so far as to say that there was no significant climatic difference between "then" and now, a position that is gaining popularity in this century. What would seem to be based on facts has been labeled opinion by one researcher (Smith 1965:634–35). There does seem to be consensus among researchers, however, that subregional variation could account for the disparate "opinions" about climatic change during the Holocene and the Middle and Late Archaic cultural periods.

The weather patterns of the central and eastern United States are determined by the mix of air deriving from the Pacific and Arctic Oceans and the Gulf of Mexico, with each moisture source distinguishable through oxygen isotopes. During the Early and Late Holocene, winds carrying Gulf of Mexico moisture prevailed over the eastern United States. However, during the Middle Holocene, drier Pacific winds dominated (e.g., Dean et al. 1996), allowing for the eastward migration of the prairie/forest border and the oak savannah, and oak-hickory forests. In central Illinois, this period of Pacific winds, the Hypsithermal, is dated from 8,000 to 6,000 years ago (museum.state.il.us/exhibits/midewin/coreact 01.html). In central Tennessee the drier conditions are evident by 8,000 years ago in animal species, tree species, and floodplain stability on the Duck River (Crites 1987). In southeast Missouri and central Ohio the new plant communities affiliated with drier conditions reached their maximum extent about 7,000 years ago (Crites 1987). This would mean that shellfishing should be concentrated in the period 8,000 to 6,000 years ago and peak between 7,000 and 6,000 years ago as well, because the rivers would have been at their lowest levels in those centuries.

Recent studies challenge the oft-cited climate characteristics. O'Brien (2001:35) says that the cooler and moister Boreal (archaeological Early Archaic period), which resides in the minds of many, was only slightly cooler and moister and only in extremely localized areas. Instead, the era was one of warming and drying. Forests retreated toward moist localities found along stream courses.

A better understanding of the rainfall pattern during the Holocene can be found in cave settings. The growth rate of speleothems in Cold Water Cave, Iowa, which reflects the amount of water infiltration, increased beginning around 5,900 years ago. This increase in moisture has been attributed to increased cool season precipitation/infiltration from elevated solar insulation, in a period of increased summer aridity (Denniston et al. 1999). The advance of the prairie is argued to be more reliant on moisture than on a uniform temperature rise (Denniston et al. 1999). In fact, for at least Illinois, while Hypsithermal summers were much drier than those of today, Hypsithermal winters were not significantly different (Purdue 1991). The mean annual temperature reconstruction also has been revised lower, indicating cooler summers than once portrayed and supporting the idea of winter-dominated rainfall patterns during the Hypsithermal in Illinois (Yu 1997).

But what happened in Illinois may have been restricted to Illinois. Incident solar radiation or insolation indirectly governs many ecological processes linked to climate (e.g., Dean et al. 1996, Purdue 1991). These processes can vary in their sensitivity to seasonal, annual, or decadal changes in insolation. This variability in sensitivity means that regional differences in ecological processes reflecting changes in climate (changing water levels, plant communities, animal communities, among other changes) are to be expected.

Evidence for a Hypsithermal interval, at least in central Tennessee, is not very convincing. The Hypsithermal causality scenario should mean that shellfishing declined in Tennessee's rivers after 7000 BP. One can see from Table 2.1 that the opposite case is true. Meeks et al. (2007) offer data that central Tennessee's rainfall and temperatures during the Middle Holocene were essentially those of today. The pollen evidence for the enlargement of the Kentucky Barrens (reflecting a drier climate) dates after 3900 BP, not during the Hypsithermal Interval (DeSelm et al. 1997). Pollen cores from southeastern Missouri and northeastern Arkansas indicate that the Hypsithermal drying was not as severe as once thought in the meander-belt portion of the Mississippi Valley (O'Brien 2001:37). The upper Tombigbee watershed was probably warmer but wetter on the western side of the river (Muto and Gunn 1981), while western Tennessee was only somewhat wetter (Meeks et al. 2007). Winters (1969:3) concluded after his review of the literature: "It is increasingly doubtful that the Hypsithermal was marked in the Midwest by drastic changes in rainfall. . . . [It is] doubtful that marked changes in river depths can be postulated for either the critical period of the Xerothermic (ca. 6000 to 4000 BP) or for subsequent millennia."

Climate Data from the Shell Sites

Given the possibility that the river valleys were insulated habitats, where Hypsithermal climate was ameliorated, much paleoclimatological data may not be very relevant to the specific rivers or the specific sections of those rivers where shells accumulated during the Archaic. In order to evaluate the climate explanation for the initiation and cessation of intensive shellfishing from the rivers between 8,000 and 5,000 years ago, data from the actual shell heaps are preferable.

This examination, like all others undertaken in this book, requires a uniform suite of calibrated radiocarbon dates, which is provided in Table 2.1. However, all work with this site type is greatly hampered by the lack of dates from most of the shell-bearing heaps. Even more of a handicap in discussing the activity of harvesting mussels is the total lack of dated shells and but a few dated human bodies. We must presume that the shells and the bodies were simultaneously introduced to these locations and that the charcoal that has been dated (albeit infrequently) is also contemporaneous with the shells and the bodies. Problems associated with dating naiads have diminished with the awareness of the potential for dating protein from shell and with the development of reservoir corrections (e.g., Claassen 1998, Moore et al. 1998).

THE BEGINNING OF INTENSIVE SHELLFISHING

But there is no doubt that the intensification [in use of freshwater resources] coincides with the warm Hypsithermal climatic episode (Fagan 2000:371).

The expectations of the Hypsithermal explanation are straightforward: if the Hypsithermal can account for the shellfishing of the Middle and Late Archaic, then there should be little to no shellfishing prior to 8,000 years ago and little to no shellfishing after 5,000 years ago.

Shellfish were recognized as a resource by some Paleoindians. There are some valves in Rodgers Shelter (Missouri) by 9500 BP (Haynes 1976:56), in Dust Cave (Driskell 1994:91), where shells may have been collected as early as 10687–9961 BP, and in several rock shelters in Texas, such as Levi (Alexander 1963). Clearly, shellfish were present in the southern Ohio Valley and in other southern river valleys shortly after the end of the Pleistocene. Malacologists believe that there has been no appreciable change in molluscan distribution since the late Pleistocene (Patch 2005:258).

It is a curious phenomenon, and one that is underexplored, that so many of the shell-bearing sites of the Archaic have Paleoindian artifacts in them. Sites that contain Paleoindian artifacts are Ervin, Anderson, 40Sm1, Robinson, Fennel, Klein, Perry, Reid, Ward, Barrett, Jimtown Hill, Indian Knoll, Chiggerville, Baker, Bowles, Read, and Carlston Annis (Herrmann 2004:52). Until we have dates on shells, we cannot rule out the possibility that shells began accumulating during the Paleoindian period at these sites.

The same can be said of Early Archaic shellfishing (10,000 to 8,000 years ago)—that it may be present in the records of Mulberry Creek, Perry, Breeden, Klein, Read, Robinson, Little Bear Creek, Ervin, and Anderson, for example. The oldest certain shellfishing is that by Morrow Mountain people (radiocarbon dated in the Tennessee Valley from 9023 to 8199 and 7453–6903 BP) at several Tennessee River sites. There are several reasons, then, to suspect that shellfishing began before the Hypsithermal. Although this early shellfishing seems to have been quite geographically circumscribed, it could have been "intensive" in those places. We simply do not know.

Instead of the Hypsithermal facilitating shellfishing by 8,000 years ago, however, the majority of shell heaps begin after the peak drying (7000 BP), as temperatures were decreasing and moisture was increasing, and even after the 6,000-years-ago end of the Hypsithermal! A look at Table 2.1 will confirm these statements.

Given that shellfishing intensified in many areas and began in others after 6,000 years ago, and given the greater number of shell-bearing sites and the quantity of shells in Woodland-era sites (Peacock 2002), a stronger case can be made that a wetter (post-4000 BP) and cooler climate, rather than the drier climate of the Hypsithermal, stimulated greater shellfishing. Just such a claim has been made for the Florida record. Thanz (1977) and Milanich (1994) see the end of the Hypsithermal (at 5,000 years ago) and, more importantly, the rising sea level to have stimulated freshwater shellfishing on the St. Johns River and in the coastal lagoons.

The End of Intensive Shellfishing in the Ohio Valley

Before declaring the Hypsithermal irrelevant to the cultural choices evident in the archaeological record between 8200 and 3600 BP, it is appropriate to spend some time examining the data derived from the final layers of these sites and the succession of sites on one river.

Table 2.1 will again serve to ground discussion of causes leading to the end of Archaic shellfishing in the Duck, Ohio, Harpeth and Green rivers. (Shellfishing did not end on the Cumberland or Tennessee rivers during the Archaic.) Considering the dates and placing the end of the Hypsithermal at 5,500 years ago, one can see that shellfishing may have ended at Barrett, Haynes, Hayes, Hornung, Reid, Old Clarksville, and Rabbit Mount during the next 500 years. But, if shellfishing ended in one place and started or continued in another place on the same river after 5,500 years ago, the Hypsithermal argument is irrelevant. Therefore, the only river abandoned by shellfishers by 5,000 years ago, according to Table 2.1, is possibly the Duck. The shell-free stratum at Hayes is dated 5317–4579 BP. Abandonment of other rivers was typically protracted, which does not support the Hypsithermal explanation. Abandonment of the Nashville Basin sites occurred over a 5,000-year period, the Green River sites over a 3,400-year interval, the Louisville region of the Ohio over 1,900 years, the Savannah River over 1,700 years, and on the Atlantic Coast over a period of 1,400 years. These ranges will probably increase with the addition of more radiocarbon dates.

The sequence of site abandonment in these various rivers also negates the Hypsithermal explanation. It is highly unlikely that living shellfish were present around the two shell-bearing mortuaries of Anderson on the Harpeth and Hart, on a tributary of the Harpeth, and not present downriver on the Harpeth in the vicinity of the shell-free Ensworth site. At Carlston Annis, on the Green, the shell-free stratum spans 4810 to 4418 BP, when shells were *accumulating* downriver at Indian Knoll. The two dates from the shell-free stratum at Indian Knoll span 4417 to 3639 BP. These shell-free dates, which seem to imply that there were no mollusks in the river from 4810 to 3639 BP, are contradicted by the accumulation of shells on the same stretch of river at Bowles and Read during this interval. Furthermore, there are later dates from shell context at Carlston Annis. Therefore, the shell-free caps at Green River sites are not the result of drowned beds or fast currents. Perhaps these heaps were intentionally "capped."

The shellfishing record from the Cumberland is equally contradictory—shells accumulated at Hermitage Springs near Nashville and on the lower Tennessee River near its juncture with the Cumberland during the Middle Archaic and Late Archaic, but not on the lower Cumberland (Nance 1986). A shell-free midden at Hayes, on the Duck River, has been dated from 5317 to 4579 BP (Table 2.1), when shells were available in the Cumberland and shellfishing apparently was underway on a tributary of the Ohio at KYANG and Lone Hill, on the Ohio River proper, and on the Green River. From the central Ohio River come dates from Panther Rock that indicate that shells (apparently) were accumulating around 3685–3473 BP, a date that is much later than most of the Falls sites. Furthermore, at Panther Rock the majority of species dwell in water two feet deep or less (Peacock 2009:199). Even with the return of mesic conditions, the water near Panther Rock remained shallow.

Hofman (1986:198) and Lewis and Lewis (1961), believed that some environmental change had precluded the collection of shellfish in the Late Archaic. Hofman suggested that Eva peoples relocated to the tributary Big Sandy River, specifically the shell-bearing Cherry aggregation camp, where they could harvest the untapped molluscan resources. But what that environmental change would have been is a mystery. Only a molluscan mass die-off could affect just the Eva section of the Tennessee River and not the tributary Big Sandy Creek. Mass die-offs, however, appear to be a phenomenon of the twentieth century (Claassen 1998:36). Again we see a tributary providing shells when a large river does not, more evidence that the end of the Hypsithermal cannot account for the shellfishing record in the southern Ohio Valley.

But dates are not the only means by which we can assess the Hypsithermal implications for water conditions. Mollusks can provide much information about water conditions and habitat, including substrate conditions, water depth, and current strength, during occupation and at abandonment. I turn now to a brief discussion of the gastropod and bivalve studies that have been conducted at some of these sites.

From an analysis of terrestrial gastropods in the shell layers at Carlston Annis, Baerreis (2005) interprets a trend from warmer air to cooler air over the centuries and an overall shortening of the growing season. (No gastropods were recovered from the shell-free stratum.) Based on a formula using the maximum length of *Carychium exiguum* from four excavation units, Baerreis (2005:252) found that there was a progressive (though insignificant) decrease in the number of days in the growing cycle from bottom to top of the Carlston Annis heap, not an increase to a peak and then a decrease, as predicted by the climate model. An uninterrupted cooling trend means that there was no Hypsithermal impact on molluscan habitat.

Baerreis also found from measurement of two land snail species that the annual rainfall throughout the occupation of Carlston Annis (from evidence in two units) was between 897mm and 796mm +/-6.8mm. Today the average annual rainfall is 1160mm in that county (Baerreis 2005:251). It is clear that the climate was considerably drier during the centuries this heap was accumulating, but it is equally clear that there was no gradual increase in surface run-off and river water volumes during the time of occupation. Given the lack of any evidence of gradually deepening water at Carlston Annis, the purported increase in moisture that is part of the Hypsithermal explanation must have been very dramatic, occurring in the space of several decades, to drown the shellfish populations and/or discourage the shellfishers in the late Late Archaic. In fact, Baerreis notes several incidences of abrupt changes in the proportions of various key gastropod species, but when these breaks are compared to the stratigraphic descriptions of each unit (various chapters in Marquardt and Watson eds. 2005), most breaks can be explained by a hard clay floor, a burial, or dense charcoal/ash.

Even more to the point, Baerreis found evidence at Carlston Annis for what paleoclimatologists have begun to uncover, that the major difference between then and now in rainfall is the greater amount of winter precipitation since the Hypsithermal (including now). Greater winter precipitation does not translate into deeper rivers in August-September-October, the period during which the shellfishing appears to have occurred (Claassen 2005). Though it does mean greater water volume in the Green River during the springtime, this flow was not so strong during the early part of the year as to scour clean the bottom and prevent naiad settlement in the summer. By late summer there would have been no more water in the river than there was during the Hypsithermal years. While it is true that "during late winter and early spring months this resource is frequently difficult, if not impossible, to obtain" because of cold water, water depth, and turbidity, such that collecting during this period "would have imposed considerable risk" (Klippel and Morey 1986:808), greater winter and spring rainfall is when shellfishing is least likely to have occurred, and is thus irrelevant to the issue of shellfishing potential in the rivers during the Archaic.

The Hypsithermal advocate is reminded that annual rainfall is much greater now (1,100 mm per year) and is winter dominant in the Tennessean province, yet there are still shallows, riffle-runs, and shellfish beds in those rivers. As Chapter 4 makes abundantly clear, even 1,100 mm per year was not and is not enough rainfall to drown the shellfish beds or prevent their harvest using a variety of techniques, including hand gathering. Morey and Crothers (1998:922) have established that shoals have probably been present on the Green River for the last 6,000 years at least. Even in the rest of the Midwest that now experiences summer-dominant rainfall, water levels are still at their lowest during the August to October period, still have shallows and shellfish beds, and shellfishing is still easiest in late summer.

Diana Patch (2005) examined 21,190 valves from Carlston Annis, found in three excavation units. She observed that 1) the same species occurred regularly throughout the depth of the heap, 2) there was a consistent predominance of certain species, 3) some species occurred in the same frequency throughout the mound, and 4) the majority of species prefer gravel-sand bottom in shallow to moderately deep water. These observations mean that there is neither evidence of overexploitation of the riffle-run nor evidence of environmental changes that affected the molluscan communities. Specifically, there is no evidence of deepening water, of water that is increasingly sluggish, or of increasing silt. I examined 5,956 shells from one column sample at the DeWeese heap, "next door" to Carlston Annis, possibly composed of shells gathered from the same bed, in the same centuries. I, too, found no noticeable change in the frequency of the top seven species over time (Claassen 2005), again negating the idea of environmental changes affecting the molluscan communities. In short, there is no evidence of a Hypsithermal influence in the molluscan record in the Big Bend of the Green River.

Winters pointed out that shallow-water species predominated throughout the Wabash sequence of 4286–2985 BP (his 1500 to 1000 BC) and dismissed the notion of catastrophic increase in river levels implied by this explanation. Malacologist William Clench found the same lack of evidence for the presumed fauna and water changes in the molluscan assemblage of Russell Cave, Alabama, which is located near the Widow's Creek site:

> So far as the land and freshwater mollusks are concerned, no climatic change of any magnitude took place during the entire occupancy of Russell Cave. If any climatic changes did occur in northeastern Alabama during this time span, such changes were not great enough to modify the molluscan fauna. The species of mollusks living in Widow's Creek and the Tennessee River today are the same as those that existed in the same situations nine thousand years ago. Even the land snails in the various layers are composed of the same species which are to be found in the immediate area of Russell Cave (Clench 1974:89).

Warren (1975), looking at the Widow's Creek site itself, said there was little change in the mollusks from the Middle Archaic to Late Woodland at Widows Creek except for greater numbers of silt-tolerant forms.

Weighing in from the lower Tennessee and Cumberland rivers, again based on the molluscan record, Jack Nance (1986:7) adds his considered opinion to the anti-Hypsithermal camp:

> I am prepared to argue that river conditions in the lower Tennessee-Cumberland region in Archaic times were similar to those in the late prehistoric and historic periods, that shellfish were available along the lower courses of the Tennessee and Cumberland rivers, and that the shellfish populations extant in Archaic times probably resembled those reconstructed from our study of Mississippian materials.

Morrison sampled several of the heaps of Pickwick Landing (1Lu72, 1Lu70, 1Lu67, Meander Scar, Bluff Creek, Smithsonia Landing, and Mulberry Creek), reporting "a slight faunal change here, without the extinction of any species since the shell mounds were built up" (Morrison 1942:382). At East Steubenville, 26 species of unios were identified, 80 percent of which can be found in water three to seven feet deep. The implied habitat is virtually identical to that present today in the Ohio River near the site (Rollins and Dugas 2007).

There is then in these various studies of mollusks, no evidence that water depths became so deep as to preclude shoals, mollusks, or their human predators. There is thin support for a climatic explanation for the end of Archaic shellfishing in the southern Ohio Valley.

Shellfishing After the Hypsithermal

The Hypsithermalists assert that there were climatic conditions coalescing around 5,000 years ago to cause the end of shellfishing. Therefore, those conditions, once in place, should have prevented shellfishing in the sub–Boreal/Early Woodland and thereafter. But shellfishing did continue on the Tennessee River, the Wabash, and the Cumberland, was renewed on the Tombigbee, and began in numerous other places, such as the Coosa River valley (Little 2003) in earnest, even as water levels in rivers continued to rise until about 2,000 years ago.

A recent examination of shellfishing in the prehistory of the Cumberland, Tennessee, and Tombigbee rivers (27 sites) by Peacock (2002) found that shell accumulation was the most intense during the Woodland period based on valve counts alone. The Elliott's Point culture of northwest Florida (4210–3036), the Colbert culture, and the Dry Branch phase of the Coosa River—all Woodland period cultural manifestations—also stand out among sites with notable shell content (Little 2003). Widows

Creek and Hamilton Culture sites indicate that shellfish were plentiful toward the upper end of the Tennessee River, and subsequent deposits of shells in the middle Tennessee valley sites indicate that they continued to be available in that region of the Tennessee River as well (Lewis and Kneberg 1970, Warren 1975).

Information on Mississippian shellfishing in the region of the lower Cumberland, lower Tennessee and Ohio rivers junction is of relevance to the deep-water issue. According to Nance (1986:7):

> Harvesting of deep-water species was not uncommon. However, collection of species tolerant of a broad range of water depths and other conditions was predominant. In no samples were shallow-water taxa found to be the most abundant. . . . the abundance of species preferring deeper water implies that water depths of over 1–2 m were common . . . the low incidence of species preferring shallow water suggests that riffle/run habitats in the area were limited in extent.

Those rivers were neither so deep that molluscs were eliminated nor too deep for humans to secure them.

While the molluscan data should suffice to squelch the Hypsithermal causality argument, it is also possible to muster vertebrate data that likewise debunk the idea of changes in landscape and resources sufficient to cause the abandonment of the rivers and these sites (e.g. Curren 1974, Glore 2005, Pipes 2007). Lewis and Lewis (1961) noted that while shellfish disappeared during the final stratum at Eva, on the lower Tennessee, the fauna remained the same so that environmental change was not the cause for the abandonment of shellfishing.

The Sea-Level Drop Stimulus

Rather than the increasing and decreasing rainfall argument, there is another way in which the Atlantic-period drying may have impacted Archaic shellfishing, and that is through sea-level rise and fall, an explanation adopted by Fagan (2000:371). The advent of oystering in the Hudson has been attributed to the retreat of saltwater/freshwater interface upriver, owing ultimately to a sea-level transgression that reached its maximum at 6500 BP (Weiss 1974). Little (2003) has made a very similar argument to explain the shellfishing record of the Tennessee Valley during the later Woodland period.

Of specific interest to Little were two late Holocene sea-level regressions and two transgressions, beginning 3,200 years ago. Although his particular study is beyond the period of interest here, the correlation he found is of interest. Little found that shellfish use apparently increased during periods when sea level was equal to or lower than that of today and declined during periods of higher sea level (Little 2003:9), although it did not cease. His work suggests that one might also find correlations earlier in the Holocene between transgressions (higher sea level) and shellfish-use decline, and regressions (lower sea level) and shellfish-use increase.

Sea level fluctuates with the speed of glacial melting, rainfall runoff, and siltation, all of which are governed by climate change. There are two models of Holocene sea-level change that vary in their ramifications for the Archaic. One model that has long been popular is that Holocene glacial melting from Antarctica occurred uninterrupted from the end of the last glacial advance until sea level reached its modern height about 4,000 years ago, when estuaries finally formed. Sea level then dropped after 3,300 years ago along the Atlantic Coast, 3,000 to 2,000 years ago on the eastern Gulf Coast, and 4,000 to 3,000 years ago in the western Gulf of Mexico (Blum et al. 2002). This is the model that Little has adopted to explain the enthusiasm of post-Archaic shellfishers.

The implications from this model are that freshwater shellfishing should have declined from 14,000 years ago until 4,000 or 3,000 years ago (through the Late Archaic and into Early Woodland) as water levels rose, and then shellfishing should have increased noticeably from 3000 to 2000 BP during the first period of regression. (Recall that the Hypsithermal affected the environment from ca. 8,500 to 6,000 years ago.) Only the increase in naiad shellfishing during the Early Woodland is substantiated by the regression/transgression model.

Saltwater shellfishing in the southeastern United States would have had to await the stabilization of sea level in order for the estuaries to form, beginning about 4,200 years ago. Estuaries or no, the accumulation of marine shells began much earlier than 4,200 years ago at Horr's Island (7649–7437 BP) on the Gulf Coast, and on the Atlantic Coast at Tomoka (5291–4883), Sapelo Island, and Cannon's Point. Shellfishing also began much earlier in the freshwater settings of the St. Johns River at Harris Creek (6486–5930BP), and on the Savannah River at Stallings Island (5466–4850 BP).

The other model of sea-level history has glacial meltwater loads causing a sea level slightly higher than today's by 6,700 years ago, or the middle Holocene, and a slight regression since that time to a height little different from today. This model actually offers a better fit to the (inferred) shellfishing record of the Archaic than the one Little has favored for the post-Archaic activity. It would have shellfishing increasing from 6,700 years ago until contact.

Summary and Discussion

The shell heaping phenomenon under study was not bracketed by the Hypsithermal climatic episode of 8,000 to 6,000 or even 5,000 years ago or created by lower sea levels. In fact, the evidence accumulated in this study and presented so far in Chapters 2, 3, and 4 actually is counterintuitive to arguments relying on environmental stimuli. I present the following points:

1. Shellfishing began on a first-order tributary of the Green River, not on the main river. This tributary is not where shellfish would first appear, remain the longest, or be found in abundance.
2. Shellfish were carried to a hilltop first (Ward), not deposited at the riverside.
3. Shellfishing usually occurred earliest midway up a tributary and never downriver on a major river (Duck, Harpeth, Green, Savannah).
4. Dates indicate that shellfishing was going on at Indian Knoll while shell-free midden was accumulating at Carlston Annis, and then resumed at Carlston Annis while shell-free midden accumulated at Indian Knoll, both on the Green River.
5. Shellfish were still available downriver on the Green, evident from the dates at Read and Bowles, just when they ceased to be collected upriver in the Big Bend. Shellfishing there apparently spanned the end of the Hypsithermal, defying expectations that shellfish beds were flooded on the Green.
6. Shells disappeared from the lower Tennessee River sites but continued on Big Sandy River, a tributary. Again, in a scenario of worsening conditions, populations in tributaries would be the first to suffer.
7. On the Tennessee River, foragers gathered only in the easiest conditions and the easiest species to find. Mollusks were not gathered from the tributaries.

Such a strategy does not suggest that that the humans were harvesting a disappearing resource.

8. Pre-Riverton culture shell-bearing sites were followed by Riverton shell-bearing sites on the Wabash River, which indicates that shellfish were readily available in the Wabash River from 3480 to 3100 BP.

9. Shellfishing disappeared over long periods on each river, again defying the expectations of Hypsithermalists.

The points that I consider most salient in this review of climate influence on Archaic period shellfishing are:

10. Shellfish were a proven resource prior to the Middle Archaic.

11. Shellfish were available in all 1000+ rivers of the Mississippi Valley, Ohio Valley, Missouri River valley, and coastal plains during the Archaic. Archaic shell harvesting did not reflect this potentiality. Instead, the sites are highly clustered and restricted geographically.

12. Wetter conditions were primarily experienced as greater winter rainfall in the Cumberland Plateau area (Green River, Nashville Basin). Rivers would still have been shallow in late summer. Where rainfall increases came primarily in the summertime, as is the case today, shellfishing was still possible in late summer.

13. Shoals, shallow water, and shellfish were clearly still available in the Early Woodland period, as was an appetite for mollusks.

14. Molluscan records do not substantiate any significant change in water conditions, river bottoms, or species mix during the Archaic or the Woodland period.

15. It is during the era of increasing moisture and cooling temperatures that most of these heaps were initiated—after 6,000 years ago. Still, others were

founded after the arbitrarily designated end of the
Hypsithermal, e.g., after 5,500 years ago.
16. The abandonment record of these heaps is not different from what would be expected from social
decisions and very different from what is predicted
by the Hypsithermalists.

Certainly the Hypsithermal effects were time transgressive (Dye
1996), but this scenario has the Hypsithermal tiptoeing through the
mid-South. It is implausible that shellfish would be accessible on the
Cumberland River from 4270 to 2068 BP but not around the Falls of
the Ohio, or that they were available in the Wabash from 4240 to 2985
BP but not in the Ohio River, or that they would be found in beds near
Read and Bowles on the Green but not in other beds on the Green after
4,000 years ago.

There should be no room left to argue that the suite of Archaic shell
mounds of the Ohio Valley and Atlantic slope flourished and disappeared because of climatic or sea-level factors. Numerous authors have
rebuked this explanation for individual sites as well, such as at Koster
in Illinois (Brown 1977) and on the Tennessee (Lewis and Lewis 1961).
Brown (1977:172) warns "the effect of climatic change on hunter gatherers in as diverse an environment as riverine areas of the Midwest is
to lead to changes in the mix of existing strategies rather than to adopt
fundamentally different strategies." If shellfish were a staple in the diets
of the few people lucky enough to have "owned" this resource, then the
abandonment of shellfish would constitute a fundamentally different
strategy given the quantities visible today in these heaps, and the fact that
all members of a community could contribute this foodstuff. In the next
chapter I will explore in depth the data from these sites that highlight
their uniqueness and set up the probability that they began and ended
for socially determined reasons, not natural ones.

Chapter 6
Ohio River Valley
Shell-Bearing Sites: Villages?

Prior to the late 1980s, the shell mounds that are the focus of this study were assumed to be villages, lived in at least half of each year. The quantity of debris and the size of some of these accumulations were just two of the lines of evidence. The types of artifacts and features found in them were even more significant in the village logic. Places such as Carlston Annis are comprised of fire-cracked rock, sandstone, ash, charcoal, shells, fractured bones, flakes, cobbles, and various bone and stone tools. DeWeese, a neighboring shell heap, is estimated to have 17 percent shell, 6 percent sandstone, 42 percent pore space, and 34 percent matrix (Crothers 1999:206). The features suggest small cook fires, earth ovens, and storage pits—all the stuff of domestic life. The presence of shells was another expectation of villages, as they were thought to be food debris only.

There are very good reasons for interpreting these Archaic shell-heap sites as more than mere habitation areas, and the shells as representing something more than daily food collected and amassed in family-sized portions over thousands of years. The evidence I have cited in the past for these ideas were 1) the disconnect between the potential for this type of site to be found on every river in the eastern United States yet their appearance on only a few, 2) the accumulation of shells into piles instead of lineal spreads mimicking the bed, 3) accumulation of shells under difficult circumstances (such as carrying them up a bluff), 4) the often voluminous strata of clean, whole shells, 5) the occurrence of paired valves, which indicated little disturbance of parts of these heaps, as well as wasted food, 6) the large number and high density of burials, and 7) the death/rebirth symbolism that is known to be accorded shells later in time. I have discussed each of these points of contention in previous publications (e.g., Claassen 1991, 1996), and some of them in Chapter

3 in this study. There are other aspects of these heaps that raise doubts about their assumed function and should be added to the list: 8) the volume and stratigraphy of the heaps, 9) the quantity of dog burials, 10) the numbers and proportions of artifacts, 11) the type of grave goods, 12) the number of violent deaths, and 13) the characteristics of the initial burials. Each of these new topics will be discussed in some detail at this time.

Heap Construction and Volume

The excavators and reporters of these sites referred to them as mounds, yet assumed that the mound shape was inconsequential. Bringing shellfish to a central spot, however, when this resource occurs linearly in beds (see Chapter 3) suggests otherwise. Both construction evidence—layers of clean, whole shells—and the monumentality of these sites have received little attention and deserve more.

Clean Shell Layers

Recent attention has been called to the intentional construction of Middle Archaic mounds using shells at several sites on the St. Johns River: Harris Creek (Aten 1999), Hontoon Island North (Randall and Sassaman 2005), and Hontoon Dead Creek (Sassaman 2005:98). Loose, clean, whole shells are also the principal constituent of Rollins, Fig Island, and many more shell rings and arcs (Ken Sassaman, personal communication, 1994). The mounds of marine shell at Horr's Island are also said to be intentionally constructed (Russo 1994a, b).

Given that shell was being used as construction material in Florida by 7,000 years ago, we must take a closer look at the midcontinent shell heaps for intentional construction clues. Layers consisting of only shell suggest little disturbance and building episodes. Such layers existed at Mulberry Creek, with four alternating pairs of shell and sand layers (Webb and DeJarnette 1942:264), as the basal layer of Long Branch (Webb and DeJarnette 1942:180), at Perry, where "layers of nearly pure shell. . . were separated by more compact layers containing silt" (Webb and DeJarnette 1942:60), and at the base of Bluff Creek (Morrison 1942) (Figure 6.1). The O'Neal site in Pickwick Basin had nine pairs of thick, clean, shell lenses alternating with ashy midden (Webb and DeJarnette 1942:Figure 37).

Figure 6.1. Bluff Creek, Alabama. 160' Profile. Human in lower right provides scale. TVA photo collection, courtesy of University of Alabama Museums, Tuscaloosa, AL.

Watson (2005) and Cridlebaugh (1986) are comfortable with shell as construction material. For instance, Watson (2005:516) offers that the "more massive shell layers [in Carlston Annis on the Green River] probably resulted from deliberate modification of the shape or size of the mound topography to improve a landing stage or to facilitate access to watercraft." Researchers need to address the question of construction activities and land modification in these sites.

Mound Volume

The largest site in Alabama on the Tennessee River covered six acres. The next largest heap covered three acres. Six sites ranged in size from two to three acres, eight were one to two acres, while 23 covered less than an acre (Morse 1967:230). But more than the area they cover, their depth and height are significant in several cases. Morrison (1942:341) describes the sites he viewed in the Pickwick Basin in northwestern

Alabama as "moderately prominent features of the river bank . . . as much as 10' higher in elevation than the surrounding land" (e.g., Figure 6.1). The O'Neal site "was a large dome rising some 8 feet above the level of the surrounding fields" (Webb and DeJarnette 1942:132). The Carlston Annis "mound is a great shell midden elliptical in outline about 350 feet maximum length and 300 feet in breadth. Its top rises to a height of 6 feet above the present surrounding surface of the valley. . . . The shell midden which is now seven and one half feet deep at the mound center diminishes in depth toward the periphery" (Webb 1950a:267).

It is appropriate at this point to raise the issue of monumentality for these heaps of shell and dirt. Mound volume is one measure of monumentality that has been applied to later earthen mounds and has been used to argue the mound-ness of the Brazilian sambaquis (Fish et al. 2006). While mound-ness has been rejected by several authors (e.g., Milner and Jefferies 1998), Marquardt and Watson (2005c:111) recently consciously chose the adjective "mounded" and listed "distinctly mounded sites" as positive support of the burial mound hypothesis.

Inspired by Blitz and Livingood (2004), who calculated and compared Mississippian mound volumes, I have calculated shell mound volume using the formula $v=.16dh(3ab+h^2)$ where a is the maximum length of the radius, b is the maximum width of the other radius, and h is height, approximating a circular or elliptical basin. (All measurements are converted into metric values.) The result is divided by 1,000 and given in Table 6.1. (Here the vertical axis is assumed to extend in only one direction from a flat top, not an entirely satisfactory solution.)

Mound volume values of between 14 (Ward) and 1.5 (Chiggerville) were generated with this formula. When we compare excavator-estimated volume with the values generated, there is satisfactory agreement. Read has a value of 4.0 (4,032 cu m), close to the volume estimated by Milner and Jefferies (1998) of 3,700, or 3.7. Likewise, the volume of Haynes in Table 6.1 is 5.1 (5,124 cu m), and that offered by the excavator is 5.3 (5,340 cu m in Crothers 1999:205). An isopach map generated by Stein (2005b) for Carlston Annis returned a volume estimate of 5,848 cubic meters (5.8), compared to the estimate of 8.4 in Table 6.1.

As seen in Table 6.1, several Archaic heaps are larger than some well-known Mississippian mounds. They are truly monumental when compared with the conical Archaic dirt mounds recently documented in Louisiana, Arkansas, and Florida of the same age and calculated with the same formula (all calculated by the author). Six of the Archaic shell heaps are larger than the largest Archaic earthen mound, which appears to be

Table 6.1. Volumes for Some Archaic, Woodland, and Mississippian Mounds (cu. m/1000) Site order is upriver.

Archaic Earthen Mounds	Vol.	Archaic Shell heaps	Vol.
Hedgepeth A	4.7	Barrett	2.8
Hillman	4.7	Bowles	6.1
Crown-Zellerbach	4.3	Indian Knoll	5.2
Monte Sano	3.9	Chiggerville	1.5
LSU Campus	3.0	Read	4.0
Frenchman Md. A	2.1	Haynes	5.1
Watson Brake Md. E	1.4	Carlston Annis	8.4
Tomoka Md. 6	1.2	DeWeese	11.0
Hedgepeth Md. B	0.2	Long Branch	9.6
Banana Bayou	0.07	Bluff Creek	6.7
Frenchman Md. B	0.06	O'Neal	8.0
Later Earthen Mounds[1]	**Vol.**	Mulberry Creek	9.6
Cahokia Monks	51.40	Smithsonia	4.0
Moundville Md. R	33.60	Little Bear Creek	3.0
Angel Md. F	20.80	Perry	5.1
Etowah Md. C	17.16	Lu86	10.8
Toqua Md. A	14.70	Whitesburg Bridge	2.2
Hiwassee Island	12.10	**Adena/Hopewell Mounds[2]**	**Vol.**
Irene primary	11.20	Chillicothe #5	19.5
Winterville G	7.70	Chillicothe #6	10.9
Anna 5	7.00	Adena #1	5.8
Lake Jackson 3	5.90	Webb & Snow #2	2.1
Hixon	5.80	Webb & Snow #3	1.1
Pevey G	3.50	Webb & Snow #4	0.1
Bear Creek	2.90	Webb & Snow #32	0.1
McKelvey	2.20		
Town Creek	2.00		

[1]Values from Blitz and Livingood 2004.
[2]Author calculated using Webb and Snow (1974:110-131) and formula of Blitz and Livingood (2004).

Lower Jackson mound at 8400m³ or 8.4 (in J. Saunders 2004). Many of these southern Ohio Valley shell heaps are also larger than the vast majority of Adena mounds recorded in Webb and Snow (1974:110–131 and Table 6.1). Given their size, it is amazing to me that a burial place on a ridgetop in Missouri with measurements of 7x9 meters "no more than 15 centimeters high" (O'Brien and Wood 1998:162) can be called a burial "mound" while we debate "mound" for these huge shell heaps with hundreds of bodies.

Based on personal experience, photographs, data in Table 6.1, and the experience of Marquardt and Watson, I retain the label of "mound" for Bluff Creek (Figure 6.1), Long Branch (Figure 6.2), Perry, Lu86, Mulberry Creek (Figure 6.3), and O'Neal on the Tennessee River in Alabama, and DeWeese, Carlston Annis, Indian Knoll, Bowles, and Read on the Green River. Based on size descriptions it would also seem that in the Falls of the Ohio River district at least Old Clarkesville, Reid, Crib, and Hornung would qualify as mounds.

I conclude from this exercise with mound volumes, and from the various excavator comments about layers of clean shell, that many of the

Figure 6.2. Working Inside Long Branch, Alabama. TVA photo collection, courtesy of University of Alabama Museums, Tuscaloosa, AL.

shell heaps qualify as monumental and have some construction phases, both of which signal a role much different than that of mundane village. Mike Russo has also argued persuasively for the monumentality of other Archaic shell-bearing sites: the shell ring complexes (2004) and the shell · mounds at Horr's Island (1994b).

Indications of Low Disturbance and Transient Use

Villages, particularly those villages occupied year-round, are scenes of a myriad of activities that churn, homogenize, break, and scatter a huge array of objects and require the construction of many different types of facilities. The shell heaps of the midcontinent, however, do not evidence the expected investment of energy into facilities observations that began with Webb and DeJarnette speaking of the Alabama sites: ·

> Such evidences [of features] were very numerous, yet there were prac-
> tically no well-constructed works which indicate any permanency of
> occupation on any small area. Fire basins were not well made or hard
> burned, but seemed to have been built to serve only the purpose of
> the moment. Areas covered with clay were not large, and the clay was

Figure 6.3. Digging Trenches in Mulberry Creek, Alabama. TVA photo collection, courtesy of University of Alabama Museums, Tuscaloosa, AL.

uneven in thickness and not very smooth on the surface. Pits containing charcoal and burned mussel shell, which may have represented "clambakes" or "barbecue holes" . . . seem to have been used only once, or but a few times at the most.

All such evidences of the use of fire seem to suggest that the type of occupancy of the shell mound might be well described as "camping." There was nothing to suggest any special care in the construction of any permanent feature in the midden. The attempt to list or describe important features in this site [Bluff Creek] emphasizes at once this transient character of all construction. (1942:104)

Webb and coauthors repeatedly attribute the disturbance of Archaic burials not to the digging of their kinsmen but to later groups (e.g., Webb and DeJarnette 1942:82). These authors offer a picture not of villages but of camps.

Villages also should show a great deal of disturbance. Despite the impression of extensive digging by Archaic users of these heaps, there are many ways in which the stratigraphy, artifacts, and features show remarkable integrity. For instance, there are only two bones with gnawing marks among the fauna examined from Carlston Annis, and only one gnawed deer bone at Read (Milner and Jefferies 1998:126). Bones also lack any signs of weathering (Glore 2005). At Bowles, only 2 percent of the fauna was classified as gnawed (Marquardt and Watson 2005a:65). These observations mean that faunal debris was not exposed on the surface for any length of time and that dogs did not roam freely over the mound. How would these conditions be possible in a village setting?

Artifact distributions also belie the image of extensive and intensive daily activities at many of these sites. Webb postulated that the atlatl parts found in general midden at Carlston Annis owed to the disturbance of graves, but the distribution of other items do not support this idea. None of the 9,679 pieces of marine shell at this site was recovered from the general midden. None of the carapace cups, none of the perforated carnassials of canines, none of the carapace fragments, none of the rostra were found outside of burials. Instead of digging distrurbance, there is a picture of much site integrity and little random digging. Again, we have evidence of short-term site use.

The numerous examples of clean, whole shell cited above mean that foot traffic and disturbance in those places were rare. The large numbers of gastropods that make up much of the matrix of the Nashville Basin, Hayes, and Ervin sites are largely whole. Archaeological excavation is identified as the source of their fragmentation in the lab (Klippel and Morey 1986:809). A number of authors have commented on finding bivalve valves still paired in lenses and in features. Warren undertook pairing in his sample from features at Widow's Creek on the Tennessee. From among 5,571 valves, 744 pairs were made for 27 percent of valves (1975:124):

> The incidence of paired valves in a unit may be taken as an indication of its depositional homogeneity; where a high percentage of pairable specimens are matched, there is reason to believe that at least part of the unit was deposited as a single, fresh accumulation with minimal post-depositional disturbance. (Warren 1975:127)

A lack of disturbance also seems evident in this remark, "At Perry some [shells] nearest the fire were burned and never eaten. The paired bivalves often remained in position above the ash layer" (Webb and DeJarnette 1948c:20).

The extent of pairing has been quantified at DeWeese (Claassen 2005), at Widow's Creek (Warren 1975), and recently at East Steuben-ville (Rollins and Dugas 2007), where 1.2 percent of the valves were paired. Pairings have been noted at Robinson (Morse 1967:137), Haynes (Morey and Crothers 1998), and several Tennessee River sites (Webb and DeJarnette 1942).

At DeWeese on the Green River, many of the shells in a 3m-long column sample were still paired when I dumped them out onto the lab table (Claassen 2005). No feature was evident at this point in the site, but the pairings in several 5cm-thick levels (25cm x 25cm) were quanti-fied. At 115cmbd, 8 of 95 values were still paired (8 percent), at 144cm 102 valves of 225 were still paired (or 45 percent), at 150cm 10 of 85 valves (or 12 percent) were still paired, and at 215cm 74 of 135 valves were still paired (55 percent). If an effort had been made to pair loose valves, no doubt the pairings would be significantly greater.

These paired individuals are not insignificant in number, accounting for 8 percent to as much as 55 percent of the shells in these proveniences. While the number of pairs appears to some authors as insignificant, it is a small miracle that any of them are still paired given the looting and bioturbation, the grave digging, and all those presumed villagers. There is no way to know now how many of the naiads were *deposited* intact. These pairs indicate that many areas of these sites saw little postdepo-sitional disturbance. How is this possible in a village? I believe they are evidence not only of little disturbance but also of wasted food.

These heaps are also not homogenized. At Read there were earth ovens and "numerous pockets of dense shell and concentrations of mostly burned and seemingly redeposited rocks" (Milner and Jefferies

1998:125). Clean shell strata have remained uncontaminated by digging or exposure at many of the sites. Differences in site contents have been noted from side to side and vertically. Webb was able to use depth below surface to examine the distributions of artifact types and burial practices at many sites. Small clay floors, large lithic workshops, and cemeteries have been defined.

George Crothers (2004:90), with a perspective garnered from excavating at several of the shell sites, describes them thus:

> Post depositional trampling and mixing of the deposits do not appear to be significant. Burial placement is random, often overlapping or intersecting earlier burials. All sites lack evidence of permanent or semipermanent structures or facilities. The two most common features are presumably the result of mass processing of resources. One is left with an impression of multiple, large-scale events, intensive collection of resources, and production and consumption of large amounts of food, but occupation that is of relatively short duration.

In a related observation, Cridlebaugh (1986) mentions a "remarkable lack of disturbed habitat species" around Penitentiary Branch that seems contrary to the expectation of a village.

This evidence, and more to be presented later, suggests to me that the activities carried out on these heaps were focused or specialized, and of short duration. In the next several sections, I will continue this line of thought through the examination of the nature of the features, the artifacts, and the fauna, and provide numerous tables and statistical tests to support the conclusions.

Features

In addition to the restricted location of these sites, mound volume, and clean shell layers suggesting construction, there are aspects of the features, the artifacts, and the fauna in these sites that also suggest that many of them were not "simply" villages where the population size and duration could explain their differences. It is unfortunate that many aspects of features and artifacts are so subjective as to mean that excavators are a weightier factor in their enumeration and recognition than is the action of people in the past.

It is often said of these shell heaps that features are few in number. The lack of features has been attributed to the homogeneous shell matrix, the homogenizing action of earthworms and other burrowing animals, to the digging activities of their residents, and to underenumeration by

WPA crews. The number of features identified at each site can be found in Appendix I. Though the number of features is higher in most modern excavations, the variety of features compares well to those identified in the WPA excavations, with the exception of postholes, which are much more commonly identified in modern excavations. Basically, old or new excavators identify lithic workshops, caches, fire features, hearth dumps, fired clay floors, limestone or fire-cracked rock clusters, several varieties of pits, and human and dog burials. Not only does this variety of features seem too narrow to encompass the activities of dozens of families engaged in dozens of household and social activities carried out over thousands of years of occupation, but the content of these features shows less variety than expected, as well. As Webb and DeJarnette noted (1942), the energy expended in the creation of facilities was minimal. Each of these feature types is suggestive of something other than villages, for they tend to be unusually frequent at shell heaps, unique to shell heaps, or occur at known ritual locations later in time. The features that are present can be interpreted as facilities associated with very short-term activities.

Anne Bader (2005:11) has concluded that two sites in the Falls area of the Ohio River were not primarily villages but were dedicated mortuary areas based on the low variety and type of features that she excavated:

> The argument for this position is based largely on the restricted types of behavior reflected by the narrow range of feature types and other material remains evident within the excavated portions of both the Meyer and KYANG sites. At Meyer, of the excavated Archaic period features, burials, smudge pits, and red stains account for nearly 75% of the total features. At the KYANG Site, burials and smudge-pits account for nearly 80% of the total features. The usual cadre of day-to-day residence-related features, such as hearths and earth ovens, storage pits, refuse pits, and other activity-specific processing areas are simply lacking or in the minority at these sites.

I conclude the same for the shell mounds in general. There is too little variety in features to convince me of village function, and the types of features found are rather unique to shell-bearing sites. One of the most distinctive types of features is the dog burial.

Dog Burials

The shell mounds contain most of the Archaic dog burials known, or 419 of 447 dogs (94 percent) and 50 percent of those dogs come from the few Green River sites excavated (Appendix I). Two late sites stand out for having 31 percent of all dogs: Read (n=65), a bluff-top site overlooking the Green River, and multicomponent Perry (n=75) on the bank of the central Tennessee River. Individually, they have more dogs than any other site anywhere in the United States during the Archaic or any other time period. (I wonder if one could not relatively date these sites within one valley based on dog burial depths.) Haag (1948:242) indicates that based on dog size alone, the Green River dogs were older than the Alabama dogs, a proposition that could be radiocarbon dated. The dogs from central Tennessee sites were not available to Haag.

Dog burial numbers and placement with human burials also suggest some site differences. Within the Green River valley, bluff-top shell-bearing sites (Ward, Baker, Jimtown Hill, Jackson Bluff, Read) have 55 percent of the dogs, while riverside shell heaps have 38 percent and shell-free mortuaries have 7 percent. Accentuating the differences between bluff-top sites and others is the fact that fewer than 10 percent of the dogs placed with a human were found in those settings, and then only at one site, Ward. In a series of Mann-Whitney U tests, the greatest number of significant differences in site traits occurs between those sites with 14 or more dog burials and those sites with no dog burials.

The central Tennessee River (Alabama) has yielded at least 129 dogs. Thirty-six dogs are known from Archaic sites on the Tennessee River in western Tennessee and 33 in the Duck, Cumberland, and Harpeth Valleys (Appendix I). There are at least five dogs in the Falls area. In addition to the dogs enumerated in Appendix I, there was one dog at Meander Scar and two dogs at Lester, one with a human, four at Black Earth without humans, and four at Dust Cave, one with a juvenile (Walker et al. 2005).

Outside the Ohio Valley, dog burials in Archaic components are uncommon. There are three dogs at Koster. There were apparently no dog burials in the Wabash, Savannah, or St. Johns sites or Atlantic and Gulf coastal saltwater shell rings. It could be that dog burial served as a cultural marker.

Given that practically no bone was reportedly gnawed at Carlston Annis (Glore 2005), where there were 29 dog burials, or at Panther Rock (Ross-Stallings 2009), where there was one dog burial, it can be assumed that dogs did not roam freely over those sites. In fact, the only localities where gnawing was noted in the original burial reports were Kay's Landing and Big Sandy, in the western Tennessee River valley, where gnawing was attributed to rodents, and on one body at Mulberry. The human burial pits were quite shallow and seemingly were within reach of a digging dog.

If Archaic dogs were kept tied up or penned, it suggests a different picture of Archaic village life than many museum displays have indicated. It suggests that breeding was controlled, a possibility noted by Warren (2004) as well, and that dogs were not serving their communities as scavengers. Even more significant, the lack of gnawing could be an indication that no dogs were kept at these heaps, that they were only buried in them. Villages without dogs?

It is also striking when examining dog burials that burial with a human is rare and seems to be confined to the Green, the Tennessee, and the Cumberland rivers. Many of these dogs show traumas that call into question their status as beloved pets. In several cases the traumas indicate that the Kentucky dogs buried with humans were pack dogs. "This mortuary treatment was preferentially applied to dogs that performed an economically important function such as pack carrying in life" (Warren 2004:247). Furthermore, differences in vertebral marginal osteophytosis in the thoracic and lumbar vertebra, and the frequency and patterning of dental pathologies, seem to indicate diet and activity differences between Illinois and southeastern dogs as well as separate breeding pools across space and time (Warren 2004:248–249). Haag (1948:211) also concluded that Green River and Tennessee River dogs came from two distinct populations.

The presence of pack dogs at riverside Green River sites and their absence at bluff-top Green River sites (where burial with a human is rare) is intriguing, as is the evidence of pack animals at Mulberry Creek, Long Branch, and Eva, but not at Perry. The two sites with the greatest number of dogs do not seem to have pack dogs. Later in prehistory and in another region, dog ownership would be exclusive to members of high-ranking lineages and dogs would be traded (Hayden 1996). Could that situation be unfolding in the southern Ohio Valley? Dog burials in quantity and burials with humans serve to distinguish the shell-bearing sites from contemporary shell-free sites.

Archaic dog burials are clearly concentrated in shell-bearing sites, particularly sites on the Green and Tennessee rivers. The large number of dogs at Read and Perry during the Late Archaic is surely suggestive of some important activity/function for those dogs and in those places. The large number of dogs in the shell heaps and not in the shell-free sites strongly suggests a significant difference in the activities conducted in those respective places.

Table 6.2 Tool Counts at Archaic Sites

Shell Site	PPk	Scrap	Pestles	Hammer	Drill	Awls	Bone/Ant. points
Tennessee River							
Eva/Eva	378	45	0	2	36	108	17
Eva/3 mile	160	16	7	2	21	110	6
Long Branch	308	?	5	?	?	?	42
Bluff Creek	268	?	3	0	?	775	511
O'Neal	259	?	1	3	0	111	12
Mulberry Creek	271	107+	5	0	15	98	60
Little Bear	433	0	10	7	0	691	132
Perry 1, 2	513+	606	?	?	?	659	713
Perry 3, 4	6,707	?	6	41	?	1,473	729
Whitesburg	1,030?	5	3	3	17	435	21
Green River[1]							
Ward	481	705	216	26	201	488	48
Barrett	253	178	58	4	61	110	11
Butterfield	252	195	55	6	38	18	1
Bowles	128	83	97	6	55	412	31
Jimtown Hill	197	165	44	77	33	?	?
Indian Knoll	9,424	?	1,439	671	?	7,338	796
Jackson Bluff	50	109	13	10	14	169	8
Chiggerville	300	x	122	30	x	635	49

(cont.)

Artifacts

The artifacts found in the Archaic Green River and Tennessee River sites, as well as in other watersheds, are taken as evidence of domestic activities at base camps. However, several authors have noted that variety in particular, and quality of some artifact categories, suggests that these loci were not base camps but were occupied for short intervals. Below, I will also point out that the proportions of tools and the quantity of tools raise problems with the village scenario, as well. Furthermore, the grave goods indicate that those individuals buried in shell mounds were distinctive from those buried in non-shell-bearing sites within the region.

Shell Site	PPk	Scrap	Pestles	Hammer	Drill	Awls	Bone/Ant. points
Read	555	350	214	39	176	607	73
Carlston Ann.	2,101	24+	284	222	18+	1,546	383
Other Sites							
Anderson	1,342	421	54	31	73	327	115?
Robinson	508	5	14	21	1	154	18
Penitentiary	294	15	0	16	43	104	14
E. Steubenvi.	201	2	8	65	12	0	0
Globe Hill	193	48	1	20	7	12	0
Riverton	161	9	65	3	11	103	11
Swan Is.	54	2	20	2	4	28	11
Robeson Hills	46	2	63	0	4	68	5
Shell-free Mortuaries							
Eva/Big Sandy	144	9	6	1	16	31	3
Ensworth	249	17	2	0	7	?	?
Parrish	587	640	123	72	175	7	0
Kirkland	70	?	21	2	?	9	0
Rosenberger	706	?	38	73	48	16	?

¹Values corrected with Watson 2005 or obtained from site files at Webb Museum

Quantities of Non-burial Artifacts

Dozens of people living in villages for hundreds of years should produce thousands of bone, antler, and stone artifacts and hundreds of pounds of manufacturing debris. The numbers of artifacts recorded in various site reports is presented in Table 6.2 by functional category. There were, indeed, thousands of items recovered. Stone bifaces total to 13,137 from the WPA reports for the Green River sites (Watson 2005:551) alone. A total of 2,058 stone tools and 1,058 bone tools were catalogued from Ward, for instance. These numbers would seem to support the village interpretation.

However, when the number of items is divided by the number of non-infants evident in the burial populations, it is hard to sustain the image of village living. For stone bifaces, the largest number of items recovered at most sites, there are often fewer than four bifaces per person (Appendix I)! Furthermore, for supposed villages with redundant activities (Pedde and Prufer 2001b:75) there are wide discrepancies between sites in the number of bifaces per adult. There are places where it is greater than 10 and other places where it is fewer than 5.2. The range at the non-shell cemetery sites is much narrower, from 4.9 to 1.6. Eva during the first component, O'Neal, Indian Knoll, Perry, Penitentiary Branch, Riverton, and particularly Anderson, have dramatically more bifaces per adult than do the other sites. If the number of bifaces is depressed significantly by collecting and removal by workmen (Phil DiBlasi, personal communication, May 2009), then the proportion of points to other tool types is even greater and the case for hunting camps made stronger. Groundstone items, discussed next, may have been subject to less removal given their weight and redundancy in form. In two cases, the number of points per non-infant was statistically significant—that of the many dog burials versus no dog burial sites, and in the case of the bluff-top sites versus the Alabama shell heaps.

Groundstone tools, essential for processing foods, medicines, and paints, are even scarcer at these "villages," particularly among the Alabama sites. When I performed the same exercise of tools per buried non-infant (Table 6.3), there was much less site variation than when bifaces were the subject, but still there was a paucity of tools. Most sites showed fewer than one item per non-infant! Considering all tools (axes, mauls, hammers, abraders, balls, pestles, nutstones, lapstones, mortars, whetstones, hoes, cylindroids, anvils, celts, groove pebbles, and bowl fragments), only four sites had more than one item per non-infant. It is a wonder that any of these scarce tools ended up in graves or caches, removed from use. Though Pedde and Prufer (2001b:75) commented that "the large numbers of pestles and their concomitant, although poorly recorded, grinding stones, indicate a heavy reliance on proto-food production" [at the Ward site] based on a count of pieces, the proportion per non-infant indicates very little individual attention to grinding. Tables 6.2, 6.3, and the ratios of bifaces per adult in Appendix I also call into question the comment by Pedde and Prufer (2001b:75) that "all major sites . . . were indeed fairly permanent settlements, representing stable and continuous communities."

Table 6.3 Groundstone Items per Non-infant.

Site	all items/	hammer/	pestles/	axes/	nutstones/	tools/
Eva/Eva	1.57	.14	0	0	.14	.93
Eva/3 mile	.50	.03	.09	0	.01	.18
Long Branch	.41	0	.06	0	0	.06
Bluff Creek	.20	0	.02	.01	0	.09
O'Neal	.25	.05	.02	0	0	.08
Mulberry	.18	0	.05	0	0	.18
Little Bear Creek	.62	.05	.08	.02	.02	.41
Perry U1	.47	0	0	t	0	.06
Anderson	2.4	.54	.95	0	.09	2.07
Barrett	..36	.01	.15	.04	.02	.28
Ward	.59	?	.39	.08	0	.55
Butterfield	.66	.04	.40	.11	.01	.62
Bowles	6.80	.35	5.70	.25	0	6.29
Jimtown Hill	8.80	4.81	2.75	.81	.06	8.50
Indian Knoll	5.24	1.10	2.30	.29	.09	4.44
Jackson Bluff		1.42	1.86	.85	0	4.14
Chiggerville	2.23	.36	1.47	.16	0	2.10
Read	1.76	.18	.99	.18	.02	1.46
Carlston Annis	3.38	.70	.87	.15	.08	2.49
Panther Rock	31.0	7.0	6.0	6.0	9.0	29.0
E. Steubenville	40.2	-	-	-	-	40.2
Riverton	34.5	.75	16.3	.25	.25	34.3
Robeson	10.9	0	7.9	.12	.12	10.7
Shell-free						
Eva/Big Sandy	.63	.05	.16	0	.03	.29
Ensworth	.33	0	.03	0	.02	.24
Parrish	1.95	.53	.96	.25	.03	1.80
Kirkland	.66	.05	.48	0	0	.56
Rosenberger	.44	.24	.02	.03	.04	.38

The numbers in Table 6.2 indicate that although these tools were types easily recognized by WPA workers in the field and lab, there were, for instance, only one mortar, two hammerstones, and no lapstones, nutstones, abrader, or axes found at Kirkland. Penitentiary Branch was excavated in 1976 and lab work was done in 1980, a time when groundstone tools were receiving much more analytical treatment than previously, yet only 3 percent of stone items recovered were groundstone tools. Few groundstone tools were recovered in other recent projects at the shell-free Ensworth (Deter-Wolf et al. 2004) and Rosenberger mortuaries (Driskell 1979:701). The SMAP project at Carlston Annis also recovered few of these items (Marquardt and Watson 2005c). Although groundstone is rare before the Middle Archaic, all of the sites in this study have Middle Archaic or later components, meaning that age of site probably is not the explanation for the differences in groundstone items. Nowhere in this set of sites are there enough tools to sustain the year-round village interpretation. Of all the criteria used to compare sites, the proportion of groundstone tools per non-infant was the single most distinctive criterion. Seven of eleven tests registered statistical significance for this proportion (see Discussion section).

Proportions of Artifact Types

In addition to the unexpectedly great numbers of bifaces found in these sites, the lithic tools and flakes do not conform to the base camp/village expectation of large tool variety and full production sequence in several of the (few) places where they have been analyzed. Eugene Futato investigated site function at Perry by examining the numbers and types of lithic tools recovered from two blocks in Unit 1, or 1,692 flaked tools. Zone E, with 658 tools, yielded 99 percent preforms, bifacial knives and points, and general bifaces. Zones D and C had only 159 items, again as preforms, points, knives, and bifaces. In zone B, points and knives are more common and other bifaces decline. Zone A, with possible post-Archaic materials, had 734 specimens, including 85 percent of the thick biface tools found in these two blocks. Based on these tool types, Futato sees a change in site function between zones C and B. "Evidence for long term, multi-purpose occupation is scarce [in the deeper zones]. The Zone A/B assemblage is much more diverse, suggesting greater residential stability. . . . 4500 BP to perhaps 3500 BP" (Futato 2002:86). In short, Futato does not agree with the standard interpretation of the Perry site as always a residential base, and hints that the same may be true of the other large shell mounds on the central Tennessee River.

Other researchers have drawn similar conclusions about site function. Germaine (1986:42) found an almost total lack of larger percussion and smaller pressure flakes in the 6,323 pieces he examined from East Steubenville, instead finding abundant cores, core reduction, and small percussion flakes in the form of expedient unifacial tools. The more sophisticated bifacial tools discarded at the site—the Steubenvilles—were not produced there. Lithic remains, then, would seem to indicate a short occupation for a few specific activities—a special activity area. Crothers (2004:93), too, remarked that there was not enough debitage given the number of finished tools to indicate on-site fabrication of them all.

The low variety of chert tools was the basis of a specialized site function and seasonal occupation interpretation for Penitentiary Branch (Cridlebaugh 1986). An expedient core and flake collection for cutting and scraping needs was seen at Carlston Annis, with no significant temporal differences (Marquardt 2005). Initial reduction and primary flaking stages accounted for 81 percent of the lithic artifacts recovered at Rosenberger, where more than 900 cores were recovered (Driskell 1979:714). Very few of the projectile points, however, showed signs of in-situ manufacture. In the few cases where lithics have been examined with site function in mind, the conclusion has been short-term, special activity loci.

In addition to the incomplete lithic sequences found at the sites discussed above, what Table 6.2 makes clear is that if the artifacts accumulated in the course of ordinary village activities, then the activities conducted at them varied considerably, contrary to the assertion by Pedde and Prufer (2001b:75) that "all the major sites . . . are to a large extent interchangeable in function." Bone and antler points were discarded/lost/cached in much larger numbers among Tennessee River dwellers in the Pickwick basin area and much less often on the Green and at sites elsewhere. Women of Alabama and Kentucky performed hide working and lost or tossed away awls more often than did their counterparts elsewhere. Women processed far more plants and minerals on the Green and men and women may have hammered and flaked there more often, as well. And everywhere, we see that men engaged rather similarly in hunting and tossing or losing their equipment. (It seems that one could make the case that during the Archaic, men's lives were far more mundane and repetitious than were women's lives.)

Activity-specific roles were accorded the Green River sites by Rolingson (1967). She saw Butterfield, with its small quantity of shells, as dominated by projectile points and therefore to be a hunting camp. Kirkland had a high proportion of milling tools (yet few in number) and was probably a nutting station. Barrett had many ornaments and milling tools, so it was likely to have been a base camp. Ward, on a bluff but with considerable quantity of shell and with its high number of perforators and its low number of projectile points, was thought to be a living site. Winters (1974) interpreted some of the Green River sites differently than Rolingson. He developed a ratio of points to processing/domestic tools for Green River sites and for several caves. Barrett, Kirkland, Butterfield, and Smith Cave all had less than one point per domestic item and were put in the habitation category. Chiggerville (2.7) and Ward (2.6) had greater numbers of points than would be expected at villages. Where Rolingson had Ward as a living site, Winters saw it as a hunting base.

Both Lewis and Lewis (1961) and Magennis (1977) interpreted Eva as a hunting camp, and the same was offered for Butterfield (Winters 1969:134). Eva has an extreme paucity of domestic and entertaining tools, lots of general utility, fabricating, and processing tools, and a lack of pits and postholes, (Magennis 1977:34). One thing that bothered Winters about a hunting camp interpretation for Eva was the number of burials. I concur.

Other than projectile points, few items of chert were found at Penitentiary Branch. Winters (1969:131) found that tools outnumbered weapons 4.3/1 to 8/1 in the four levels of Robeson Hills. Swan Island and Riverton were 2.2/1 and 1.2/1, respectively. Eva and Modoc rock shelter were swamped with weapons, their ratios being 0.3/1–0.8/1 at Eva, bottom to top, and 0.8/1 to 2.6/1 to 0.3/1 at Modoc, bottom to top. At Stanfield-Worley there was nothing but weaponry by Winters's definition.

In many cases, then, the proportion of artifact categories, as well as their numbers, does not support the idea of villages. (Believing as I do that there are no "villages" in the Archaic, there are no "villages" to use for comparison.) Instead, we have the basis for interpreting most of the shell heaps as special activity areas. Burial was one of the consistent activities. It is possible that, rather than many different site functions (nutting, hide processing, hunting base, etc.), these shell-bearing sites had but one function: world renewal. The variability in artifact numbers and proportions from site to site would reflect not different on-site activities but differences stemming from offerings and ritualized tool renewal activities. That is to say that most of the items found in these places were simply discarded at them. I am proposing that rather than constituting largely primary refuse, the artifacts found in these sites are a mixture of both secondary "refuse"—offerings and cleanings—and primary refuse generated during short-term encampments. The archaeological practice of deducing on-site activities from discarded artifacts may be inapplicable in these settings.

It was the analysis of projectile point styles that led Martha Rolingson (1967) to conclude that the large number of styles must mean short occupations over hundreds of years. Little time investment in tool shaping, a narrow range of tools, and the implied activities do not support many authors' vision of the large shell heap sites as year-round villages.

Grave Goods

Another category of artifacts, for which the shell heaps have been scrutinized over the decades, is grave goods. Confusion abounds over what is and is not a grave good, what was and was not intentionally associated, and what was and was not embedded in the body at the time of burial. Webb discussed the evidence for atlatls (e.g., 1939) and medicine bags (1950a:336–343) in burials. Other authors have struggled to find social meaning in the presence and absence of items and concluded contradictorily that Indian Knoll society was "egalitarian," or that there was ascribed status given that infants were buried with exotic grave goods.

Rolingson (1967) commented that it was typical in Green River sites to find a single "rich" burial, not a multitude, and my own evaluation supports that observation. Appendix I presents the percentage of burials with grave goods for each site, as well as the average number of grave goods when they do occur. Not only does the number of grave goods serve to distinguish an individual at each site, this number was statistically significant in six comparisons (out of 11) of various groupings of sites.

The most distinctive grave goods when comparing regions or types of sites (rather than the typical comparison of individuals at one site) were items of marine shell, the use of heavy items (groundstone items), and projectile points. These traits in grave goods distinguished the large riverside shell heaps from shell-free sites and bluff-top sites, as well as sites with no dog burials and sites on tributaries.

Perhaps distinctive grave goods served to distinguish social differences not at the individual level, within burial populations, but groups of individuals, those buried at monumental riverside shell heaps, and those buried elsewhere. Perhaps the grave goods reflect particular rituals held at the time of burial. Rather than assume that marine shell, for instance, found with infants signals ascribed status, it is possible that ceremonies conducted for rainfall or cave-dwelling spirits required both shell and infant sacrifice.

Burial Populations and Practices

A remarkable aspect of the sites on the Green, the Tennessee, the central Ohio, and the St. Johns rivers was their use as repositories for the dead over presumably long periods of time given their depths. In contrast, none of the coastal shell rings contain bodies and none of the Archaic shell heaps on the Hudson River have revealed skeletons. (Several heaps on the Tennessee in Alabama, many of the bluff-top sites, and a few shell-bearing sites on the Ohio have very few burials, and several riverside sites on the Savannah have no more than two burials.) In addition to riverside shell-bearing sites, the burial needs of these people were also met with the use of shell-free mortuaries, often situated quite near the shell-bearing mortuaries (e.g., Rosenberger, Kirkland, Ensworth, Meyer). The number of dead, the amount and type of violence, and the characteristics of the initial burials further the point that these places were not ordinary villages.

The Number of Dead

The Tennessee River and Green River shell-bearing sites and mounds are world famous for the number of dead interred in many of them. Nevertheless, calculating the actual number of bodies is not a simple act. It is possible to say that there was a minimum of 2,699 bodies accounted for in published Green River sites during WPA work (Watson 2005:519) and at least 1,386 shell mounder bodies removed from Pickwick Basin and from Wheeler Basin sites, for a published WPA total of 4,085. Hofman (1986) offered a total of 3,139 bodies, of which 2,497 had useful data. Since the WPA and TVA excavations, there have been new excavations at old sites and new sites and laboratory analyses that have identified additional skeletons. Based on the numbers of burials given in Appendix I, I can offer a minimal count of 7,259 people in shell-bearing sites and 616 in the shell-free sites I have used for comparison.

This figure for the shell-bearing sites is still a gross underestimate of the number of dead interred in them, even admitting that some of those included in the count are not Archaic in age. (I have omitted non-Archaic bodies in the counts where that number was evident.) Bodies were viewed but left undug and uncounted in several places. Meindl et al. (2001:102) project a possible 2,300 bodies left at Ward, 500 at Read, 1,100 at Butterfield, 1,850 at Carlston Annis, 1,950 at Indian Knoll, and 1,950 at Barrett, a total of 9,650 estimated bodies. The 62 bodies removed at O'Neal were "but a very small part of the hundreds that were evidently in this huge midden" (Webb and DeJarnette 1942:135). Bodies remain unexcavated and uncounted at Ervin (100 to 135 more, Hofman 1986) and Anderson. The count of bodies in Widow's Creek and in most of the Falls of the Ohio sites is unknown. No counts are available for several sites in Appendix I. The count does not include the unreported number of bodies uncovered by the excavations of Funkhouser and Webb (1928) and Moore (1916) (296 bodies from Indian Knoll, 17 from Bluff City, 16 from Yankee, five from Smallhous).

Subsequent WPA laboratory work seems to have tallied not the 667 Archaic bodies reported in the two Perry site reports (Webb and DeJarnette 1942, 1948c) but 1,027 bodies judging from the burial cards, an addition of 360 dead, although many of these may not be Archaic. I will assume that half of the additional bodies (n=180) are Archaic for the purposes of constructing a count. Burial cards for Ward also indicate an actual count of 465 bodies, not the 433 reported, augmenting the count by 32 more bodies.

Since those counts were made, new excavations have increased the counts on the Green River by 11 from Carlston Annis, five at the Bowles site (both sites reported in Marquardt and Watson 2005b), and by 11 at Whitesburg Bridge on the Tennessee River (Matthew Gage, personal communication). Newly recognized skeletons have emerged from recent reexaminations in the Green River site collections. From Read come 21 more bodies (Herrmann 1990) and four more in the analysis of Ward (Meindl et al. 2001:91).

Finally, there are dozens of shell-bearing Archaic sites on the Green River, in Ohio and Indiana, and on the Tennessee River that surely incorporate bodies but have never been tested, and shell-bearing sites with reports that I have overlooked or chosen not to include, such as Calhoun (16), Barnard (150), Smithsonia Landing (six), Meander Scar (two), Union Hollow (16), Georgetown Landing (nine), Pride 1Ct17 (nine), and Mason 1Li36 (28).

Adding the additional 829 known burials gives a new total of 8,188 known bodies in shell-bearing sites. Adding the estimated 9,750 missing burials tallied here moves that count to more than 17,938 bodies! Thousands of bodies remain uncounted. Can there be any doubt that shell-bearing sites were the primary mortuary facilities for people during the Archaic in the southern Ohio Valley? They even may have been the mortuaries for people living beyond this region.

Calculation of burials per square meter was usually dependent on my estimation of the area excavated (Appendix I). Burial densities in the shell-free mortuary sites, particularly at Ensworth, Meyer, and Rosenberger, ranged from one burial every seven square meters to one per 35 square meters, generally lower than in the Green riverside shell-bearing mortuaries. Riverside shell-heap densities were as high as one body every three square meters to one every 15 square meters. The lowest density was found at bluff-top shell-bearing sites with a range of one to four square meters up to one to 176 square meters. The densities are quite low for the Wabash and upper Ohio River shell-bearing bluff-top sites as well.

The number of dead occasionally served to distinguish, statistically, the large riverside shell heaps when compared to sites with no dogs, bluff-top sites, and shell-free sites. The numbers of dead also differed significantly when bluff-top sites and shell-free sites were compared. Burial density was one of only three traits that differed between early and late shell-bearing sites and one of four traits of significance when comparing Green and Tennessee riverside shell heaps.

Demography of the Dead

Many archaeologists have noted different burial programs at much later Mississippian ritual precincts versus village cemeteries with infants absent in the former but present in the latter. Our understanding of Mississippian social stratification is predicated on these differential burial programs. Archaic societies, however, are assumed to have been "egalitarian" within each group and basically undifferentiated among groups. There are numerous examples in the skeletal populations of shell-bearing Archaic sites, however, of populations that have fewer than the expected number of infants. This suggestion of a differential burial program is most intriguing and suggests that these heaps received a subset of the dead.

When a burial assemblage deviates from the expected demographic profile, bioarchaeologists typically have attributed the problem to preservation, often infant underenumeration. In published mortality-centered approaches to demography like all of those published before 1998 (McCaa 12003), which are based on life tables, the perceived "problem" with the age pyramid is "corrected" mathematically. It is a misapplication of uniformitarianism, however, for workers to fit a prehistoric population to a model life table (typically a demographic profile from a village from later times) because deviations from the expectations tell us about population differences.

Earlier applications of aging criteria and the life tables have flaws. Aging criteria based on cranial sutures is now known to be unreliable and incapable of identifying individuals older than 50. Mortality-centered tables like the Kohl and Demeny life tables of 1983 or the West models rely upon regressions that force the data into a preponderance of deaths between ages 35 and 50 that will mirror the village population reference sample.

Herrmann (1990) found an additional 21 bodies, many of them infants, when reexamining the Read skeletons. When he recalculated ages, most of the deviation from Webb (1950b) was in the infant and the young adult categories. There were, therefore, two sources of the increase in the number of infants: skeleton discovery in the lab and the application of modern aging criteria. These modes of correcting infant underenumeration are far preferable to mathematical manipulations that make it impossible to identify the social processes at work. Until skeletal populations are reexamined, modern aging criteria employed, and a fertility-centered approach (McCaa 2003) applied, it will only be possible to highlight suggestions of burial programs.

The suggestion of selective criteria for who is buried in a shell heap is quite strong at several sites. Harris Creek on the St. Johns yielded no fetuses, newborns, or toddlers (Aten 1999). Meindl et al. (2001:92) said "there is no reason to suspect a differential loss of skeletons by age class" at Ward, on a tributary of the Green River in Kentucky, where "there was relatively lower infant mortality and higher adult mortality" than predicted (Meindl et al. 2001:94–95). The skeletal analyst at Anderson, in central Tennessee, where special care was expended to recover infants, concluded that the recovered population did not represent a general cross section of the population who probably used the locus (Joerschke 1983:29). Magennis (1977:137) concluded that Eva did not have not a representative population, given the few infants. Lewis and Lewis (1961), in fact, found a statistically significant difference in age groups represented in the Big Sandy component at Eva, caused by a marked decrease in infants. Negligible infant underenumeration was asserted for the skewed older population at Indian Knoll (Mensforth 2005:461). We have several highly suggestive cases that the people brought to these places for burial were not a random cross section of those who died. There are other indications that this was the case, to which I turn now.

Table 6.4 Site-Specific Evidence of Violence (Number of bodies; blanks indicate no examination to date)[1]

Site	scalp	decap.	trophy taken	trophy deposit	embed	CDI	fractures
Eva/Eva		0	0	0	0		
Eva/3 mile	1	0	2	0	1		6
Big Sandy	1	2	8	2	0	1	
Cherry	0	0	0		2	0	
Kay's Lndg.	1	1	8	2	0	4	
Long Branch	1	3	1	1	2	4	15
Bluff Creek		3	1	1	4	7	
O'Neal	0	0	0	0	2	0	22
Mulberry (MA)	0	0	1	0	4	0	1
Mulberry (LA)	1	2	1	0	2	10	
Perry U1	0	8	2		1	2	
Lu86		4	0		0	4	
Hayes		0	0	0	0		
Anderson		0	0		1		22
Hermitage Sp.		0	0	1	2	2	15
Robinson		2?	0	0	0		
Ward	3	6	3	0	6	1	2
Barrett	0	0	0	0	2	13	3
Butterfield	0	0	0		0		

(cont.)

Violent Deaths

Violent deaths—individuals who were headless, missing body parts, or with embedded points—have recently been recognized at several of the shell heaps. Maria Smith (1993, 1995, 1996) and Robert Mensforth (2001, 2005, 2007) have investigated violence on the lower Tennessee River and the Green River, respectively. Violent deaths were tallied for 11.3 percent of Ward, 6.5 percent of Indian Knoll, and 5 percent of Carlston Annis burials (Mensforth 2005:467). These percentages are relatively high for Archaic populations and suggest, along with the other phenomena discussed prior to this section, that the shell heaps were often the burial locus designated for those killed at the hands of others. In the

Site	scalp	decap.	trophy taken	trophy deposit	embed	CDI	fractures
Jimtown Hill			1	1			
Chiggerville	0	3	2	1	0		
Bowles		2	3	0	1	1?	
Indian Knoll	1	13	12	30	8	2	72
Jackson Bluff		0	2	1	0		
Baker		0	0	3?	0		
Read	0	2	2	1	0	0	?
Carlston Annis	1	10	8	0	5	10	11
KYANG		2	0	6	3		
Panther Rock	0	0	1	0	1		
McCain		1	0	0	0		
E. Steubenville		0	0	0	1		
Robeson Hills		1	0		1		
Riverton		0	0		2		
Shell-Free Sites							
Eva/Big Sandy	0	1	1	0	1	0	0
Ensworth	0	0	1	0	0		
Meyer		1	0		1		
Bluegrass		1	?	1	1		1
Parrish		1	3	2	1		

[1] I have made my own counts from Alabama sites, so the figures here will differ occasionally from those offered by Mensforth (2007). Chiggerville and the lower Tennessee River sites are judgments based on NAGPRA files or WPA burial forms.

pages that follow, I will outline the types of violence and the numbers of people so treated, and look closely at the affected burials to uncover several new indications of violent deaths. Table 6.4 has been prepared to summarize the data of Smith and Mensforth, augmented with my own interpretation of the burial descriptions from the various reports and burial forms. In numerous cases, it is clear that the interpretation of these burial populations and sites as highly disturbed by WPA excavators comes from a failure to recognize that the bodies were missing body parts when interred. Because of the general confusion about bodies missing parts, site disturbance, and bundle burials, I have chosen not to deal with "secondary burials" in this study.

TYPES OF VIOLENCE

Skull injuries (CDIs) that were lethal are rare in those groups that have been investigated—one being recorded at Indian Knoll. Instead, many people survived skull injuries, as seen in the Green River populations, where men were twice as likely as women to experience this trauma, and in two sites in the Tennessee River valley where women were so injured more often. CDIs were found in 14.4 percent of the 443 Indian Knoll skulls examined, 9.2 percent of Ward, and 4.6 percent of Carlston Annis crania, for a grand total of 10.7 percent of the 917 skulls examined (Mensforth 2005). Because the majority of cranial depression injuries were trivial ones, in Mensforth's estimation (2001:121–122) the implied violence appears to have been well controlled.

Evidence of scalping, which usually was lethal, has been gathered by Smith and Mensforth for Tennessee, Kentucky, and Ohio groups (Mensforth 2005:467). One individual each from three Late Archaic sites appears to have been scalped, out of a cranial sample of 201 adults from seven populations in western Tennessee (Table 6.4). These victims were three males: one 25–35 years old, one 50+ years old, and one of indeterminate age. This latter individual from Big Sandy also lacked forearms (Smith 1995:63–64). The single scalping victims at Indian Knoll and Carlston Annis were both male. One subadult at Long Branch showed scalping marks. Two scalped females were identified among six Archaic burials in Watts Cave in Kentucky (Mensforth 2007). To date, the number of scalping victims identified in the sites covered here are but ten.

Bone fractures of the face and lower arms can be evidence of violence. Many of the bone fractures were healed when burial occurred, however, suggesting that attacks potent enough to result in death were uncommon.

Missing body parts from a skeleton in a grave could be the result of trophies taken by the murderer before burial of the victim. Trophies were taken as part of torture, proof of victory, to enhance prestige (Smith 1996), and as amulets. Trophies taken from victims of Green River and Tennessee River folks were heads, entire limbs, partial limbs, all limbs of one side, hands, and feet. In some cases only a torso was interred (e.g., Read, Bowles). Isolated body part disposal such as that of skulls and long bones, may reflect trophy decommissioning. These victims and body part disposal may most often be reflected in the WPA burial category "disturbed" (e.g., Webb and DeJarnette 1942:244).

Embedded points, both stone and antler, are the clearest evidence of a violent death. Webb (1974:204) observed that flint or antler points were positioned in the grave to suggest the cause of death for 23 Indian Knoll individuals. Mensforth discovered 44 penetration or puncture wounds in the Green River sample, 37 of which had no bone healing (2001:120–121). Two percent of Archaic Perry site individuals had embedded points (Bridges et al. 2000). Many more examples are tallied in Table 6.4.

Statistically significant differences in number of bodies with embedded points were found in tests of several pairings of sites. Differences were noted between the Alabama heaps and those sites grouped as Nashville Basin, lower Tennessee River, bluff-top sites, and shell-free sites. Significant differences in embedded point occurrence was also noted when the monumental sites (Table 6.1>4.0) were compared to the small sites.

Group burials often prove to have at least one member with an embedded point and or missing body parts, suggesting that all members of the group died violently. At Cherry, a multiple burial of three adults contained two with embedded points (Magennis 1972:78). Violent deaths were evident in 33.3 percent of Indian Knoll multiple burials, in 46.2 percent of Ward multiple burials, and in 36.4 percent of Carlston Annis multiple burials.

> The ratios of definite victims relative to the total number of individuals included in each multiple grave for these three sites are as follows: IK 1/6, 1/4, 2/4, 2/2, 2/2, 2/2; Ward 1/6, 1/4, 2/5, 2/4, 4/5, 2/2); Carlston Annis 1/3 and 3/4. Nine of the 14 (64.3%) multiple graves listed here for the three Kentucky Late Archaic sites contained two or more definite victims of violent death. Among the 53 bodies interred in the 14 multiple graves of interest, 26 (49.1%) exhibited clear evidence of lethal perimortem violent injury. (Mensforth 2001:117)

Group burials are common in the shell heaps and suggest a large number of unrecognized victims.

REGIONAL AND TEMPORAL PATTERNS IN VIOLENCE

While Smith found that Cherry and Eva displayed evidence of violence, the other six sites combined that she examined from western Tennessee had but 1.2 percent violent deaths (Smith 1996:144). None of the Early Woodland components in this area showed much evidence of violence, either. Farther upriver, Perry, a multicomponent site with one of the highest counts of violent deaths, had decapitations throughout the deposits, but with a number of cases coming from Mississippian burials.

From upper Ohio River Archaic sites (159 bodies) came two scalpings (a male and a female), a few cranial injuries, no decapitations or dismemberments, and nine extra skulls, eight occurring as grave goods. At Frontenac in New York (4930+/-260 rcy, but generally 4700–3200 for Mast Culture, Fagan 2005), four males had projectile point injuries, four males had CDIs, two male skeletons consisted of torsos only, and seven males were missing both their heads and some limbs. Like the situation at Carlston Annis, two women were missing heads but no other body parts (Mensforth 2007).

Bridges et al. (2000) looked at northern Alabama skeletons for evidence of violence. Two percent of Archaic Perry burials, 8 percent of Late Woodland individuals from 1Pi61, and no individuals from either of two Mississippian sites had embedded projectile points. Farther up the Tennessee River, Smith (2003:311) found six individuals from Late Mississippian–era levels in the Chickamauga Reservoir to have embedded projectile points. Violence was far more obvious in the Archaic sites.

Other Possible Indications of Violent Death: Body Positioning

Not all violent deaths will be evident—marked by head wounds, missing body parts, or embedded points. There is some suggestion that body positioning is also a clue to violent death (raiding, sacrifice, or family decree) or status as Other. Burial positions of interest are on the back flexed, on the face flexed, headfirst into a pit, stacking, and the extended position. Many bodies with embedded points are buried in these postures.

FLEXED ON THE BACK

Watson (2005:557) counted 458 bodies on their backs from seven Green River sites, to which should be added 24 from Chiggerville, for a total of 482. This number amounts to 36 percent of the 1,336 Green River burials with positioning information (excluding infants). At least two circumstances related to death seem to warrant burial on the back, and those are violent death, per se, and childbirth deaths. There is apparently at least one other situation that accounts for placing a flexed body on the back that is unknown at this time.

Looking at Table 6.5, we see that 40 percent of the violence obvious on Indian Knoll and Carlston Annis burials is found on bodies interred on their backs. Moore (1916) describes seven bodies, all with something or someone included in the grave and one lacking several body parts. Jackson Bluff's Bu12, the only body found there on its back, was missing the right hand.

Flexed burials on the back are also found in the other river valleys under discussion. Bluff Creek's Bu60 was headless, flexed on back with human awls, human teeth, and fox jaw inclusions. At Vaughn Mound (shell bearing) in Mississippi, there are two flexed on-the-back burials, both men. One had a twisted head and the feet were missing (Atkinson 1974:124). Other examples of violence associated with this position could be mustered, but the conclusion remains the same—the on-the-back position has strong associations with violent death, including death in childbirth. For example, all five of the adult women with fetal remains at Indian Knoll were placed on their backs, a woman with newborn at Hayes was on her back, and a woman with infant at Rosenberger was extended on her back.

EXTENDED ON BACK OR ON FACE

Extension is a rare burial position in Archaic sites of the southern Ohio Valley. One possible explanation for its occurrence among infants is the use of the cradleboard, suggested by Lewis and Lewis (1961), as well as others before them but negated by Dowd (1989:78). If burial on a cradleboard is the reason behind extended burials, then this device was possibly present as early as the Hayes site's burials.

There is also evidence that corpse extension of adolescents and adults during the Archaic, in either the face-down or face-up position, was a sign of violent death. Ten extended bodies were noted at Mulberry Creek. Three of them had been thrown into a pit (Shields 2003). Each had an embedded point. Among the other extended bodies were several headless ones. Seventy percent of the extended bodies had grave goods, whereas most bodies at Mulberry Creek did not.

Unit 2 of the Perry site contained four extended burials between 4.5'bs and 5.5'bs. Two bodies had grave goods and one also lay face down and lacked feet (Bu305). From Robeson Hills, on the Wabash River, comes one record of a male extended on his back with an embedded point. Another male was found extended in a large refuse pit. The single extension at KYANG had been decapitated and the head placed on the ground, the legs splayed, and the vertebrae scattered in an arc

Table 6.5 Burial Positions of Violent Deaths at Indian Knoll and Carlston Annis[1]

Position	decap.	scalp	embed.	dismem.	CDI	Total violence	percent of treatment
Indian Knoll (counts)							
Flexed on back	7	0	2	5	0	40%	14/162=9
Flexed on face	0	0	2	0	0	6%	2/38=5
Flexed on right	2	0	3	3	0	23%	8/183=4
Flexed on left	1	0	0	1	0	6%	2/158=1
Sitting	0	0	0	0	0	0%	0/3=0
Extnd. on back	1	0	0	0	0	3%	1/9=11
Unknown	1	1	1	3	2	23%	
Totals	12	1	8	12	2	100%	
Multiples	2	1	2	5	1	31%	
Carlston Annis (counts)							
Flexed on back	3	0	3	3	1	40%	10/55=18
Flexed on face	0	0	0	0	0	0%	0/1=0
Flexed on right	4	1	1	4	0	40%	10/118=9
Flexed on left	2	0	0	0	0	8%	2/91=2
Sitting	1	0	0	0	0	4%	1/7=14
Extnd. on back	0	0	0	0	0	0%	0/2=0
Unknown	0	0	1	1	0	8%	
Totals	10	1	5	8	1	100%	
Multiples	1	1	3	1	0	24%	

[1]Infants are deleted from number, found in Watson 2005:556.

outside the body. Lacking evidence of violence in Tennessee River sites are the three extended bodies at O'Neal, five bodies at Lu86, one in Perry U3/4, two at Whitesburg Bridge, and one at Eva.

Extended bodies also appear in several Green River heaps. Records from Read indicated that in a group of four bodies, three (one male and one female at least) were extended on their backs; none had grave goods. The fourth member of the group, a subadult, was extended on the face in shell. Three extended non-infants at Barrett were annotated. One was approximately three years old, with shell beads and red ocher. An extended adult about 21 years old had a plethora of grave goods (Bu1) and from the photo, appears to be lacking the right hand. The third extended person was 30 years old, male, with an embedded point and several offerings.

At Indian Knoll four males 25–28 years old (Bu 611–612–613–614) were extended and in a group, with many goods. One was headless. The age distribution for extended bodies at Indian Knoll is almost the opposite of that for the flexed on-the-face position, suggesting that age may have figured in at least these two burial positions.

In summary, there is reason to consider the on-the-back position—extended or flexed—as one reflecting a violent death. Looking at Table 6.5, we see that there were a total of 35 violent acts recorded at Indian Knoll (omitting fractures and assuming that missing heads resulted from violence), and 40 percent of those are registered on bodies buried on their backs, whether extended or flexed, 9 percent of all bodies in that posture. Twenty-five lethal acts of violence are recorded for Carlston Annis (Table 6.5), also with 40 percent of those acts registered on bodies reclining on their backs, or 18 percent of all bodies buried flexed and on the back. Furthermore, at Indian Knoll, 31 of 108 bodies in multiple burials were placed flexed on the back and four more were extended on their backs. Multiple burials have been shown to be highly suggestive of violent deaths. One type of multiple burial is the mother and fetus. Five adults found with fetal remains in the WPA excavations were buried on their backs, presumably childbirth deaths.

From Carlston Annis come 81 bodies buried on their backs. Ten, or 12 percent, are bodies with clear indications of violent deaths, another 12 percent are women who may have died in childbirth, 29, or 36 percent are infants possibly buried on cradleboards, while two others were on their backs in groups who had evidence of violent death. Omitting the infants, at least 12, or 15 percent, and possibly as many as 27 percent of the bodies placed on their backs derived from violent deaths, including

Table 6.6 Additional Possible Violent Deaths (Body Counts)[1]

Site	# obvious[2]	# extended	# flex face	# flex back	multiples	# other[3]	% total
Eva/Eva (14)	0	1	1	0	1	0	21
Eva/3 mi. (82)	4	1	11	9	8	2	43
Big Sandy (55)	11	1	4	2	0	2	36
Kay's Lndg. (74)	10	0	1	19	6	0	47
Cherry (?)	2	1	?	?	10	?	?
Long Branch (77)	7	4	6	23	0	1	52
Bluff Creek (110)	8	1	6	32	0	0	43
Mulberry MA (11)	5	1	0	0	0	0	55
Mulberry LA (64)	6	0	0	0	0	0	9
O'Neal (48)	2	2	0	4	3	0	23
Perry U1 (113)	11	2	3	43	18	1	69
Little Bear (116)	0	2	?	?	6	?	7+
Hayes (3)	0	0	0	1	0	0	33
Hermitage (223)	2	10	18	?	24	1	25+
Robinson (51)	2	0	1	3	0	0	12
Penitentiary (16)	0	0	1	3	1	0	31
Anderson (57)	1	0	1	5	2	0	16
Barrett (91)	2	19	1	32	0	0	59
Bowles (17)	6	0	0	0	4	0	56
Butterfield (40)	0	1	0	8	0	0	21
Jackson Bluff (6)	2	0	0	0	0	0	33
Indian Kn. (617)	34	8	36	151	24	0	41
Chiggerville (72)	5	2	0	12	10	2	43
Baker (4)	0	0	0	1	0	0	25

(cont.)

Site	# obvious[2]	# extended	# flex face	# flex back	multiples	# other[3]	% total
Read (217)	4	6	0	55	?	0	30
Carlston An. (318)	24	2	1	37	8	0	23
KYANG (28)	5	0	0	2	9	0	57
Panther Rock (1)	1	0	0	0	0	0	100
McCain	1	0	0	6	6	0	67
E.Steuben-ville(6)	1	0	0	0	0	0	17
Robeson Hill (8)	2	1	0	0	3	0	75
Riverton (4)	2	0	0	0	0	0	50
Shell-free Mortuaries							
Eva/BS (38)	3	0	3	4	0	0	26
Ensworth (47)	1	0	2	7	4	0	30
Parrish (132)	5	0	0	?	26	2	25+
Rosenburger (174)[4]	0	6	0	0	49	0	31
Meyer (27)	2	0	2	?	0		15
Railway (17)[5]	?	?	?	?	?	2	12+
Habich (27)[5]	?	?	?	?	11	?	40+
Bluegrass (19)	1	3	0	?	11	0	79+

[1]Percentage does not include burials lacking information about position, trophy part deposits, or infants. No body was double counted.
[2]Includes embedded points, scalping marks, missing trophy parts. Does not include body part deposits.
[3]Dismembered, stacked, headfirst, grave too short, or head/torso twisted. Will not be double counted.
[4]Count includes indeterminate positions and infants in groups. Groups of Adult+infant excluded.
[5]Percentage includes bodies with no information.

childbirth deaths. Childbirth deaths are themselves a category of violence given the blood and pain associated, and were equated with death in battle by the Aztecs (Furst 1995:178–179).

An anomalous observation is the high frequency of extended burials found at (shell-free) Carrier Mills among the Middle Archaic burials. Thirty-eight of 124 non-infant individuals (31 percent) were in this position. No other Archaic population in this study has this high a percentage of extended burials (Table 6.6). Given that 1) 50 percent of the Woodland-period burials at Carrier Mills were interred in the extended position, 2) two-thirds of Woodland burials at Carrier Mills were found on their backs, and 3) that the percentage of Archaic extended burials is highly unusual, I suspect that a significant number of the Middle Archaic extended burials may actually be post-Archaic burials. For this reason, Black Earth/Carrier Mills data are not included in this study.

THE FLEXED AND FACE-DOWN POSITION

The "frog" position, as Webb refers to it, or squatting position, also bespeaks submission, disrespect, rejection, and a possible position for sacrifice. Long Branch and Indian Knoll stand out for their high percentage of individuals buried in this position, as does the shell-bearing Vaughn burial mound in northeastern Mississippi (Atkinson 1974). The case for an association of this burial position with violence or death at the hand of another person can be made with several examples. Eva's Bu75 and Bu102 are head down or face down, with body parts missing. Long Branch's Bu36 is headless and Bu2, a woman in this position, had two broken arms, nine broken ribs, and a CDI. Bowles Bu4, a male 25–29 years old, was flexed face down and partially dismembered. Grave goods were plentiful (Marquardt and Watson 2005a:61). Bluff Creek had four such burials, two of whom were in a multiple burial. No violence is apparent in several other face-down burials, such as the four flexed, on-face burials found in Unit 1 at Perry. Bu38 at Long Branch was part of a deposit that contained a cremation with many grave goods.

Moore annotated four bodies at Indian Knoll (Watson 2005:617–619) lying on their fronts while flexed, all four with grave goods (Bu160, 161, 164, 170)—two with atlatls, one with clay, coal, and carapace, and one with lots of shell beads and hairpins. When combined with the data recorded by Webb, there were 54 bodies at Indian Knoll found squatting on their faces: eight were in group burials and one had an embedded point, suggesting that nine were associated with violence. Among the remaining bodies, two individuals were buried with dogs, 16 had grave goods, and one had red ocher (one body double counted).

HEAD-TWISTED POSITION

Attention should be called to burials in which the individual had been placed on the back but then either the skull or the spine had been turned 180 degrees, forcing the face down. Examples can be seen at Long

Branch, Mulberry Creek, Anderson, Vaughn, and Indian Knoll Bu93 (Moore 1919). Bu194 at Eva (Three Mile) was also twisted, the skull was reversed, and the right arm and leg were missing. All of these cases appear to be Middle Archaic or early Late Archaic in age. Again, I see a symbolic act, possibly one of violence associated with the treatment of at least the corpse, if not the live person. I will return to this burial type in Chapter 8.

Revised Counts of Violent Deaths

In the previous section, I have proposed that various minority burial positions—burial on the back, flexed burials on the face, and the head-twisted position—often resulted from violent deaths. To this list should be added all members of group burials (including stacked bodies), for they often include at least one member who has obvious evidence of violence. That would leave the flexed-on-left or -right as the "normal" burial positions, a regularity suggested by other authors as well, such as Magennis (1977:79), for Eva/Big Sandy level and Cherry, where 79 percent and 70 percent, respectively, of burials were buried in these positions. I am proposing that burial positioning is often related to the circumstances at the time of death during the Archaic. To the estimate of individuals whose burial treatment reflects their cause of death for each site given in Table 6.6, I could also add those who have been cremated, those with red ocher, and those weighted down with rocks.

I believe that all of the bodies treated in the above-mentioned ways have a burial procedure determined by their cause of death or circumstances surrounding their deaths. Such association between burial treatment and cause of death is prevalent in ethnographic accounts. Throughout Mexican cultures, individuals who died before the soul had entered, by drowning, by accident, in warfare or raiding, in childbirth, during extreme anger, or who had defiled public morality by being thieves or adulterers, were marked for differential treatment just before their deaths and/or in burial and/or in the destination of their souls. So were sacrificial persons and venerated elders. Archaeologists have been struggling to explain all the variation in burials in terms of occupation, wealth, and ascribed or achieved social statuses when much of it may have to do with events at the time of death.

Considering the element of body position significantly increases the counts of people buried in these sites who died violently, casting a very different light on the burial programs than previous contemplated (Table

6.6). Sixteen percent to 69 percent of the people buried in the shell-bearing sites may have died at the hand of others. A much smaller range of violent deaths appears to be registered in the few shell-free burial sites with sufficient information: 15–31 percent. There is, in fact, a statistically significant difference between the projected number of violent deaths in central Tennessee and the Alabama sites and between the shell-free sites and the Alabama sites.

These deaths were spread out over centuries. At Carlston Annis, where the radiocarbon dates are the most abundant and show artifact accumulation occurring over a 1,500-year period, someone was buried every 3.8 years. The 66 potential deaths from violence and childbirth (Table 6.6) amount to approximately one death every 23 years. Eleven hundred years are bracketed by events at Indian Knoll. The 880 bodies enumerated in WPA excavations mean that someone was buried every 15 months and the 254 possible victims of violence, once every 52 months. The multiple burials at both sites indicate that in some years, up to six people were killed at once, however.

Are the possible high numbers of victims of violence consistent with the notion of villages, or contradictory to that idea? It is true that in historic times, captives were taken to villages and tortured; however, given that there are numerous other reasons for thinking that these places were not villages, I think that the burial of a non–cross section of people, including those who died violently, suggests that these activities were not conducted at what were viewed primarily as villages. I want to add one more piece to the puzzle before exploring further the function of the large shell heaps: the possibility that there were consecrating burials at some of these sites.

Initial Burials

Violence and the richest burials are often registered on the deepest burials. Depth below surface information provided by the WPA has not figured prominently in analyses of these sites, no doubt owing to an assumption of disturbance so great that such attention would be wasted. Nevertheless, there are more reasons than not to believe that the depths below surface are largely usable as proxies for the sequence of burial and that the deepest burials may well have been the first burials. Primary among these reasons is Webb's and coauthors' own belief in the usefulness of the depth data. Webb and DeJarnette (1942:72) write that "experience has demonstrated that studies on depth distribution are much more accurate when made from data taken by the 'block' method rather than by trenching." For this reason, they conducted most of their excavations using blocks. They published numerous tables of artifact styles (e.g., throughout the 1942 Pickwick Basin report, or Webb 1950a:332–334) and burial styles according to depth, and thus implied age. Furthermore, in spite of presumed digging disturbance, several artifact types are found only in burials (see earlier discussion of artifacts).

While depth of burial below mound surface was diligently collected by fieldworkers, those data were typically published only for burials with associated grave goods or who had interesting physical characteristics. An analysis of burials by depth is also hampered by a lack of published information on depth below datum and on their place in the grid with respect to the center of the mounds. The following cursory analysis of the burial program (Table 6.7) is then tentative, relying as it does, in

Table 6.7 Initial Burials in Shell Mounds of the Southern Ohio Valley

Site	Depth	Position	Comments
Big Sandy	15.0'	flexed/right	mature woman, healed CDI
Kay's Landing	13.4'	on back	woman 16–20 years old. Gnawing, no hands.
Eva	St IVB	on face	two males in same square, broken point
Long Branch	10.7'	extended	mature male, 2 points, antler tool
Bluff Creek	17.0'	extended	point on chest
O'Neal	8.0'	flexed	two at this depth; one is the richest burial, juvenile, other—mature woman with 4 items
Mulberry Creek	13.8'	tossed	four men, shot, with grave goods
Little Bear	9.5'	flexed	2 people—atlatl weight and coal.
Perry	7.5'	on face	dismembered, stacked, face down, goods
Anderson		head-twisted	19-year-old man in refuse pit, 6 slabs on top
Robinson	4.7'	sitting	woman, richest burial with cache
Barrett	4.6'	flex L, R	3 adults at this depth, each with a good(s)
Butterfield	6.0'	on back	young man, richest burial in site
Chiggerville	4.2'	on back	with an awl and marine shell
Jackson Bluff	1.6'		long bones only—trophy part deposit?
Bowles	6.6'	flex R, L	3 people, spear, shell, puddle clay object
Indian Knoll	8.5'	on back	male 19–20 years old, grave goods
Read	5.0'	on back	mature woman with child
Carlston Annis	7.7'	flexed on L	mature woman, no trauma, no grave goods

some cases, on incomplete information. In other cases either all of the information necessary is available in the report or I was able to examine the burial forms.

Reviewing the data summarized in Table 6.7 for 19 sites indicates that the deepest burial is an actual victim of violence (one case), a possible victim of violence given the body position (11 cases), and the richest burial at the site (three cases). Some are possible trophy part deposits or cremation (two cases). A few examples are illustrative.

At Perry the deepest burials annotated were Bu6, dismembered with three points and a broken slate gorget, and Bu 73 and 74, who were flexed and stacked one on top of the other with no grave goods. The deepest burial at Butterfield may be the young adult six feet deep on his back with eight leaf-shaped blades, 18 flint projectile points, one drill, and two scrapers, the richest burial at the site. The deepest burials at Robeson Hills, a bluff-top site on the Wabash River, are the two extended males between 36 inches and 50 inches in two pits, one in a pit too small, with an embedded point, and the other with an antler item. Hayes, on the Duck River in Tennessee, had two equally deep burials, a man and an unknown. The man was on his back, head up, with several grave goods. The unknown adult had three broken blades, limestone, awl, naiad valve, and a Ft. Payne chert point and was tightly flexed on the left. The deepest individual at East Steubenville, on the upper Ohio River, was a "disarticulated jumble" of bones showing postmortem burning, accompanied by 122 flakes, nine burned rocks, and 11 naiad shell hinges.

Thirteen of the 19 cases in Table 6.7 have grave goods, or 68 percent of the deepest burials, a percentage that is much higher than the general population at any one of these sites. Are these consecrating burials? Are they indications of founding rites? If we imagine that a "village" develops only over a considerable amount of time and without intention beginning in the Middle Archaic, why would consecrating burials be present? It is possible that these places began as villages and evolved into mortuaries and ceremonial centers and were then consecrated with a very deep burial. But to ensure that this burial was the deepest one would mean that the burial depths were known at all times. Or are these places intentionally founded as ritual sites?

Summary and Discussion of the Shell Mound as Village

The shell heaps of West Virginia, Indiana, Kentucky, Tennessee and Alabama have long been considered to be habitation sites. For some archaeologists, the use was but short-term while hunting, while for others they were cast as long-term residential places. Either scenario has people converging at the banks of rivers, harvested whatever was obtainable from the forest and river, bringing the foods and products back to camp, and living atop the accumulating garbage of daily life. Those who died there were buried there. Although archaeologists of old pointed to the jumble of shells, bones, sandstone, charcoal, and burials as evidence of habitation, archaeologists of today point to the evidence of tool production and maintenance and the consumption of low-quality foodstuffs such as snails and bivalves as evidence of mundane daily activities. Contributing greatly to the presumption of the residential function of these heaps has been the old view of Archaic social and ritual life as underdeveloped, with little need for intergroup meeting places. Late Archaic marine shell and soapstone trade, domesticates, village creation, and pottery adoption merely hinted at things to come in the more socially sophisticated, ritually complex, Woodland period.

It has been my purpose in this and previous chapters to raise doubts about the interpretation of the shell heaps of the southern Ohio Valley as primarily villages, and mundane villages at that, as asserted by Milner and Jefferies (1998). In addition to their concentrated, rather than widespread, occurrence, and to their association with natural features known to be considered the dwelling places of various deities and spirits (topics covered in Chapter 3), I have, in this chapter, highlighted their monumentality, possible construction, evidence of transient use, and numbers of victims of violence.

A review of the distribution of the artifact classes, burials, profile maps, Webb's reports, and his use of depth below surface indicate that there is far more integrity to these sites than has been appreciated. There is evidence of Benton point workshops, burial and nonburial caches, repeatedly used fire loci—a few that burned intensively—possible feasting food-preparation areas, and cemeteries. Dog burials are a distinctive feature of Tennessee River and Green River heaps. There seems to have been a dearth of work tools, but abundant projectile points. Large numbers of points might indicate that these shell heaps were hunting camps; however, when the number of points per adult is calculated for each site, there seem to have been varying needs for points, as there are wildly varying ratios. Perhaps instead of viewing these items as discarded or lost in great numbers they are better understood as offerings left in acts of renewal.

At least 8,483 bodies were placed into these shell-bearing sites, with an estimate of more than 17,938 and at least 616 in the shell-free mortuaries used here for comparison. The reporting on burial positions and conditions, grave goods, and depth below surface is uneven and frustrates analysis. Many who were buried in these places suffered painful, fearful deaths at the hands of others, as victims of ambushes, tortured as captives, punished by peers, or selected as ritual participants. Death by scalping, decapitation, trophy part taking, stabbing, and clubbing is more evident at shell-bearing than at the shell-free mortuaries. Subadults were rarely victimized and women commonly showed clubbing or decapitation but not shooting, trophy taking, or amulet taking.

Although there are obvious signs of violent death, it has also been proposed and documented in some cases that body positioning in the grave, whether on the back or on the face, either while extended or flexed, also marked death at the hand of another or during childbirth. Combining counts of obvious killings with suspicious body positioning indicates the possibility that 16 percent to 69 percent of the bodies in each site were victims of violence or were women who died during birthing. This analysis suggests that cause of death had a significant role in decisions about how to place a body in burial and probably what to place with the body. Finally, most of these sites with adequate depth information and skeletal analysis reveal that the deepest burials, presumably the first burials, were distinctive among their peers and were often positioned in one of the attitudes that I have suggested reflects violent death. I have interpreted these burials as consecrating burials, a necessary step in founding a mortuary/ritual site.

Shell-bearing sites were not functioning primarily as villages but rather were ritual loci for sponsored ceremonies, large and small, where hosts and guests camped during the ritual gatherings. As Jack Hofman suggested in 1984, these places were aggregation camps for ritual observances and, I would add, camps in ritual precincts. Bodies for cremation were brought to these places, and other bodies may well have been brought as well. In Chapter 7 I will offer a more nuanced interpretation of this type of site and a look at a regional ritual site typology.

I will now focus on the differences between the shell heaps in the various regions, and the differences between shell-bearing and shell-free mortuaries.

Regional Differences in Shell-bearing Sites

Statistical testing (Mann-Whitney U) and cursory perusal of the data presented in this chapter indicate both differences and commonalities in the shell sites of Alabama and sites in Kentucky. Several of the observations that follow have been in the literature for years, while others have not.

The differences uncovered between Alabama and Kentucky shell sites are:

1. Islands, shoals, and confluences were criteria in Alabama for locating shell heaps; shoals, confluences and bluffs were favored in Kentucky. Although islands of suitable size are lacking on the Green River, bluffs are abundant around the Alabama sites, leaving unexplained the lack of their use.
2. There are no clearly associated shell-free mortuaries in the Alabama section of the Tennessee River, whereas Parrish, Kirkland, and Morris are near the Green River sites.
3. Burial density in Alabama is greater than in the Green River sites (Appendix I).
4. There were significantly more pestles in Kentucky heaps. There is the appearance of great difference in the number of hammers and drills (Table 6.2). Accordingly, there is a significant difference in the number of groundstone tools per non-infant in these sites.
5. There were many more lithic workshops in Alabama sites.
6. Cremations were common in Alabama but absent in Kentucky. Red ocher on burials only occurred in Kentucky.
7. Paleoindian components are more common in Kentucky sites.
8. Kentucky shell mounding ends. Tennessee shell mounding continues.

These differences strike me as pertaining largely to some specific ritual practices that will be explored in later chapters. Perhaps the most significant differences between the two regions is the last observation, that the shell mounding ends on the Green River by Early Woodland times but does not end on the Tennessee. It will take well-dated contexts and additional study to determine if the site functions changed in the Woodland period.

Differences aside, the commonalities evident between the two regions indicate that they were part of the same supraregional culture focused on the Tennessee and lower Ohio rivers, practiced many of the same rituals,

Table 6.8 Types of Grave Goods as Percentage of all Burials

Site (#bodies)	teeth	M.shell	carap.	atl.	ocher	awl	jaw	antler	heavy	points
Big Sandy (59)	1.7	1.7	0	3.4	1.7	0	0	0	0	3.4
Kay's Lndg. (76)	0	0	6.6	0	3.9	1.3	0	0	1.3	0
Eva/Eva (17)	0	0	6.0	0	6.0	0	0	0	0	0
Eva/3 mi. (102)	0	0	1.0	2.0	10.0	3.0	0	3.0	2.0	13.0
Long Branch (94)	0	16.0	1.0	1.0	0	3.2	0	1.0	0	2.1
Bluff Creek (176)	1.7	7.0	1.7	0	0	4.5	3.4	4.5	.01	4.0
O'Neal (61)	1.6	12.0	0	0	0	0	1.6	1.6	0	4.9
Mulberry (133)	2.2	5.0	1.5	0	0	3.0	0	2.2	2.2	5.3
Little Bear (136)	2.2	11.0	2.9	0.7	0	3.7	0	1.5	1.5	5.1
Perry (351)	0.2	x	1.1	0.2	0	6.3	0	4.0	2.8	15.1
Whitesburg (117)	0	x	0	0	0	0	0	2.6	6.0	5.1
Hayes (6)	0	0	0	0	0	17.0	17.0	33.0	0	17.0
Anderson (74)	1.4	19.0	4.1	4.1	8.2	0	6.8	1.4	9.6	7.0
Hermitage (339)	3.2	10.0	3.2	0.9	2.7	3.0	0	1.2	6.9	13.8
Robinson (51)	2.0	2.0	1.6	0	3.9	47.8	2.0	2.0	2.0	5.9
Penitentiary (16)	0	0	0	0	0	0	0	0	0	0
Ward (433)	1.1	3.9	1.6	1.6	0.2	0	0.9	1.2	1.2	1.2
Jackson Bluff (7)	0	0	0	0	0	0	0	0	0	0
Jimtown Hill (14)	0	0	0	0	0	0	0	0	0	0
Baker (4)	0	0	0	0	0	0	0	0	0	25.0
Barrett (412)	1.0	10.0	1.5	2.4	1.7	8.5	0.7	0.5	2.4	3.4
Butterfield (153)	0	0	1.3	0.6	0	2.0	0	1.3	2.6	3.9

(cont.)

Site (#bodies)	teeth	M.shell	carap.	atl.	ocher	awl	jaw	antler	heavy	points
Indian Knoll (880)	2.7	20.0	2.6	5.0	3.9	4.4	1.4	2.8	1.2	3.3
Bowles (24)	0	12.5	0	0	4.0	0	0	4.0	21.0	12.5
Chigger-ville (114)	2.6	20.0	6.1	3.5	3.5	0.9	0	0.9	0	0.9
Read (247)	1.6	3.6	1.2	4.8	1.2	4.8	0.8	2.0	2.8	8.9
Carlston An. (390)	2.8	18.2	4.6	1.2	2.0	8.2	2.3	4.1	2.3	6.2
KYANG (37)	2.7	0	0	0	0	0	2.7	0	2.7	0
E. Steuben-ville (6)	0	0	0	0	0	0	0	0	33.0	0
Robeson Hill (9)	11.0	0	0	0	11	0	0	22.0	0	0
Shell-free Cemeteries										
Ensworth (60)	1.7	0	3.3	1.7	0	3.3	0	1.7	1.7	16.7
Rosen-berger (185)	.01	0	1.1	1.6	3.8	4.9	0	3.2	4.3	22.2
Bluegrass (82)	1.2	1.2	1.2	6.1	6.1	8.5	7.3	7.3	0	7.3
Parrish (133)	.01	2.0	0	0	12.0	3.0	0	3.0	8.3	21.1
Kirkland (70)	0	3.0	0	1.4	0	0	0	1.4	1.4	2.9
Eva/BS (58)	2.0	0	2.0	0	2.0	12.0	0	7.0	3.0	16.0

and suffered the same violence. There are insignificant differences in the numbers of dog burials and in the number of dogs buried with humans. There is no significant difference in the percents of graves with grave goods or in the types of grave goods, with the exception of the atlatl that occurred more commonly in Green River sites (Table 6.8, 6.9). In both regions, sites are found in clusters that alternate banks along the river course, indicating that the heaps were functioning in the same way socially in the two areas. I conclude from this exercise that there is no reason to think that the monumental shell heaps of the upper Tennessee River and those of the Green River were functionally different kinds of places, and will therefore continue to treat them as a single group. There is too little data available from sites in the other regions to conduct a similar comparison.

Comparison of Shell-bearing and Shell-free Mortuaries

There are significant differences between shell-free and shell-bearing mortuary sites. The most obvious of these differences is the absence or presence of freshwater shells, which I think (and will develop in the following chapters) reflects differences in group size and some rituals performed. There are other points of comparison, as has been obvious in the various tables accompanying this chapter.

Among the differences between these two types of sites are:

1. Shell-free sites not only lack freshwater shells, but also they lack marine shells.
2. Dog burials are rare and dogs buried with humans even rarer at shell-free sites.
3. Graves and grave goods with infants were uncommon in shell-free sites.
4. Grave goods are quite different between the two types of mortuaries with few or no human bone objects or marine shell, rostra, heavy items or points at shell-free mortuaries.
5. Both the numbers of dead and burial densities are lower at shell-free mortuaries.
6. There are far fewer victims of violence at the shell-free sites and fewer burial postures used. Group burials, suggestive of violence, are largely absent at shell-free sites.

These differences serve to highlight the nature of the burial programs enacted at the shell-heaps where infants were placed in graves and given goods, often exotic in origin. Such a differential distribution of exotic, expensive items—present in shell heaps, absent elsewhere—at any later point in prehistory would strongly support an interpretation of a settlement hierarchy. It would mean that Indian Knoll was a "central place" and that Rosenberger and the shell-free non-mortuary sites were one or two tiers lower in a hierarchy of places. I will return to this subject in Chapter 7.

An even closer comparison can be made between the shell-bearing mortuary sites of the Green River and the non–shell-bearing burial sites in the Green River region, particularly Kirkland. Kirkland was located away from the main river channel on a tributary. This site had fewer fire features, awls, bone points, the fewest projectile points per adult, fewer groundstone tools per adult, the lowest mean number of grave goods, no outstanding burial, fewer animal teeth, and fewer shell beads. There was an extremely low obvious violent death count and low possible deaths from violence, based on body positions.

Other Comparisons

There are other site groups for which statistical analyses were conducted (Mann-Whitney U, Table 6.9). Central Tennessee (Nashville Basin) shell-bearing sites differed from the Alabama sites in the number of dogs, the average number of grave goods, expressions of violence, and the use of red ocher. Lower Tennessee River sites differed from upper Tennessee River sites on metrics related to grave goods. Tributary sites versus main river sites had some differences in grave goods and monumental sites versus small sites had differences in numbers of bifaces, average number of grave goods, and violence.

The least distinctive pairing among shell-bearing sites was that of early and late sites. Here the differences in groundstone per non-infant may be related to site age. The only other statistically significant differences found were in burial density and the percentage of burials with grave goods. The early sites had lower burial density but greater numbers of burials with grave goods. The large number of commonalities (21/25) may be capturing two tails of a phenomenon that peaked in the early Late Archaic or it may indicate that few significant changes in the practices centered upon shell-bearing sites occurred over the course of 4,000 years (or after the establishment of loci such as Anderson, Ervin, Eva, and Mulberry Creek). This finding may also simply be pointing out the inadequacies of the radiocarbon database.

The greatest number of differences among shell-bearing sites was found between those with 14 or more dog burials and those with no dog burials and between those on bluff tops and those in Alabama. This latter comparison will be discussed in Chapter 7. As for the dog burial differences, 15 of 25 criteria were found to be distinctive. While their settings, the presence of freshwater shells, the number of victims of shooting, and several types of grave goods were similar, they differed on numbers and density of burials, the presence of dog burials, the quantities of grave goods, the proportions of graves with marine shell, atlatls, heavy items, and points, the number of bifaces, and the bifaces

Table 6.9 Statistical Tests for Significance of Differences between Types of Sites (numbers entered refer to the levels at which the difference was significant)

Criteria	Green vs. Ala.	Shell-Free vs. Ala	Shell-Free vs. Green	Cent. Tenn. vs. Alab.	Lower Tenn. vs. Ala.	Early Sites vs. Late Sites	Tributary vs. Main River	13+ Dogs vs. No Dogs	Shell-Free vs. Bluff-top	Ala. vs. Bluff-top	Large vs. Small
# burials		0.10	0.10					0.01	0.05	0.01	
burial density	0.02	0.10				0.15		0.02		0.10	
dog burials		0.02	0.05	0.15				yes			
dog/humans			0.10					yes			
# bifaces			0.10	can't test	0.15			0.02	0.15	0.10	0.15
# bifaces/ non-infant				can't test		can't test		0.10	can't test	0.15	
% grave good					0.15	0.10		0.05			
X# grave goods		0.10		0.15	0.15			0.02	0.10		0.15
# embedded pt		0.05	0.10	0.15	0.15					0.02	0.01
# obvious violence		0.15	0.05	0.05				0.05		0.15	0.01
# position violence		0.15		0.10							
# with ocher	0.02	0.15		0.15	0.02						0.15

ground tools	0.01	0.10	0.05	can't test	can't test	0.10	can't test	0.10	0.05	0.02	
monumental		yes	0.02		can't test			yes	can't test	yes	yes
naiads present		yes	yes								
setting			yes				yes		yes	yes	
Grave Goods											
teeth gg											
marine shell gg	0.02	0.02	0.10			0.05	0.01	0.02		0.02	
carapaces gg							0.05			0.05	
atlatls gg	0.10					0.15		0.02	0.15		
awls gg				can't test						0.05	
jaws gg				can't test			0.15				
antler gg				can't test			0.15	0.15		0.15	
heavy items gg		0.15		can't test					0.05	0.15	
bifaces gg		0.15		can't test	0.15			0.05	0.05	0.15	
Total Differences	4	12	9	6	7	3	5	15	7	15	5

and groundstone per non-infant. Dog burials, much more than human burials, serve to distinguish the shell-bearing sites in the lower Ohio Valley. The meaning of dog burials will be explored in Chapter 8.

For all of the reasons covered in this chapter, I continue to reject the idea that many of these shell-bearing sites were primarily villages throughout their use lives. Some may have begun as villages but then passed into ritual use and were either abandoned most of the time or possibly had a resident keeper group. It could be that those sites with consecrating burials were founded as something other than villages, however (Eva, Long Branch, Bluff Creek, Mulberry Creek, Flint River, Perry, Barrett, Indian Knoll, Read, Anderson, Robeson Hills, East Steubenville).

If the reader remains convinced that these sites were villages, then one must answer why *village* life came to such a conclusive end during the Late Archaic with the demise of the shell-bearing sites on the Ohio, Green, Harpeth and Cumberland rivers. This would be the only time in the prehistory of North America where village living was adopted and then abandoned. Numerous authors have argued that people did not live in villages during the Adena and Hopewell eras, and not until the Late Woodland period in the Ohio Valley (e.g., Anderson 2002:258, Clay 1998). To push the village interpretation for these large sites is to raise far more significant issues about early Woodland social life than have yet been contemplated.

Rather than villages, what I envision were places where major short-term gatherings were held to conduct significant rituals during which or for which captives and transgressors of mores were dispatched and buried, and where a subset of the dead from several social groups were interred ceremoniously. Archaic social life was made up of many parts, the most significant of which were these ceremonial aggregations.

Unlike the possible demise of village life, the waxing and waning of a ritual expression is a common phenomenon in North American prehistory, even constituting a pattern in eastern U.S. prehistory. Significant ritual locations were being created in the northern Ohio Valley at the same time they were developing in the southern Ohio Valley and on the Gulf coastal plain. The accumulation of burials in a mortuary facility is a common phenomenon, and this type of facility was used not only in the southern Ohio Valley but on the Savannah River and in Florida on the St. Johns River. In the following chapters, I will develop this idea of the ritual site and its place in the ritualized landscape, as well as explore particular rituals completed in these places.

CHAPTER 7
CEREMONIAL DISTRICTS
OF THE SOUTHERN OHIO VALLEY

It may be said that this is a group of peoples of rather
simple culture, living in rather small groups, being primarily hunters and fishers, with deer, shellfish, roots and
berries constituting their main diet, building only rude
habitations, perhaps holding together as family groups but
with little regard for the dead (Webb and Haag 1940:109).

In previous chapters I have argued that the interpretive tag of "village"
does not do the Archaic shell-bearing sites justice. But, if the huge shell
sites at the riverside were not the places where families resided, dogs
scavenged, children played, and from which gathering and hunting parties left and to which they returned, for what were these places created?
If the amassing of shells was not part of daily dietary solutions, why
were they piled in such great numbers or harvested at all? If the Hypsithermal does not account for the demise of shellfishing on the Ohio,
on the Green, and in central Tennessee, why were shellfish, and the
practice of accumulating shells, abandoned? If shellfish were a dietary
staple and the population was growing, why was this easily harvested,
fast-replenishing food abandoned?

The answers to these questions will be provided in some detail in
this chapter. I believe that the shell-bearing sites were aggregation camps
used on a variable basis, where significant group rituals were hosted for
the populace as well as for outsider guests. Furthermore, these camps
existed in ritual precincts, specific segments of river courses believed to be
auspicious, and were but one type of sacred site. The shell-bearing sites
on top of the bluffs and knolls appear to have served ritual purposes as
well, but perhaps for a different audience or for different rituals. Other

types of sites also served ritual and gathering needs, such as some caves and rock shelters, shell-free mortuary sites, and burial-free shell sites.

The persistent point of difference about these Archaic shell sites and other Archaic sites is the presence of millions of shells. What the millions of shells offered were food, building material, visual marker, height, depth, pearls, and a direct encounter with elements of the Underworld. As extrapolated from later beliefs, the Underworld would be the source of life as a watery place and the origin of rain and winds. Shells were a visible reminder of that place and of water. Shells signified renewal of the group and of the individual (Baillou 1968, Claassen 2008).

Furthermore, shellfish provided an abundant, transportable, storable, and predictable food supply that came with its own container—precisely what would be called for when a feast was to be held (Hayden 2001, Russo 2004, Saunders 2004, Sassaman 2006). And feast they did, for weeks on end, dozens if not hundreds of times at Anderson, Hayes, Hornung, Old Clarksville, Reid, Perry, Mulberry, O'Neal, Long Branch, Indian Knoll, Carlston Annis, DeWeese, and Haynes, to name a few of the monumental feasting locations. The big feasts were occasioned by the founding of a new ceremonial center, a directional ceremony that required the killing of four individuals, performance of earth renewal/world renewal ceremonies, water cleaning, rebalancing ceremonies, and rain calling as needed. During these gatherings the participants made sacrificial offerings, buried many of their dead, and attended to social needs.

For these big events it was necessary for the hosts to spend some time at the ceremonial center to prepare the grave goods, the burial facility, the gifts, and the feast. The latter activity would require the gathering of mollusks, deer, turkey, raccoons, fish, and turtles, all while awaiting the arrival of other participants. Once the groups had assembled—hosts and guests—the rites appropriate to the occasion were performed, the dead were prepared and then buried, and feasting commenced. This sequence of events may well have required up to two months of preparation and habitation at the center, with the event perhaps unfolding over several weeks.

A mortuary center was founded when a new group wished to establish direct communication with deities through the medium of their own ancestors. These founders selected a new location in a particularly auspicious place. Where possible, a location near another center could "borrow" some of the accumulated power, and allow historically important guests to find the location easily while flaunting the spiritual favoritism of the new group's founders. A new center needed to be dedicated with a ritual involving the killing of captives or the internment of honored ones.

The shells are the key to understanding the different places used in the ritual cycle. Shellfish are an ideal feasting food. The presence of some shells may well be signaling the gathering of small groups of locals and their guests, while the presence of millions of shells would signal large groups of hosts and guests gathering multiple times. The absence of shells signals mortuary rituals that were held among kin, without foreign guests, and without the feasting food of shellfish.

Sacred Landscapes of the Southern Ohio Valley

Archaic rituals, like Paleoindian rituals, were conducted at numerous natural places, such as caves, rock shelters, sinkholes, ridgetops, bluff tops, and rivers. Evidence of the ritual use of these natural places can be seen in the deposits of sacred bird bones at Dust Cave (Walker and Parmalee 2004), Modoc Rock Shelter (Kelly and Kelly 2007), and Rodgers Cave (Kay 1982), in the manufacture of red ocher pigment at Rodger's Shelter (Kay 1982), in the human burials at Lawrence sink-hole site (Mocas 1985), Russell Cave, Dust Cave, Mammoth/Salts Cave, Stanfield-Worley, and elsewhere, and in glyphs inside Adair Cave. We do not know where Paleoindians of the southern Ohio Valley habitu-ally went for riverside rituals, but we do know where they habitually went during the Middle Archaic and the Late Archaic. We can identify these places by the thousands of shells and the hundreds of bodies and by their spatial clustering.

Unlike Paleoindians, Archaic people of the eastern woodlands began to enlarge upon elements of this sacred landscape by *creating* places to conduct rituals. Though some ridgetops and bluff tops had been ven-erated in earlier centuries, peoples of the lower Illinois River, Fishing River, and Salt River (the latter two both in Missouri) began enhancing these places with spiritually significant remains (burials, grave items) and artificial height achieved by mounding dirt and rock (Charles and Buikstra 1983, O'Brien and Wood 1998), substances from the Earth and Underworld. Along some southern tributaries of the Ohio River, people began mounding freshwater shells taken from the Underworld. They essentially created facilities for ritual and, I believe, specifically for renewal. They permanently marked these homes of the spirits with the human presence.

I think of the monumental shell-bearing mortuaries as ceremonial centers clustered into ritual districts where host groups and their guests jointly buried, feasted, and exchanged gifts (which may have ended up in the concurrent burials) while participating in renewal, rebalancing, and kinship rituals. The size of an accumulation reflects the number and size of these gatherings. Under this scenario, a site like Butterfield, for instance, on the Green River, which is small and linear rather than mounded, was in the beginning decades of hosting such gatherings when it was abandoned. Carlston Annis or Hornung or Long Branch, on the other hand, were used for hundreds of years for these types of gatherings and indicate, through the size and the number of burials, social groups that long enjoyed spiritual and social well-being in auspicious places.

In the following section I will explore the classes or types of sites that are a part of the proposed sacred landscape in the southern Ohio Valley. Each river valley that I have been discussing had a somewhat different combination of shell-bearing and shell-free ritual sites.

The Green River District

The Green River valley had what appears to be a sacred site system with three human-created elements—the large riverside shell feasting center, the shell-bearing bluff-top site, and the non-shell mortuary on small streams. People also possibly utilized at least two types of natural places: caves and rock shelters (Claassen 2006a, 2006b) and most probably waterfalls and sinks. Mundane camps may be seen in the shell-free and burial-free Reynerson site in McLean County (Webb and Haag 1947:39) and numerous places elsewhere in the vicinity (Hensley 1994).

The riverside feasting-with-shellfish centers were DeWeese, Haynes, and Carlston Annis (all in the Big Bend) as well as Chiggerville, Indian Knoll, and Bowles. (Barrett is an enigma, with its tributary location, and may have undergone a change in site function over the course of its uselife.) These shell sites are monumental in size, having grown through incremental feasts and renewal rites. They have numerous human burials and relatively large numbers of dog burials. There are victims of violent death buried in them, a number of whom appear to have been killed onsite. There are graves with marine shell items. Infants were given burial in accord with that of adults. The collection of people buried in these sites shows some selectivity. The exoticness of some of the grave goods and the unusual treatment of some of the dead suggest that the rituals conducted here had audience members who needed impressing.

Shell-bearing sites were also located on bluff tops. Webb (1950b:357) described the setting of Read as "located on top of a V-shaped bluff or promontory, which is several hundred feet long. The precipitous walls of the bluff limit the midden on the two sides of the V" and the access to the river (Figure 7.1).

In spite of their problems with accessibility, Hensley (1994) observed that Jimtown Hill (Figure 7.2, 7.3) and Jackson Bluff were among the five sites with the highest shell density in the district. Shells are abundant on top of these bluffs, nonetheless, and represent extraordinary effort to get them into place. Here is even more support for the ideas that shellfish flesh was part of a feasting menu rather than an ordinary daily meal and that the shells were a symbolic part of the feasting and ritual acts. There was ample room to have left the shells on the floodplain below Baker, Jimtown Hill, and Jackson Bluff.

These places, too, I see as feasting locations for a different suite of rituals. The bluff tops were particularly auspicious or appropriate places to bury dogs, more so than humans. In the bluff-top sites, ratios of humans to dogs range from 0.6 to 4.0, while that figure at riverside sites ranges from ten to 38 humans per dogs. The 24 total human burials found at Baker, Jimtown Hill, and Jackson Bluff, with a single exception, had no grave goods. Few burials, low burial density, little marine shell, a greater proportion of dog burials, and the dramatic settings of these sites clearly mark bluff-top shell-bearing sites as a different type of place from that of the riverside site.

I wonder about the activities at these bluff-top feasting locales. One possible role might be the mortuary processing camp (e.g., Abel et al. 2001, Buikstra et al. 1998, Jefferies 2006). A mortuary camp was a place where activities and ceremonies addressed the processing of bodies before moving them on to a separate burial location. "Presumably, many activities associated with preparing the deceased for final disposal would have taken place not at the immediate gravesite but at a nearby location" (Jefferies 2006:163). In fact, description of the Williams Mortuary complex in Ohio (Abel et al. 2001) seems very applicable to the configuration of sites on the Green River. Though very few bodies were left in the bluff-top locations, those that were may differ from those found in the riverside mortuaries in ways detectable in the skeletons. On the Green these possible mortuary camps are spaced between larger shell mounds located on the river below. Baker could pair with Chiggerville, Jackson Bluff with either Indian Knoll or Bowles, and Jimtown Hill with either Butterfield or Bowles.

Read and Ward, though both on bluff tops, are most unusual among bluff-top sites for their large number of human burials, artifacts, grave goods, etc. They are characteristic bluff-top sites in the high number of dog burials. It appears that both places functioned in both capacities during their biographies. Given that the decision to utilize the bluff top was made before the materials were deposited there, it is probable that both were founded as bluff-top sites, whatever that purpose. Read, for some reason, became the focal place for the dog ritual among Green River social groups. Both loci subsequently grew into major feasting-with-shellfish ceremonial centers. Literally tons of shells were hauled to the top of those bluffs. One should keep in mind that Ward was located on a bluff top far up a small tributary, where shellfish populations may have been quite small, and the effort expended to provision the eaters quiet evident. The animals may have been harvested even from the Green River. (As dual-function sites, neither Ward nor Read has been included in the statistical tests.)

The final class of created ritual site in the Green River drainage is the shell-free mortuary. I propose that Kirkland was a private burial area where the type of feast, or size of feast that required shellfish on the main river, did not occur. The utilizers of this mortuary, no doubt, were part of the social group aggregating at the big ceremonies. If one attributes extreme tooth wear to shellfish consumption and auditory exostoses to diving for shellfish (Mensforth 2005), both of which were found on Kirkland skeletons, then the users of these shell-free private mortuaries did indeed participate in the great rituals and feasts held at the riverside ceremonial centers.

Significantly, the private mortuaries seem not only to have lacked the big gatherings and feasts but also were located away from the main river, in secluded locations. Morris and Parrish (Rolingson and Schwartz 1967), outside even the Green River valley, were even more remote. They were truly private. Differences between the shell-free mortuaries and the main river shell mounds have been detailed in Chapter 6, but in short, the most significant ones are their lack of marine shell and lack of violent deaths.

The transition from shell-bearing to shell-free deposits at some river-side sites takes on new import under this scenario of a sacred site system. It might mean that heaps such as Carlston Annis moved from public to private mortuary function. The idea that major ritual sites were decommissioned (buried) should be explored. Until there is greater clarity on just how many burials are contained in the shell-free zones of Green River sites, and better chronological control over strata, speculation on the meaning of a shell-free zone should wait.

Figure 7.1. Excavation at the Bluff-top Read Site, Kentucky. TVA photo collection, courtesy of W. S. Webb Museum of Anthropology, University of Kentucky.

Caves, rock shelters, and sinks in the Green River valley were also utilized in what may have been an annual ritual cycle. Radiocarbon dates from Mammoth and Salts Caves indicate Late Archaic knowledge of that cave system and a possible concentration of activity in the lower passages (Kennedy 1996:67, 78). Probable activities involved the burial of some individuals in the sink outside the mouth, the deposition of numerous disarticulated and burned human and animal remains inside the Salts Cave vestibule, and mining of cave minerals. I have pointed out elsewhere (Claassen 2006a, 2006b) the evidence for cave rituals in this and other districts and will repeat some of that information in Chapter 8.

One rock shelter of import may have been the Read Rock Shelter (15Bt18), at the base of the bluff the Read shell deposit was on. An extremely deep, three-layer hearth was one feature found, as was a possible trophy part disposal of skull and long bones. Two of three burials were on their backs but appear to have been buried after the Archaic (field notes, Webb Museum).

Figure 7.2. Jimtown Hill Excavation. TVA photo collection, courtesy of W. S. Webb Museum of Anthropology, University of Kentucky.

Marquardt and Watson (2005b) report on investigations into several other rock shelters in the vicinity of Carlston Annis, some with petroglyphs and bedrock mortars. The Newt Kash Rock Shelter east of the Mammoth Cave vicinity has yielded much support for an interpretation as a women's menstrual/medicine retreat where fibers were woven and nut oils produced (Claassen 2007).

Central Ohio River District

The Falls district has three of these classes of made ritual sites, the riverside shell-heap mortuary, the shell-free mortuary, and the bluff-top shell-bearing site. The shell heap mortuaries are poorly reported and poorly dated. The collections are largely unstudied and sample sizes quite small. Nevertheless, their visual appearance and reports of work indicate that they are functionally and visually equivalent to the monumental shell mortuaries of the Green River and Tennessee River.

Figure 7.3. Bluff setting for Jimtown Hill Site. TVA photo collection. Courtesy of W. S. Webb Museum of Anthropology, University of Kentucky.

The Bono and McCain sites (Miller 1941) may be the only bluff-top site, per se, in the area. Instead, several knoll-top sites in the marshland of Jefferson County, Kentucky, are somewhat similar, primarily in their height above the floodplain, in the similar effort required to get the shells to the top of the landform, and similar to Read and Ward in their number of human burials. Knoll-top sites are KYANG, Lone Hill, Minor's Lane, and Fenley's Knob (15Jf6), all now destroyed (Bader 2009).

> The Lone Hill site was located on and around a 650-foot long hill standing 54 feet above the surrounding marsh. A midden varying between three to six feet covered the hill and during grade and fill operations 250 to 300 burials and numerous deep storage pits and hearths were exposed. (Bader 2007:53)

Minor's Lane was situated on a small knoll, two miles south of Lone Hill, with a three-foot-deep midden and several burials. There have been no reports of dog burials at any of these sites, marking them as different from the bluff-top sites of the Green. Incidentally, shellfish populations could not have survived in a marsh and were either harvested from the Ohio and carried inland to the knolls, like the situation in the Green River bluff-top sites, or a stream ran through the area during occupation of the knolls.

KYANG is the only one of these knoll-top sites to have been excavated professionally, although not reported. Anne Bader (2005:5) suggested "that portions of the Meyer [shell-free] and KYANG [knoll-top] sites were dedicated primarily to mortuary activity, with relatively short-term, non-sustained residence, and a restricted range of day-to-day activities."

Rosenberger, the largest non-shell mortuary in the vicinity of the Falls, is located only a few kilometers from contemporary shell mounds. Rosenberger individuals showed excessive tooth wear—usually linked to consumption of naiads (Wolf and Brooks 1979:915). Other smaller, shell-free mortuary sites are Bluegrass, Little Pigeon Creek, Habich, and Meyer (Bader 2007, 2009). Smaller still are the burial populations at Railway Museum, Shadow Wood, and Townsend. The shell-free Hedden site, to the south on the Ohio in McCracken County, may be related to the Falls activities as well (McGraw and Huser 1995), with its minimum of eight burials.

A different class of site present in the Falls area is the shell-bearing but non-mortuary site. Paddy's West and Breeden have shell but only two burials total (Bader 2009). There are no dog burials. If the paucity of burials persists in future excavations, then these places would be feasting localities as well but with different rituals than were conducted at the large mounded mortuaries.

This area of the Ohio River is notable for caves, rock shelters, sinks, and shoals. In Jefferson County, Kentucky, McNeeley Lake Cave (15JF200) and Durritt Cave (15Jf201) have been investigated. Hearths and human burials were encountered, as were large numbers of ground-stone tools (Bader 2009). Squire Boone Caverns and Wyandotte Cave, as well as others in southern Indiana, are prime candidates for Archaic ritual localities by the users of Falls shell mounds. Wyandotte, in fact, has evidence of Archaic use and penetration of the dark zone up to two kilometers (Crothers et al. 2002:509). Rock shelters of note are Miles (15Jf671), with more than five feet of deposits, and Ashworth shelter (15Bu236) with a dog burial (Bader 2009).

Upper Ohio River District

Bluff-top sites have been the most important of the site classes in defining the Panhandle Archaic (Mayer-Oakes 1955b). Hudson Farm (46Hk35),

Watson Farm (46Hk40), New Cumberland (46Hk1), Globe Hill, East Steubenville, the M&M site, Monahan, and possibly Marrtown (the latter three discussed in Mohney 2002:21, who says they have no site numbers) are bluff-top shell-bearing sites, with New Cumberland and Monahan offering the most dramatic demonstrations of shell transport. At Monahan, shells were hauled up a bluff face 500 feet above the Ohio, while at New Cumberland they were carried 310 feet upward. The M&M site offers a commanding view of the Ohio River along a relatively narrow ridge spur. Mayer-Oakes (1955b:132) described the setting of East Steubenville as

> situated on a small shelf projecting from a steep hillside rising from the east bank of the Ohio River. . . . While the site is about 250 yards away from the river it is more than one hundred feet above the present water level and the trail leading up to the site is quite precipitous. The site is located in such a position that it is very unlikely that it was ever used by more than one group of people.

Like the situation at the East Steubenville site, a shell midden rings the M&M site, although midden development appears more limited than at East Steubenville (Mohney 2002:21). So little excavation has occurred that dog burials have been noted only at East Steubenville (GAI 2007) but not at Globe Hill. The strong association between Late Archaic Steubenville points and shell-bearing sites and the lack of Steubenville points located away from the main river indicate that the Steubenville creators of these sites were closely tied to the Ohio River. Mayer-Oaks (1955a) recognized shell-bearing and non–shell-bearing sites as distinct entities.

Two other site classes can be identified in the district. Riverside shell sites that are unexplored at this time are Fish Run (46Mr118), Conner Run (46Mr88), and Sheet Creek (46Br24) (all mentioned in GAI 2007). The Half Moon site (46Br29) was a shell-free riverside site with an Archaic component below Adena mounds (Mayer-Oakes 1955b:132). Barking Road site on the Allegheny River just upstream from Pittsburgh is a shell-free site showing few features. Scenery Hill site (36Al75) is on another tributary of the Ohio and is yet another shell-free Steubenville point site (all mentioned in Mohney 2002).

This area also has numerous caves and rock shelters that would be part of the sacred site system and ritual round. The longest cave in the northeast, Harlansburg Cave, Pennsylvania (Fowley and Long 1997), is approximately the same distance from East Steubenville as Mammoth Cave is from the Big Bend sites of the Green River.

Wabash/White River District

There are far more shell-bearing sites on these two rivers than are summarized by the Riverton culture description of Winters (1969) or adequately published. This publication has but three sites, two riverside shell sites and one bluff-top shell site. Riverton and Swan Island are on the first terrace of the Wabash. Both have very few burials but have evidence of ritual activities. Robeson Hills is the bluff-top site. None of these sites has dog burials.

Other bluff-top sites exist on the White (e.g., 12Gi31), as well as at least one site with a dog burial (12Vi122), and there are riverside shell-bearing sites such as Point-o-Rocks (12Fo13) (Anslinger1986:27). I do not know the extent to which sites on the White River are mortuary sites or have dog burials.

Harpeth River District

In the Harpeth valley, Ensworth is a shell-free private mortuary, while the public shell mortuaries are Hart and Anderson. The shell mortuary of Hermitage Springs (Dan Allen, personal communication, October 2009) on the Cumberland River near Anderson may also be included here. Bluff-top sites or their counterpart seem to be absent.

A fourth ritual site type is the shell-bearing riverside non-mortuary site (with few burials). Yet a different set of rituals may have been undertaken at these non-mortuary loci. Included here is Mizzell (Aaron Deter-Wolf, personal communication, November 2007) and possibly the two Duck River sites of Ervin and Hayes. These two gastropod heaps are located near Big Falls in Coffee County. Big Falls and numerous caves/ rock shelters are located in this district.

Tennessee River Districts

Tennessee River sites show a different ritual site system from those to the north. The system was apparently quite simple, with only two classes of made ritual site: the riverside shell-heap mortuary and the riverside shell-heap non-mortuary, such as 1Ct17 and 1Lu86, in Pickwick (Webb and DeJarnette 1942) and Wheeler basins (Webb 1939). Meander Scar appears to have been a short-lived mortuary, like Butterfield on the Green River, where gatherings were insufficient to create a mound. There are apparently no shell-free mortuaries in the Alabama district. Downriver, in western Tennessee, there are shell-bearing mortuaries and later shell-free mortuaries such as the Big Sandy component at Eva. This loose cluster may constitute a district.

Several caves of importance in Alabama are Stanfield-Worley (DeJarnette et al. 1962), Dust (Goldman-Finn and Driskell 1994), and Russell (Griffin 1974). Russell Cave may be paired with Widow's Creek, Dust Cave with Perry, and Stanfield-Worley with several heaps in Lauderdale County, Alabama. Each of these caves has dog burials, human burials—some of which are suggestive of violent death—naiads, and freshwater gastropods. Numerous rock shelters also show Archaic use (e.g., Webb and DeJarnette 1942) and may have been the source of the crinoids found in matrix and burials of the riverside mortuaries. For the lower Tennessee River sites, Big Bone Cave may be relevant.

Statistical Analyses of Differences

Table 6.9 presents the statistical results of comparisons between classes of sites: the bluff-top shell site, shell-free mortuaries, and riverside shell mound mortuaries. (Sufficient data are available for six bluff-top sites: Robeson Hills, East Steubenville, Globe Hill, Baker, Jimtown Hill, and Jackson Bluff.) Shell-free mortuaries included were Rosenberger, Ensworth, Kirkland, Eva/Big Sandy, and Parrish, and others where possible. In addition to the dramatic difference between sites with more than 13 dogs and sites with no dogs is that difference between bluff-top sites and the Alabama riverside mounds. Fifteen elements of difference were noted, including grave goods, violence, and burials. Distinction was maintained when comparing Green River shell heaps and bluff-top sites, although to a lesser degree than when comparing the Alabama sites and bluff-top sites. Marine shell items were found significantly more often with burials placed in the large riverside shell heaps.

It should be noted that Lewis and Kneberg (1959:174–180) offered a similar statistical evaluation. They used a Z-coefficient of sites in the Green River, lower and upper Tennessee River, and Savannah River districts based on 83 traits. Their midcontinent tradition with Eva, Three Mile, Big Sandy, and Indian Knoll phases was distinguished by dog burial and notched projectile points from the Eastern Tradition with Stallings, Lauderdale, and Kays phases.

It could be that migration to the rivers in the Middle Archaic was not spurred by the climatic optimum but by the social environment where easy travel routes were available and where larger groups could congregate. Shell accumulations began to spread eastward slowly and began to cease in nearly the same order. The Harpeth/Duck River system faded first, by the close of the Middle Archaic. Next to fade was probably that system in the Falls of the Ohio district. The bluff-top sites of the upper Ohio seem to have dropped out of use as feasting and ritual locations about the same time as events ended at Indian Knoll on the Green. The Green River system faded several millennia later than the Harpeth group. Green River mounds ceased to attract burials or be the staging places for rituals by the end of the Archaic. They may have been capped with shell-free dirt as a final act of containing and decommissioning their power.

The Pickwick and Wheeler Basin group(s), as well as the St. Johns and Florida coastal groups, retained their charters to maintain their centers, while new families using new centers emerged in the Guntersville Basin and upper Tennessee River (Sassaman 2006), and in the northern Ohio River valley. Feasting with shellfish would become commonplace in the Southeast as seen in Woodland-period sites with shell debris (Peacock 2002), as would earthen mounds. The descendants of the Late Archaic Green River system would regroup and emerge as Adena and Hopewell, mounding not shell but earth, an indication of a significant change in the way earth and group renewal rituals were conceptualized. The Archaic social groups flowered and faded from west to east, not because of climatic circumstances (which changed throughout this era of feasting with shell) but because of social forces that resulted in the dissolution of groups and the end of active use of ritual facilities.

This sacred site system concept offers an interpretive framework for several aspects of the shell-bearing sites in the southern Ohio Valley. 1) It offers an explanation for the differences between shell-free and small and large shell-bearing mortuaries. Shell mass reflects the number of feasts sponsored. 2) The clustered nature of these sites and the resulting redundancy of sites is explained. The clustered nature of these sites indicates that many generations of people used the feasting-with-shellfish protocol and these designated districts for ritual renewal enactment. Clusters on different sides of a river were created by different social groups. 3) The system offers an interpretive framework for the grave goods of variable quantity and elaborateness, the variation in burial density, and in the number of violent deaths between shell-heap mortuaries and shell-free mortuaries. Culture-wide public renewal ceremonials and burials were made at shell sites, while smaller, more private rituals and burials occurred at non–shell-bearing sites.

A few additional comments on the sociality of these sacred districts in the Late Archaic are warranted. The clusters of sites suggest repetitive use by historic family groups, maybe clans. The distance between some districts (e.g., Green and Alabama districts) suggests moieties or phratries or even cultures, but the proximity of other pairs of districts is contradictory (e.g., Falls and Green districts, Green and Cumberland). It is possible that there might have been one culture group, observing a major ritual with component rites observed by clan-based priesthood groups in each district. Many other scenarios are also possible.

Feasting with shellfish is obviously a key component of the system just outlined. In the following section, I will explore the evidence for and nature of feasting at these sites.

Feasting

Feasting has only recently been recognized for its importance in social life. It is now seen as the impetus behind plant and animal domestication, pottery adoption, developing social hierarchies, and all of the ramifications of social difference that individuals are motivated to express.

Feasts are vital to the goals of showing spiritual favor and for conducting social transactions, such as attracting marriage partners. Feasts among modern Native Americans are generally occasioned by a ritual sequence that is spread over several days, such as mortuary ritual.

Hayden (2001), Russo (2004), and R. Saunders (2004), among others, have convincingly argued that the Archaic shell heaps and shell constructions of the Atlantic Coast and Florida were feasting locations. I am sorry to have come so late to the same realization for the contemporary southern Ohio Valley shell heaps. These authors, and others working on Woodland and Mississippian databases (e.g., Jackson and Scott 2001, Pauketat et al. 2002), have provided a wealth of criteria and test implications for feasting debris.

Feasting with the dead has been proposed as the cause of the San Francisco Bay shell heaps (Luby and Gruber 1999). Sassaman (2004:248) believes that Luby and Gruber

> provide a reasoned argument of the cosmological integration of food and the deceased, primarily through the practices of mortuary feasting. Together, the deceased and their food "stretch across generations in their accumulation, signifying the successes of people's ancestors in the amassing of food and other resources." (Luby and Gruber 1999:105)

The Food for Feasts

Invertebrates are the perfect feast food. They can be harvested by the thousands, can rapidly replenish their numbers, and can be harvested by all members of the host group, even the very young and the infirm. When they and the sandstone needed to steam them were hauled up the high, steep bluffs in their shells, the guests must have been impressed. Snails were apparently prepared in a broth and bivalves eaten raw, steamed, or roasted.

Paired valves, presumably unopened shells, are excellent evidence of food wastage, a by-product of feasting (Russo 2004:47–48). Shell-filled pits at Widow's Creek, on the Tennessee River (where 3 percent of the shell is attributed to Archaic activities), show remarkably high frequency of paired valves, indicating the primary deposition of great quantities of fresh specimens. One pit contained an estimated 16,025 individual naiads apparently deposited en masse and never opened (Warren 1975:312). Uneaten mollusks have been frequently noted in the literature at other shell heaps (see Chapter 6 discussion). Webb and DeJarnette (1942:106) observed about Alabama sites that "the number of mussels cooked was in excess of the demand for immediate consumption."

Other observations at Widow's Creek are relevant to the feasting scenario. Modified valves were rare, and consistent with shell as food debris. Specimen density was fairly high, in keeping with the expectations of unusually large meals. Shells were left in the site rather than at the stream. The clean shell layers and large accumulations of unbroken shells, and thus undisturbed lenses of shell, are evidence of rapid accumulation, single deposit episodes. Feasts were building this mound, just as they were building the shell rings of the Atlantic and Gulf Coasts (Russo 2004, Sassaman 2006, Sassaman and Randall 2006, R. Saunders 2004).

Morrison (1942) pointed out several aspects of the shell debris in the Pickwick Basin sites that are additional expectations for feasting with shellfish. Of greatest relevance were his observations that the majority of individual bivalves had been gathered in shallow water, and in the river at hand, and thus were the easiest species to find. Mollusks had not come from the tributaries or from deep water. In fact, the most prolific species in the Tennessee River today buries itself in the substrate in deeper water and was not among the naiads in the site samples taken by Morrison. This collecting strategy of targeting shallow-water species not only rules out long-term occupation (which surely would have resulted in the collecting of deeper-water species) but also suggests that collecting occurred rapidly and sporadically. The collection of approximately 22 species of aquatic snails further indicates a desire to get as large a quantity of molluscan meat as rapidly as possible. The Duck River sites of Ervin and Hayes and the initial levels of Anderson on the Harpeth River are entirely comprised of very easily harvested and processed gastropods. They were probably cooked for a soup broth.

The best source of vertebrate food information from the riverside shell sites, where the largest feasts were held, comes from Carlston Annis. Mandibles and limbs of deer were the most common parts, so Crothers assumes that meat fillets and organs were returned to the center (2005:312). These extra steps of bone removal and organ isolation would require more preparation time before the event and make for a finer presentation of food, part of the feasting protocol. Off-site dressing of deer would also make for a neater staging place for the feast. Leg of deer apparently was on the menu, as probably were brain and tongue.

Other possible menu items in this small sample found in general matrix and features at Carlston Annis were squirrel, rabbit, raccoon, turkey, and possibly opossum, groundhog, wapiti, black bear, and dog. Wapiti and black bear are candidates for feasting foods, requiring as they do danger in their capture, and providing large quantities of meat. Among the turkey bones, the wings and vertebra were noticeably absent, again suggesting extra effort expended in preparation and presentation of this food, as well as the possible removal of wings for fan and feather uses.

Although fish occupy a lower trophic level than do the mammals just mentioned, if one wanted to impress guests, one would present fish that had to be caught by hook and line rather than those captured in a mass gathering technique such as netting. In fact, the majority of the fish bones from the Carlston Annis sample are drum and catfish, taxa taken with hooks from river channels, not the shallows. Drum, which can achieve impressive size, peaked in levels 2–5 and levels 13–19.

Finally, faunal remains from Zones II and III at Carlston Annis were larger in size. The shell-free midden and Zone III had the least taxonomic diversity. Larger size and lower taxonomic diversity (see also Russo 2004:46) support the idea that in Zone III, debris derived from feasting, as does the complete lack of worked bones and cut bone in Zone III. Ritual activities (which would spawn feasts) are suggested by the bird variety found in the Operation C squares: one duck, goose, bobwhite, pileated woodpecker, and other waterfowl (Glore 2005:323).

The number of deer found in the excavations of Anderson and Indian Knoll was very high. At least 125 deer were recovered at Anderson and more than 1,551 at Indian Knoll, primarily as foot bones. These remains suggest field dressing and a great number of deer hides. There was an apparent preference for the delicacy of deer tongue at Little Bear Creek (Curren 1974). Although no screening was used to recover the material from Little Bear Creek, Curren was comfortable saying that the lack of ribs and vertebral fragments indicated that the deer were field dressed and mandibles and haunches brought to the site for consumption of the tongue and meat (1974:159).

Feasting at bluff-top sites may have been different from riverside sites, as seen in the East Steubenville remains recently gathered and analyzed. Shellfish consumption and fish consumption occurred (it would seem) in measured amounts, given the rarity of wasted animals (Rollins and Dugas 2007), and deer consumption may not have occurred. The deer body parts most common at East Steubenville were feet, head, lower hind leg, and lower foreleg (Pipes 2007), suggesting processing of deer rather than feasting on meaty deer parts. (The lack of meatier body parts of deer also suggests that this location was not primarily a family camp.) Marrow appears to have been a target product. Shellfish were collected below the bluff top from the Ohio River itself in water three to seven feet deep, showing more difficulty in gathering (Rollins and Dugas 2007:349). It is possible, then, that bluff-top shell-bearing sites were the places used for processing deer meat or hides for riverside feasts, but where fish and shellfish were consumed in small feasts related to rituals.

Food Preparation and Disposal Features

The obvious food preparation and disposal features for a pre-pottery–using people were the clay floors, storage and refuse pits, and fire pits. Large feasts required large preparation facilities and discard facilities.

Shell-filled pits with the valves still articulated suggest that mollusks were typically prepared at riverside heaps during the feast in roasting pits and occasionally not needed. Characteristics of cooking at the Widow's Creek site on the Tennessee River were noted by Warren (1975:171). Charred and partially charred valves were found in features as well as in general midden. The incidence of charred valves was proportionately greatest in features associated with evidence of fire, areas of concentrated food preparation. Bell-shaped and basin-shaped pits showed moderate to high specimen densities, moderate concentrations of charred and modified valves, and moderate to high concentrations of paired valves.

Pits containing food debris and earth ovens were repeatedly found throughout the region. The largest measured pit in these shell-bearing sites was found at the bluff-top Ward mortuary. This huge pit (23,524 liters) was dug into yellow subsoil and contained black earth, charcoal, ashes, fire-cracked rock, considerable shell, bones, antlers, bone needles and pins, and several projectile points. Other large pits were excavated at Kirkland (13,942 liters), with a dog skull at the bottom, and two at Parrish, (13,462 liters each), both empty. Sassaman (2006:110–111) calls large pits at the shell-bearing Victor Mills site on the Savannah River "silos" with volumes of 1,083 liters. The report of work at Perry gave pit dimensions for only two pits, but they were large. One pit had a volume of 1,012 liters and the other 610 liters, both filled with uncharred midden debris. The pits and basins at Penitentiary, with shells both paired and single, were also quite voluminous. They ranged from 774 to 71 liter capacity and would seem to represent waste greater than that for a single family. The largest pits at Robinson had 760 liter and 746 liter capacities. Two pits at Riverton, where ritual evidence is abundant, were smaller at 469 liters and 520 liters.

These pits are all large enough for cooking and waste disposal related to feasting events. Pit features at the bluff-top East Steubenville site were found to be distributed in the shell area and were used as shellfish processing facilities (GAI 2007). Each of three sizes of pits at East Steubenville had distinguishing characteristics, but all seemed to have animal butchery, dietary waste, or processing waste (Pipes 2007). In contrast, the largest pit at the non-shell habitation site of Longwood-Glick, in the Falls district, offered only 148 liter capacity.

Clay floors found in southern shell heaps and caves have attracted archaeological curiosity and are another potential feasting facility. Once argued to be house floors (Webb 1939) in shell-heap "villages," recent analysis has interpreted them as cooking griddles (Sherwood and Chapman 2005), particularly well suited for nut toasting, fish cooking, and tuber cooking. These floors are often found near ritual evidence, such as was the case at Riverton (Winters 1969) and 1Ct17, where five burials were found in association with clay floors (Webb 1939). A portion of some burial rites seemed to involve the clay floor or stone pavement, a fire, food consumption, and a nearby burial. I draw the reader's attention to this set of features at Read (Webb 1950b) and to Sassaman's (1993b:104) discussion of graveside feasting at Mims Point on the Savannah River. Association with ritual makes these surfaces candidates for feasting facilities, either as cooking areas, food preparation areas, or guest seating, given both their sizes and their extra effort to prepare. Renewal of these floors, and their paucity in most sites, suggests to me that they were special-use features. There is also evidence that the floors were larger later in time, which would correspond with the documented greater population sizes in the Late Archaic and presumably larger feasts.

Two aspects of fire features at shell-bearing sites suggest that they were not the fireplaces of houses. Most of the features appear to have been only temporarily used, not repeatedly used, as one would expect from an established household. Often fireplaces were superimposed (site reports in Webb 1939, Webb and DeJarnette 1942) rather than being spread out over the site, as we would imagine households would locate themselves. Instead, several burned areas suggest short burn fires, such as those associated with funeral feasts (Bader 2005). Fires would have been useful in both cooking and cleanup.

Feasting activities have been cited as a cause for the development and adoption of pottery (Clark and Gosser 1995). Feasting may have motivated the adoption of stone and clay vessels in the Tennessee River valley. These large feasts created a need for larger vessels and for direct-heat cooking. They were new items for the display of wealth/health and ethnicity.

The Setting of the Feast

The feasts were held where the shell accumulated. At some sites this was also an area of burial, but in a number of sites, burials occurred away from shell as well as in the shell. The scene of the feast may have been punctuated with surface features. I suspect that in all of these heaps the burial area, and possibly individual burials, were marked in some way. Marking has also been suggested by Athens (2000) for the Lawrence site burials, which were undisturbed by later digging. The high frequency of disturbed infants rather than other age groups must mean that the infant burials were either separated from the rest of the burials or marked. "Mothers often visited the graves of their children and noticed the least change in the appearance of the enshrouding earth; sometimes they identified the spot of an unmarked grave after years of absence" (Wallace and Steen 1972:94). The superpositioning of fires and clay floors at several sites (e.g., Riverton, Chiggerville) also suggests rather permanent installations for these facilities. The fires may have been located with respect to something else that was fixed and durable, like a shrine, making the location for a new fire obvious.

Seating at the public feasts may have relied upon an uneven surface of shell to create higher and lower areas. Russo (2004:53) has argued that "asymmetrical social relations are legitimated in the spatial arrangement of horizontally distributed shell (height) and vertically distributed shell (height/volume/thickness/depth)." Furthermore, "distribution of shell reflects social relationships that were isometric from initiation to abandonment of the site." Perhaps future mapping at these shell heaps can provide the type of evidence Russo has found for the shell rings, indicative of temporary social hierarchies.

The reliance on shellfish for feasting, a low trophic food, indicates that the nature of these feasts was that between more or less equal social units recognizing only a few levels of social differences (Hayden 2001, Saunders 2004). Feasting among unequal social units would require far more impressive foods—those rare and dangerous (Hayden 2001, Russo 2004:45). The remains of the southern Ohio Valley feasts were concentrated as markers of the rituals, and sacred space, and made the largess of the hosts conspicuous. The shell debris, however, may have been obscured from river and overland travelers, situated as it was on elevations, even bluff tops. A domed shape would have belied their presence only late in their use histories. Were these ritual loci meant to be secret places, or were they marked by visible shrines or standards and kept cleared of overgrowth? Medicine societies, priesthoods, warrior societies, or families could have been their caretakers and feasts the opportunity to recruit work crews.

The Social Landscape

George Crothers (2004) asked the question, "how do we define an Archaic public?" My answer is that the public was created through ritual and feasting and consisted of the universe of potential invitees to these annual events. So who were the hosts and who were the guests? The hosts were the people with a mortuary place and resources sufficient for hosting an annual renewal ceremony. The guests were those people who were actual or fictive kin, trading partners, former hosts, and others worthy of an invitation or whom the hosts wished to impress.

Contemporaneity of Mortuaries

Clustering and pairing, which reflect social concerns, were detailed in Chapter 3. These social phenomena also suggest contemporaneity of heaps between clusters. Unfortunately, there is not a single pairing with radiocarbon dates and only two clusters with dates.

Haynes, DeWeese, Carlston Annis, and Rayburn are all located on the western side of the Big Bend (Figure 3.2b). Radiocarbon dates (Table 2.1) indicate that Carlston Annis, Haynes, and DeWeese were contemporaries for 600 years from 5,600 to 4,983 years ago. These dates for three shell mounds in one meander raise the possibility that what we are really observing here is a four-mound multimound complex like those now recognized for the Gulf coastal plain (e.g., Saunders et al. 2004). These dates also indicate a founding of a new ceremonial center approximately every 300 years and use of each center for at least 900 years. After the decommissioning of these centers, Read, the next site downriver, which may have started as a mortuary camp, developed into the sole feasting-with-shellfish ceremonial center in the Big Bend area. This suite of dates also indicates possibly that length of use is not directly responsible for the volume of these mounds, because DeWeese, a very large mound (Table 6.1), was utilized for 900 years, while Carlston Annis, with less volume, was employed for 1,800 years or more.

Crothers, too, pointed out the contemporaneity of Haynes and DeWeese but noted that the two deposits were opposites in shellfish use. Where the first and third levels of Haynes had much shell, DeWeese's second level had the most. Other categories of artifacts showed no corresponding increase and decline with shell at either site (Crothers 1999:244). Alternating feasting locales is a presumption of this sacred site system.

Turning to the Ohio County sites of the Green River, there are dates only for Indian Knoll and Bowles. Indian Knoll may have been founded about 5,585 years ago and was in use until at least 3,639 years ago. Bowles was founded 500 years later and was utilized until 3,481 years ago, and maybe as late as 2,060 years ago. Again we see two monumental ceremonial centers overlapping in time from at least 5033 BP until 3639 BP, or 1,600 years.

Recently acquired radiocarbon dates from sites in the Falls district indicate that a number of sites were possibly in use simultaneously. Breeden, Reid, Hornung, and Miller all appear to have been contemporaries with one another and with several shell-free mortuaries (Table 2.1). Although dates from KYANG and Lone Hill, two neighboring knoll-top sites, overlap by 400 years, they may well have been largely sequential sites. Can the artifacts and physical characteristics of skeletons tell us in greater detail who feasted with whom?

Biological Evidence of Interactions

Biodistance studies are about genetic exchange through sexual encounters. While it is possible, and even probable, that in the Archaic some of this genetic exchange happened among enemies through capture of women who came to be wives of their captors, more of the indicated sexual exchange in the midcontinent certainly came about through marriages between friendly groups—allies, trading partners, neighbors. Although true biodistance estimations are not possible with these burials because they cannot be parceled into generations and they may well not represent populations because of issues of preservation, recovery, sample size, and selective burial, bioarchaeologists have nevertheless conducted such studies.

Biodistance was explored first using the skeletal collections from Indian Knoll, Eva, Kay's Landing, and Big Sandy (Lewis and Lewis 1961). The variability of the Eva population was approximately that of Indian Knoll, and both populations were somewhat inbred. Other measures of similarity within the collection from the Eva site alone indicated that the Three Mile component males were more variable than the Eva component males. The Three Mile females were still more variable than the males on many traits, suggesting that they came from outside the site catchment area. Examination of bodies from the Big Sandy site indicated general similarity to the Eva series in cranial observations (Lewis and Lewis 1961). Kay's Landing was singled out as "different" from the other skeletal series of the Archaic by several authors (e.g., Brendel 1972, Lewis and Lewis 1961) for the head shapes and stature. It has been said that this skeletal population is most like that of Stallings Island (Brendel 1972, Lewis and Kneberg 1959:169).

Carlston Annis and Indian Knoll burials appear to have been drawn from different populations based on dental metrics (Ward 2005). Furthermore, the Carlston Annis "dentition is larger in all measurements than those of males and females in the Glacial Kame, Fort Ancient, and Ohio Hopewell samples" (Ward 2005:391).

At Rosenberger the R distance between males and females was least pronounced, indicating that they resembled each other in body-facial shape. Men and women were also similar in body size, indicating inconsequential sexual dimorphism. Neither situation was found at Indian Knoll (n=76), where there were pronounced size and facial differences between men and women. "Furthermore, the distance between the group [site] centroids indicates considerable genetic distance between these two populations [Rosenberger and Indian Knoll]. . . . In short, there is a strong indication that the [Rosenberger] group is very homogeneous and the Indian Knoll group is very heterogeneous" (Wolf and Brooks 1979:945).

The conclusion of greater heterogeneity among Indian Knoll burials supports the idea that more foreigners may have been buried in the Indian Knoll ceremonial center, where there are numerous bodies that died violently. Bodies in Rosenberger, a shell-free mortuary, did not show much indication of violence, suggesting that few foreigners were buried there. Greater homogeneity at Rosenberger is expected under this interpretation.

Ward (2005) concluded that Carlston Annis people were distinct from those contemporaneous groups north of the Ohio River, an interpretation that is supported by the conclusions of Powell (1995), studying genetic distance between groups in the eastern United States. Herrmann (2004:175) found that Eva was distinct from the Green River sites. Several of the regions I have isolated in this discussion were, not surprisingly, also gene pools by Powell's results. For instance, dentitions from Tennessee and Illinois were more similar to each other than they were to Florida dentitions.

"Within Powell's (1995) analysis, the correlation of temporal and spatial distance with biological distance does indicate some level of gene flow between the spatially distant samples" (Herrmann 2004:175). But Herrmann thinks that Powell's findings do not mean long-distance migration, and rejects an Illinois to Florida immigration, or even frequent immigrants between major river valleys.

> Down-the-line exchange of trade goods and marriage partners between proximate groups spanning the Southeast could have facilitated the level of gene flow evident within Powell's analysis. I envision a similar level of social interaction as hypothesized by Jefferies (1997) within the Green River drainage where there is a potential for mate exchange across the entire region. (Herrmann 2004:175)

Looking only at Green River crania, Herrmann found 1) cranial samples from Read, Carlston Annis, Ward, Barrett, Chiggerville, and Indian Knoll were significantly different from one another, but 2) the people buried in the shell-free zone at Indian Knoll were indistinguishable from those buried lower, and 3) the Green River burial population appears to be a breeding isolate, although the data available from elsewhere are limited.

To summarize the few relevant studies, one researcher says Eva and Indian Knoll are similar, another says they are distinctive. Powell sees reason to posit a migration corridor for people between Illinois and Florida, while Herrmann attributes similar variation to marriage among neighbors. Lower Tennessee groups were patrilocal. Groups in the northern Ohio Valley were distinct from Carlston Annis.

Future tests need to isolate the burials of possible victims of violence and compare their genetic markers to the burials of those placed in the "normal" burial position of flexed on a side. I suspect that "foreigners" will be among those meeting a violent death.

Artifactual Evidence of Friendly Interactions

The peoples of the Tennessee and Green rivers were suffering the loss of loved ones and experiencing the thrill of revenge from "mourning" and revenge warfare at least by 6,000 years ago, possibly earlier. Alliance making is a common motivation for feasts and would seem relevant in the social milieu of the southern Ohio River valley at the time, when several of the feasting-with-shellfish ceremonial centers were first established across the region. An integral part of the feasting would be gift giving and spouse exchanges.

SOUTHERN RELATIONS

As expected, exotic goods were moving around the eastern United States as early as 6,000 years ago, and further intensified in the South with the development of the Poverty Point network about 3700 BP (Jefferies 1996:222–223), near the end of the history of the Green River "peoples" as envisioned here. Movement of groundstone artifacts such as celts, bannerstones, pendants, and beads out of Florida began during the Mt. Taylor period, the earliest shell-mounding culture in that area (Wheeler et al. 2000). Ovate bannerstones have been found in mounds in northeastern Florida, the shell mounds of the Tennessee River, and in northeastern North Carolina (Sassaman 2006:66). Two individuals at Perry, one who died violently, were given sandstone bannerstones. This sandstone is possibly from Clark County, Mississippi, approximately 150 kilometers to the southwest of Perry (Shields 2007). Gulf Coast whelk shells in Green River graves indicate relations even farther to the south.

The Benton interaction sphere existed 5,600 to 5,000 years ago. It is indicated by its large- and medium-sized Benton points and Turkey Tail–like points found in numerous caches in many sites of the central Tennessee, the Harpeth, and Duck River shell sites, and sites on the upper Tombigbee River. "Bifaces collected from Savannah River Middle Archaic sites, as well as from caches and isolated finds, conform in both age and morphology to Benton points from the Tennessee-Tombigbee region" (Jefferies 1996:230–231). A banded slate bead found at Carlston Annis is similar to banded slate points found at east Aberdeen, also in the Tombigbee region (Watson 2005:531).

Dentalium shell was acquired by central Tennessee River groups from at least two locations, one of them the Florida Keys and West Indies (author's observations of collections). People of these regions appear to have been associates in the late Middle Archaic, and judging from continued similarities and flow of goods—marine shell, steatite, ceramic vessels—they remained friendly for 2,000 years or more. Mention should also be made of the abundant "Poverty Point objects" found at sites in the southern Falls region, which suggests contact along the Mississippi River.

The fact that the only gastropod heaps of the midcontinent are the three Middle Archaic heaps found on the Duck and Harpeth rivers in central Tennessee and the basal layer of Old Clarksville on the Ohio is highly suggestive of a kinship relationship or even multiple ritual loci for a single social group. This anomaly also suggests that there may have been a relationship between Duck River folks and the other Archaic gastropod mound builders, the families of the St. Johns River.

The social associations between northern Alabama clans and those on the Gulf/Atlantic Coast appear not to have been alliances for safety. The evidence of violent deaths is missing (so far) at Stallings Island and Lake Spring, both on the Savannah, and in the St. Johns River mortuaries. The shell arcs/rings and shell works of coastal Florida and the southern Atlantic lack burials altogether. Those feasts would not have been connected to safety alliances but rather were possibly related to trading and renewal rituals.

NORTHERN/WESTERN RELATIONS

The carved bone pin region stretches 500 kilometers from the Falls of the Ohio to eastern Missouri and seems to implicate contact 6,000 to 5,000 years ago, among local groups who also maintained alliances, obtained mates, and exchanged goods, services, and information (Jefferies 1997:482). The Falls pin styles, however, are not found above the Falls and differ from those found in Green River valley burials (Jefferies 1997). "The small number of exotic items found [in the bone pin zone] suggests that while the exchange of nonlocal materials took place, the frequency and volume of this exchange were very limited" (Jefferies 1997:469).

Like the bone pin region, there appears to be a naiad-valve-in-grave region. The Falls-area sites such as KYANG, a shell-bearing mortuary, and Meyer, a shell-free mortuary, frequently have graves with one or more bivalve valves or aquatic gastropod shells included. This burial practice is also seen in one burial at Hayes on the Duck, in numerous burials at Kay's Landing on the lower Tennessee, and in a few burials on the Green River at Chiggerville, Barrett, Ward, and Vaughn in Mississippi. The sporadic appearance of this practice suggests something like the out-marrying of individuals from the Falls district.

Fishhook manufacturing styles recently have revealed similar relationships between peoples of the southern Ohio River, according to Moore (2008:13):

> Review of the existing fishhook literature indicates that the Green River type is widespread in both space and time. In addition to the Pickwick Basin and Eva sites, Green River fishhooks are found in significant quantities in Middle to Late Archaic contexts at the Anderson site in Tennessee and at the McCutchan-McLaughlin site in Oklahoma. Green River hooks were also found at the Rosenberger site in Kentucky, at Black Earth in Illinois, Crib Mound, [and] Russell Cave in Alabama.

Other social relations with groups to the north of the Ohio River valley may be indicated in the large, highly polished granite bannerstone piece from Perry and similar ones from Wisconsin (Lindstrom and Steverson 1987). Two percent of the stone used at Globe Hill in West Virginia is from the Flint Ridge quarries of central Ohio (Mayer-Oaks 1955a:17). The presence of rostra and jaws of martens and fishers, for example, could have come only from the far north (Marquardt and Watson 2004:13). Wabash sites and Green River sites shared the same turtle shell rattle style and the use of red ocher (Winters 1969:76).

INDIVIDUAL RELATIONSHIPS

It is also possible to suggest contact between or contemporaneity of individuals in specific sites. For instance, there are very similar copper pendants in Bu103 of Indian Knoll and Barrett's Bu1. There are single examples of a rather unique necklace—bannerstone strung with beads—at Indian Knoll and Carlston Annis (Kwas cited in Lindstrom and Stevenson 1987). *Busycon* shell wall pieces were carved to look like turtle shells at Indian Knoll and at Whitesburg Bridge on the Tennessee River (Morse 1967:194). The deepest burials at Little Bear Creek, a pair of individuals, possibly had associations with the Green River as reflected in a lump of coal, an atlatl weight, and two projectile points, goods frequently seen in Green River burials. At Long Branch one burial had two atlatls, a bannerstone, shell beads, and shell pendant, also more like the grave goods of a Green River burial than a Tennessee River burial. Several Anderson burials had coal and shell beads that make these burials appear far more like Green River burials than western Tennessee River burials. The segmented shell weights found at Indian Knoll, Bowles, and 1Lu67 on the central Tennessee River also suggest social contact. Perhaps the *Dentalium* shell found at Indian Knoll was gifted by a member of a central Tennessee River clan from 1Ct17, Long Branch, or Perry, where *Dentalium* shell necklaces are more common. Trumpeter swan bones, a species found today in the Mississippi River valley, suggest that guests from the west, perhaps from Arkansas, attended feasts held at Long Branch and Anderson. Nearly identically worked human bone femur tubes come from the Snideker site in Arkansas and Indian Knoll, further hinting at social interaction spanning the Mississippi River (Morse 1967). The bone tube from Arkansas was found with a headless adult male buried below a skull cache.

POSSIBLE HOSTILE RELATIONSHIPS

The Tennessee, Kentucky, and northern Ohio Valley social interactions were apparently different in nature from the southern ones. The presence of violent deaths among the southern Ohio Valley populations is the most obvious difference. Jefferies (1997) thought the bone pin zone of the Ohio Valley was ringed by a border, beyond which the groups were probably "alien." Groups identifiable as possible sources of the victims of violence buried in southern Ohio Valley sites appear to have resided north or west of the Tennessee River, possibly in southern Illinois, Indiana, Ohio, Pennsylvania, and New York. A brief review of the evidence for conflict with groups in the northern Ohio River valley is possible.

Mohney (2002:29) points out that Brewerton eared-notched points are associated with shell middens on Martha's Vineyard and at the Falls of the Ohio. They are prominent in the Hudson River shell heaps as well (Claassen 1995). The distribution of Brewerton points in the Ohio Valley suggests an Archaic population migration from the New York coast and the Hudson River down the Ohio River. Along the route is Frontenac Island, New York, an island mortuary with several violent deaths. Four males have projectile point injuries, four other males have clubbing injuries, two males are torso burials, one has a female skull, one has the skull of a three-year-old, nine individuals are headless, and three skulls were found as isolated elements. (Seven of these headless burials are males who are also missing limbs and two of the headless are women. Again we see the pattern of taking only skulls from females.) In all, 19 of the 159 bodies (12 percent) have obvious evidence of violence in a mortuary dating to 4930+/-260 rcy (Mensforth 2007) or 6206 to 5061 BP. Were they the enemies of the southern Ohio Valley peoples?

Though there are violent deaths in several sites in Ohio and in New York (Mensforth 2007), there are few among Glacial Kame people of northwestern Ohio. Among 120 bodies from four Glacial Kame sites there were two scalpings, and a few cranial injuries, but no decapitations and no dismemberments (Ward 2005).

A group using a Scottsbluff-like point (which could have come from Missouri) apparently attacked members of the group(s) using Cherry and Eva mortuaries in Tennessee (Lewis and Lewis 1961:138). Nevertheless, it seems that most embedded points fit comfortably within the local point styles, given the lack of comments to the contrary, suggesting that the victims were shot locally. For instance, Riverton culture Merom/Trimble point was found in the ribs of a Panther Rock burial on the Ohio River (Bader 2007:50) and in the hand of Bu1 at Riverton.

The End of Shell Mounding in Tennessee, Kentucky, West Virginia, and Indiana

Taçon (1999:40) writes about natural places that humans convert into social landscapes and points out that "this connection did not end with death for an important feature of secondary mortuary ceremonies . . . [and] is the reintegration of the deceased with the special, more sacred parts of the land." Viewing these shell-bearing sites as primarily places to conduct rituals and burial means that changes in religious beliefs and practices explain the end of the shell-mounding phenomenon. In particular, the changes of greatest importance seem to be 1) the abandonment of a shell context within which to ensure renewal of individuals and groups by burying some of the dead, 2) the abandonment of rites focused on human sacrifice, and 3) a temporary interruption in the power of priests to conduct these rites around 3,500 years ago. The public feasting with shellfish stopped even where burial continued—in sites such as Eva. In earlier centuries the rites and feasts probably ceased at particular heaps because of changing priests and their devotees and changing social needs while new locations were founded and rites continued to evolve.

Public feasting with shellfish continued on the Tennessee River in the Guntersville area and on the St. Johns River in Florida. New centers were founded on the Wabash River contemporaneous with Read on the Green River, the latter a converted bluff-top ritual location. Robinson was founded on the Cumberland. Even in those new locations the rites rapidly declined. Although the various districts seem to have had similar motivations for mounding shell during the Middle and early Late Archaic, by 3500 BP the relevant cultural practices and attendant beliefs had diverged between the various districts.

But the last heaps ceased for reasons owing to more than changes in charismatic priests or water depth. For some reason, perhaps associated with changes in beliefs about Mammoth Cave and the Green River, or the birth and life of a great visionary, or the disenfranchisement of the ritual district, the large feasts and human sacrifices ended at Read and Bowles, the (presumed) last heaps on the Green to be utilized. Perhaps the families or priests of the Green River suffered a social blow from which they could not recover.

Conclusions

This chapter has presented an argument for subdividing the category of shell-bearing sites into several classes based on the quantity of dog burials, quantity of human burials, quantity of shells, and elevation/location. Shell-bearing riverside mortuaries, shell-bearing bluff-top sites, which are possible mortuary camps, and shell-bearing non-mortuaries are furthermore argued to be three classes of sites in a sacred site system that also included shell-free mortuaries. Each district in the southern Ohio Valley that had shell-bearing sites had a different combination of these made ritual loci, but all districts offered large public rituals and feasts at the shell-bearing mortuaries.

When I began formulating my questions about the social significance of these sites in 1982, I was not the first to assert the overlooked social importance of these locations. Hofman (1984) referred to several of the midcontinental shell mounds such as Hayes, Ervin, Eva, and Indian Knoll as "aggregation centers." Granger (1988) called the heaps of the Falls district "tribal mortuaries." Rolingson (1967) warned that Green River culture was far more complex than was being acknowledged. We have chosen to emphasize the burials over the artifacts, while for nearly a century the artifacts have been emphasized over the burials. Artifacts, shell debris, and burials fit comfortably with most archaeologists' conception of a village and villages are, with few exceptions, otherwise noticeably absent on this landscape. Nevertheless, in this study I propose that the artifacts, shells, and burials, as well as the fauna, flora, and features, fit comfortably within known ritual/feasting practices.

Critics of the ceremonial center/mortuary argument have claimed that these heaps could not be mortuaries because mortuaries would not be composed of domestic debris (e.g., Marquardt and Watson 2005a, Milner and Jefferies 1998, Pedde and Prufer 2001b). Numerous contradictory examples can be mustered of midden material as a source of mound building material, however. For instance, midden material was used in the St. Johns River shell heaps, in Adena mounds (Webb and Snow 1974:38–39), and in Mound A of the Middle Woodland Mound House site in the lower Illinois River valley (King and Buikstra 2006). "Domestic refuse" is also common on mounds such as McKeithen mound, whose top had "numerous small fire pits, a central hearth, two red ocher deposits, two refuse deposits with hundreds of sherds and deer bone" (Knight 2001:314). On Stage 2 of the (Woodland) Walling platform mound "were surface hearths, small pits, midden areas, stone tools, and abundant bone" (Knight 2001:316).

"Trash" is also the building material of the Puebloan mounds and berms. Mounded trash has been regarded as part of sacred space and renewal ritual possibly as early as Basketmaker III times and continues to be so regarded today (Cameron 2002:683). The great house trash mounds of ancient Puebloan culture have a much lower density of vegetal material and less ash and charcoal, than do the shell heaps, reminiscent of the shell-free cap at Carlston Annis (Wagner 2005). Toll (2001) pointed out that the quantity of ceramics and of lithics found in the great house mounds far exceeded the quantity expected from the number of people thought to live in the associated community.

I am not, however, arguing that the Archaic shell heaps are secondarily deposited village debris. Instead, it seems that the debris is, in fact, primary, even though much of it may never have been used at the heaps, or used only for the short encampment necessary for the completion of the rituals. The primary lithic manufacturing material found in shell heaps, as well as the discarded items of bone, groundstone, and chipped stone, is easily related to renewal rites, involving the discard of the old and the making of the new. In stating that the artifacts in the Mississippian-era submound 51 pit at Cahokia might be mistaken as domestic refuse, Pauketat et al. (2002) specifically drew attention to the debitage and high number of points in the huge submound pit. Renewal of lithic toolkits has been identified frequently by archaeologists looking at quarry sites. Later mounds and other sacred places were the scenes of cooking, tool maintenance, and food discard (e.g., Knight 2001:319). Furthermore, the discarding of all items used in rituals and during ritual feasting is commonly recorded, and such was the situation during Mississippian feasting at Cahokia (Pauketat et al. 2002).

Proof of habitation in these mounds—great variety and number of features, large numbers of animals, housing, wide diversity of artifact types—is missing, while clear evidence of ritual exists. To claim that the burials are mingled with the habitation area is moot, as there are no verifiable habitation areas on any of these heaps. Some habitation areas have been identified adjacent to shell mortuaries on the Tennessee River, such as those at Cherry (Magennis 1977), Kay's Landing (Lewis and Kneberg 1947:4), and Whitesburg Bridge (Gage 2008). It is possible that there is a village (15Bt91) associated with 15Bt12 on the Green River (Hensley 1989), but such findings are rare.

This lack of village sites creates a significant theoretical problem for students of the Archaic who have largely accepted the proposition that sedentism was well underway by Middle Archaic times and evident all around in Late Archaic times. Sedentary populations worry about the abundance of resources around them, and create boundaries to protect those resources that they mark with cemeteries and mounds. Sedentary populations have aggrandizing individuals and families who hoard resources and engineer indebtedness (e.g., Hayden 2001).

The people of the Middle and Late Archaic in the southern Ohio Valley were not sedentary. They did not have villages. They may not have had trading networks. The violence, the exotics, these large sites, and the sacred site system provided their needs for ritual. This situation is not unique and is, interestingly, characteristic of the Adena cultural manifestation that followed the shell-mound–using groups of the late Late Archaic. Adena ritual sites were not connected to residential sites and Adena earthwork ceremonial centers were used by multiple groups (Clay 1998:15). The Hopewell also lived in dispersed hamlets and made regular trips to "free-standing" mounds and earthworks year-round for feasting, adoption, mortuary rituals, exchange, and social interaction (Carr and Yerkes 2005:246).

Similar to the situations of the Late Archaic and Adena peoples, there are at this time no known residential sites or houses for the sambaquis users of Brazil, those other giant heaps of shell, that are now interpreted as mortuary centers made up of "domestic" debris (Fish et al. 2006). Food refuse is present in sambaquis, along with a set of several feature types that are commonplace in residential occupations. Furthermore, arrangements of features and distributions of artifacts indicate domestic activity. Expediently produced chipped stone objects, groundstone objects ranging from informal pebble and cobble forms to well-shaped and polished axes, and shell and bone implements such as hooks, points, and needles, are commonplace. However, archaeologists attribute this domestic debris to graveside mortuary feasts. During the interment ceremonies, and also during later visits to the grave, fires surrounding and overlying the burial pits were lighted and large quantities of food were consumed and deposited with the dead.

It is clear that sambaquis do not represent ordinary habitation loci, but rather are specialized elements of settlement systems—very little is known about the other kinds of sites. Like southern Ohio Valley shell heaps, sambaquis frequently terminate in capping deposits of dark soil that are structurally similar to previous shell strata and also contain burials, but contrast in having only minor shell inclusions. After some period of time, an affinity group ceased to add burials to its funerary area and it was then "closed" by covering it with dirt and large quantities of shell, so much shell, in fact, that it had to be procured elsewhere and transported to the site. Subsequent funerary areas were established on new surfaces atop previous deposits such that the heap grew horizontally and vertically. This process of burial, feasting, and covering a former funerary area was reenacted over centuries, incrementally and ultimately giving rise to their huge volume and monumental appearance (Fish et al. 2000:13–14). Like the case in the Late Archaic of the southern Ohio Valley and the following Adena period, Fish et al. believe that the evidence indicates that all of this feasting, construction, and ritual occurred without the emergence of explicit mechanisms for rank and hierarchy (Fish et al. 2006:20).

We must seriously consider ritual behavior if we are to grasp the lived lives of our subjects. Writing about Plains Indian rituals and ritual sites, Linea Sundstrom (2000) takes to task archaeologists who stare ritual behavior in the face yet cannot see it because they insist that tools are always already only domestic items (see also Pauketat et al. 2002). We also obscure ritual when caches and feature contents are divided into their raw-materials categories or species rather than being considered as a set (Osborn 2004). Sundstrom attributes this blindness to a failure to read anthropology. The task before us is to separate domestic debris from feasting/ceremonial /ritual debris, but this will not be achieved with artifact typologies and laboratory sorting into raw material categories. It can and is being achieved with attention to context, through quantitative characteristics of "domestic debris," with qualitative characteristics, with attention to groupings of artifacts and features of landscape, and with study of modern and pre-Columbian ritual practices and places. Pestles and broken projectile points are legitimate offerings that might have little to do with the sex, age, or status of the dead person. The same can be said for a turkey bone, a human jaw, a rounded pebble, a plant stem, or seeds. The residue from council fires, smoke lodges, feasts, projectile point production, the hunt, or production of craft items is residue with a soul, residue to be tended to and cared for. A pit full of unopened shells or a large number of deer bones can be feasting debris, a pit with an odd assortment of animal parts can be an offering, and a pit filled with charcoal and fire-cracked rock can indicate a ritual deposit of the living spirit of a sweat lodge.

Numerous archaeologists working in the Southeast are now comfortable with Archaic-aged dirt mounds, Archaic shell monuments in Florida, and even Archaic ceremonial shell rings, yet still are not comfortable with the idea that there was anything special about the height or depth of shell mounding achieved in the midcontinent and the hundreds of bodies put into them. The observations recorded in this and other chapters should at least challenge the idea that these sites are uniformly simple villages or base camps where only mundane activities occurred. They should also challenge our assumptions about Archaic social and political simplicity, and even the degree to which there was complexity.

The mere existence of private mortuaries suggests that those people buried in the riverside shell heaps—where most people were buried—differed in some way from those who were not buried in such a location. Maybe those people placed in shell-free mortuaries died at the wrong time of year, were born to the wrong lineage, or died without achieving a particular status in their communities, or any number of other "causes." Rather than looking for social differences among the burial population of one site (Rothschild 1979) or one class of site (e.g., Magennis 1977, Winters 1974), tests should investigate the differences in bodies and grave goods first within class and then between these different classes of ritual sites. Several such studies have been conducted without the investigators recognizing that they were dealing with different site classes (e.g., Driskell 1979, Mayes 1997). I offered such an investigation here and in Chapter 6.

I do not expect to be right in all of the particulars or avenues that I pursue in this study. But, I believe with great confidence that those who think that the Hypsithermal or overexploitation of shellfish or busy gardeners account for the end of shell mounding are wrong. In the following pages, I further explore the rituals conducted at these and other locations.

CHAPTER 8
ARCHAIC RITUALS AT
SHELL-BEARING SITES

Archaic rituals and beliefs are the frontier in the study of the past in North America. Woodland period ritual beliefs have been tackled in two recent compendia (Charles and Buikstra 2006, Carr and Case 2005) and Mississippian beliefs continue to attract scholarly attention (e.g., Reilly and Garber 2007). Webb (1950a), Winters (1969), and Blitz (1983) offered thoughts on Archaic beliefs and ritual paraphernalia. Numerous people have discussed the cache blade phenomenon as well (e.g., Deter-Wolf 2004, Futato 1983, Johnson and Brookes 1989, Sassaman et al. 1988). Burial ceremonialism has been explored by Mires (1991) and Bader (2006), among others. Understanding caves as ritual places has been the focus of work in the past decade (Claassen 2006a, 2006b, Lockheart et al. 2007, Simek et al. 2007).

The shells, the burials, the dogs, the caches, and the artifacts found in the shell-bearing sites of the southern Ohio Valley leave us tantalizing clues as to the types of rituals enacted in these settings and the beliefs that motivated them. In the previous chapter, I proposed a set of sacred sites for each district of the southern Ohio Valley, including bluff-top shell sites, riverside shell-heap mortuaries, shell-free mortuaries, and natural features, particularly caves. The bluff-top sites in the Green River district were scenes of numerous dog ceremonies and were possible burial processing locations. The large shell heaps found there and elsewhere were places for staging rituals important to groups of people and holding feasts of regional scope.

In addition to feeding an audience, making a show of Other World favoritism, and communicating social information to attendees, feasts are the primary means used to mobilize labor (R. Saunders 2004). Labor would have been needed in the production of the feasts but also in the maintenance and "feeding" of shrines, idols, fires, and other ritual facilities and utensils (e.g., Brown 2005). What rituals may have been held that would have precipitated the great and small feasts indicated by shell accumulation?

Based on the evidence available from excavation reports, it is possible to propose that one key ritual observed was earth renewal where priests addressed the moon, sun, thunder, lightning, rain deities, and ancestors to petition them for fertility of women, families, game, and plants. These renewal rites involved bone caching, shell accumulation, human sacrifice, and stone deposits. Another important ritual may have been a community rebalancing rite, the most severe of which involved a distinctive type of burial. There is also a hint of going-to-water rites, which may have focused on either a river-keeper sodality and/or cleansing mourners of corpse sickness. It is these rites that I will focus on in this chapter. In addition, I will present evidence of the symbolic importance of shell and stone.

In addition to the public rites at the shell-bearing sites, there would also be rites conducted by individuals held at natural features and the private mortuaries making requests for aid and thanksgiving for aid in courting, hunting, fishing, trading, dreaming, fiber arts, lapidary arts and other such skilled endeavors, traveling, alliance making, and seeking lost items and people. Those prayers would be delivered by aromas, sounds, animal others, spirits, and deities. Individuals performing birthing rites, naming rites, first craft production/kill rites, completion or achievement rites in craft production or hunting, or fishing (e.g., Schaefer 2002) are to be anticipated as well, each with aspects of fertility, health, and thanksgiving. Curing and well-being rites with protection from witches, malevolent spirits/airs, and powerful priests would be important.

The material manifestations of these ritual actions and prayers that are apparent in the North American ethnographies, and in the Archaic, Woodland, and Mississippian sacred sites and ritual deposits, are tool, craft, and animal part offerings, human and animal sacrifice, ocher, cremation, rite paraphernalia (e.g., pipes, beads, shells, rattles, stones), and indications of directionality and numeracy. But there were many more elements that were perishable, or intangible: gender; water; smoke; smells, sounds, color; time; solar, astral, and lunar alignments; feasting and fasting. Because the various rites and their elements are so intertwined in meaning and staging, and because analogy and metaphor are essential elements of native perception (Hall 1997), my discussion of artifacts, features, postures, associations, context, and meaning will be hopelessly reductive. A rich world of pageantry, prescription, dancing, singing, feasting, learning, emotion, and drama will be reduced to paper and limited in scope.

Earth Renewal Rites

Assuring that the deities would continue to provide water, children, and essential animals and plants is of great concern to many modern American groups (e.g., Chickasaw, Creek, Cherokee) and apparently was so to many ancient groups. Individuals often conduct private renewal acts such as the deposition of shells (Halperin et al. 2003) or animal bones in caves and personal hunting shrines (e.g., Brown 2005), but rites of renewal are also performed by priests on behalf of entire communities. It is earth renewal rites that I believe were the primary rituals conducted at riverside shell heaps, evident in caches, offerings, shells, burials, human sacrifice, and stone items.

Bone Caches

There are several candidates for renewal rite caches/offerings in the riverside shell-bearing sites, shell-free sites, and caves. These rites apparently involved the "return" of one or a few bones of key species to an earth deity as thanks and prayer for continued abundance of each species. I have highlighted several renewal offerings from Archaic strata in Roger's Shelter, Russell Cave, and Modoc Rock Shelter in previous papers (Claassen 2005, 2006). Shell-bearing sites were also appropriate places to leave these offerings.

Riverton, on the Wabash River, has three possible renewal offerings in Features 18, 22, and 11 (Winters 1969:101). Feature 18 contained more than 200 bones of 19 animals (Table 8.1). The artifacts included were two cut antler sections, two splinter awls, and one triangular chert blade, leaf-shaped blade, blade fragment, shell paint cup, shuttle, canine pendant, and Riverton point fragment. The artifacts may have been items used in the accompanying ritual that were also put away/decommissioned at the conclusion of the ritual. Feature 22 contained 49 bones, including several different species than were included in Feature 18. Although Feature 22 was found in the area of much burned sandstone and a fired-clay floor, none of the bones was burned. No artifacts were included. Feature 11, called a "storage pit," had several layers of soil over a plug of yellow clay that covered 13 large mammal bones, and those of five other creatures, one Robeson point, and one cut section of antler. Below these items ("Riv 11lo" in Table 8.1) was more clay, then 12 bones of at least four species.

Offerings typically have high species diversity, and but a few bones from each animal. Small animals are particularly common, those species that zooarchaeologists often label intrusive, and immature animals are popular inclusions. Burned bones are also common. The bones present are often from the left side or the fore quarter (Claassen 2006a, 2006b, Pohl 1983).

Feature 18 also indicates that the tools used to hunt and the tools derived from the bones and antlers of the prey were similarly featured in the supplicants' prayers. Feature 11 suggests that, at least in the second layer of bones, there may have been a concern on the part of the supplicant to include representatives of the lower world (fish), this world (deer), and the upper world (bird), a distribution that can also be seen in the other proposed renewal offerings. Riverton emerges, then, as a place where earth renewal rites were conducted.

Bone caches, also probably for earth renewal, are found in the much older Middle Archaic Ervin site (Hofman 1986) on the Duck River in its Features 22, 35, and 36 (Table 8.1). Feature 22 contained a cremated human along with 18 other species. A few bones of deer, raccoon, rabbit, mole, and turkey were burned. Feature 35 contained bones of *Homo sapiens,* striped skunk, and four other species with burned bones from fox squirrel and human. Feature 36 again contained burned human bone and 16 additional species. Some of its rabbit, woodchuck, squirrel, and gar bones were burned (Hofman 1986:112). In these offerings we see the use of fire, the inclusion of humans, and the importance of small animals (Table 8.1).

It is interesting that these so-called "riverine exploitation bases" have renewal offerings that lack water birds and most fish species. Ironically, where there *is* a possible bone soul/earth renewal offering with fish and naiad remains is at the *shell-free* Rosenberger site. Feature 31 contained burned rock, five bones of deer, one bone each of drumfish, turtle, and a large mammal, two other fish bones, and 58 pieces of naiads (Driskell 1979). A wealth of aquatic fauna was found whose quantity and variety increased with depth also at the base of the Archaic earthen mound called Watson Brake in Louisiana, as though the gifts of the Underworld were the spiritual foundation of the mound (Jackson and Scott 2001).

There is one other ritual act that is evident in two sites that may be an aspect of earth renewal if the turtle was viewed as the representative of this World. Eva's feature 2 was a prepared bed of mussel shells, four shells arranged "tulip fashion," and a small terrapin shell placed top down in the middle of them (field notes). At the base of the bluff upon which accumulated the Read site was a "circle of large rough stones carefully laid to enclose two carapace of terrapin at the center" (Webb 1950:362). At the least these two features suggest a common ritual was practiced for which either stones or shells could be used during the period bracketed by the Eva/Three Mile component.

Renewal with Shell

But more than the caching of individual bones, the millions of shells can also be seen as renewal offerings and collectively creating renewal contexts (Becker 1988). I have, as yet, said little about the symbolism of shell, whether marine or freshwater. In numerous papers, I have explored this symbolism and conclude, in accordance with the knowledge of others (e.g., Baillou 1968, Ceci 1989, Hall 1997), that shell, whether a single item, three dozen beads, or a mass of valves, was understood throughout North and Central America as symbolic of rebirth and rejuvenation.

Mollusks and their shells are of the Underworld. Mollusks were present in the primordial sea when the deities created the island Earth, at the beginning of time and history. The spiraling form of the gastropods, particularly the large marine whelks and conchs, was emblematic of the Winds, eternity, and the turning movement of the world at the dawn of creation (e.g., Bassie-Sweet 1996, Schaefer 2002).

> The inner spiral of the conch shell we see often used as a pendant and the spiral probably represented eternity. . . . It can be assumed that the function of . . . a conch shell mask was to assure eternity or rebirth. . . . Several times we found infant burials . . . buried by squeezing the scanty remains of bones in the opening of the shell. One should not wonder that the opening and its coloration reminded man of the female sex organ, therefore, he buried his premature infants in another mother shell. (Baillou 1968:14)

The flesh of many naiads strongly resembles the genitalia of women, evident not only in many scientific names, but also in native use and beliefs, clear evidence of their procreative function. Gastropods have caves, women have caves, and caves are a known portal to the Underworld, where reside earth deities and ancestors, many groups believe (Claassen 2008). Deities such as Quetzalcoatl and Changing Woman, and humans, in some cases (Northwest Coast groups), emerged from shells. To drink from a gastropod cup, to dig a grave with bivalves, to look through a shell maskette, is to go back to the Beginning, to be in direct contact with Underworld powers, to ask for fertility and continuance.

As renewal symbols, shells were suitable offerings to rain deities or to the ancestors and earth lord/mother to ensure human fertility. A Cherokee priest told trader Alexander Longe in the 1720s:

> when our 4 days of fasting is ended, we go out into the wood unto some solitary place to keep us from distraction and then we open our [shell] beads which we throw towards the south to that white petty god that

is there and implore the great king to tell him to send us rain. (Corkran 1969:34)

Shells were used by Ohio Valley medicine societies for the initiation of new members and used in adoption (Hall 1997). The Tlingit of the Northwest Coast had a single word for womb, bivalve, and coffin (Ceci 1989). The Seneca thought a soul could be purified by placing a body in a shell (Ceci 1989). Shells were given to returning warriors both in eastern North America (Corkran 1969:46) and in central Mexico (Emiliano Melgar Tísoc, personal communication, 2006).

Most Native Americans believe(d) in reincarnation that is/was achieved through resemblance, naming, offspring, and adoption. Shell shooting/bead spitting initiation ceremonies enacted the rebirth of the initiate, and strings of shell beads were used to forge fictive kinship among the Iroquois League. The placing of the corpse of the older male on a platform of shell beads in the shape of a falcon in Mound 72 of Cahokia was a preparatory act for reincarnation. (Other examples of shell use related to birth and rebirth can be found in Hall 1997 and in Claassen 2008.)

Beliefs similar to those specified above may well explain the following examples of Archaic shell/human associations. Infant Bu308 was placed in a shell at Hermitage Springs (burial data file in possession of Dan Allen), in a shell "casing" at Perry (Bu53), under an inverted shell at Perry (Bu237), and with a conch shell at Mulberry Creek (Bu94). A conch shell sat in the center of cremated remains and contained the calcined skull fragments of Bu166 at Bluff Creek. A marine shell was placed over the face of Ward's Bu175. The skull of Bu24 at 1Lu86 was resting in a large bivalve (Webb 1939a). A missing skull was replaced with a shell at Widow's Creek (Warren 1975). (Both of these last bodies may be post-Archaic in age, however.) Ocher powder was found in a shell valve in a group burial of women at Bluegrass. The only gastropods found in graves at Bluegrass were found with women (Mayes 1997:86).

One or more shells were present as digging implements for many graves in Falls district sites, particularly at Meyer (Bader 2005) and Black Earth (Nance 1986), both shell-free mortuaries. They may have served as the digging tool in the symbol complex of shell=cave=pit=womb. Unutilized valves were often included in burials in the Falls district and occasionally found elsewhere. East Steubenville's Feature 62 was a body with 11 naiad hinges. Four infants at Chiggerville had from nine to 17 pairs of valves, while seven women's graves at Ward (Watson 2005), one grave at Barrett, and graves at Bowles contained valves. The practice occurred with two newborns and six adults at Indian Knoll. Big Sandy had one such grave, but farther up the Tennessee River, Widow's Creek had at least five Archaic graves with valve inclusions (Warren 1975). Extremely large valves were found near the bodies of a couple at Vaughn (Atkinson 1974). Though whole shells are different from shell beads or shell pendants, the purpose behind including them was probably the same. "These contextual associations [of shells] with several . . . burials suggested at least a peripheral role in the ideological sub-systems of the [Widows Creek] occupants" (Warren 1975:169). About the practice at the Black Earth site, Nance says valves "must be assigned some kind of ceremonial status" (1986:11).

More so than individual graves or a handful of shells as grave goods, the hundreds of thousands of shells at these feasting loci created a renewal *setting*. Whole families and entire lineages could seek renewal/continuance through burial in a shell heap. These shell mountains would have been identified as aquatic realms linked to supernatural Underworld domains. "[They were] situated metaphorically in the Underworld, reinforcing their aquatic setting" (Brady and Ashmore 1999:133). By incorporating Underworld creatures with artifacts, it was possible to blur the distinction between the natural and the artificial (Brady and Ashmore 1999:132) and humanize the landscape of both the Underworld and This World. The accumulation of shells moved the Underworld into This World. At the least, we should expect that lineage/moiety heads and elders, clan heads, and family heads were buried in these renewal places.

Human Sacrifice for Renewal

Human sacrifice for Earth Renewal purposes is potentially evident in the offerings with burned human bone, detailed above (Table 8.1). Smell is an integral part of offerings and the smell of burning flesh and the smoke from the fire are highly appropriate means of communicating with deities. As a minority burial practice, cremation needs to be understood as appropriate in certain, special settings. I leave to others an extended study of cremation during the Archaic.

Human sacrifices may also be seen in the mass burials with evidence of violent treatment, particularly the ritually important combinations of four to six skeletons. When looking at groups of four or more simultaneous burials, different ages are often included, suggesting ritual disposal.

Table 8.1. Fauna in Proposed Renewal Offerings (x=present)[1]

	Features						
	Riv 18	Riv 22	Riv 11up	Riv 11lo	Erv 22	Erv 35	Erv 36
Animal (NISP)							
Deer	40	3	3	1	x		x
Elk	1						
Bird	12	5		1			
Turkey	5				x		
Fish	9	2	3	2	x		x
Turtle	11		3		x	x	
Snapping turtle	1	2			x	x	x
Woodchuck	1				x		x
Raccoon	2	1			x		
Opossum	3	1			x		
Squirrel	10				x	x	x
Beaver			1		x		x
Mink	1				x		x
Otter					x		
Porcupine	1	1					
Grey fox	1						
Rabbit	1				x	x	x
Frog			1		1		
Snake	2						
Human					x	x	x
Mollusks							

[1] Winters 1969:101

These significant age categories are infants, juveniles, adults, and old adults in proportions approximating 1/1/1 or 1/1/1/2. Group renewal rites could well call for the sacrifice of one person of each age of life. Many Indian groups associate each stage of life with a cardinal direction (dioramas in the Museum of the American Indian, Washington, D.C.), suggesting that the relevant ritual in this case would be one that invoked the four/five/six directions, as a renewal rite might do.

At 1Ct17, a shell heap on the Tennessee River, there were five bodies laid on top of the shell, including one infant, one child, one adolescent, one adult, and one cremated child. The only bodies within the shell matrix were an adult, an adolescent, a child, and an infant; the combination I am suggesting is ritually significant. The infant had hundreds of shell beads, and a second burial had a terrapin bowl that contained a bear jaw gorget, bone awl, and bone spatula. In each subset of bodies, each body was buried in a distinctive manner—one flexed, one extended, one bundled, and one partially flexed, lending further support to the idea that burial posture has ritualized significance, and that these foursomes were ritually constituted. Although these burials did not register with the excavator as simultaneous, this age distribution is suggestive of two ritual events, one during and one after, shell collecting times. The event after shell-collecting times may indicate a closing or decommissioning event.

In addition to this evidence from 1Ct17 for ritual burial numbers and a site closing or decommissioning ceremony, there is evidence that a number of feasting with shellfish ceremonial centers were *initiated* with a ceremonial burial rite of one to four bodies, as was proposed and developed in Chapter 6. Consecration rites are also a form of renewal rite. In this place the lineage will continue, prosper, and gain power as the ancestors accumulate.

Not all group burials were consecration burials (Table 8.2). One of the most interesting group burials was found at Ward, where four flexed adults were arranged around a central flexed adult. Judging from the photo (Webb and Haag 1940:90), two bodies were head to head, two were foot to foot, and the central individual was headless. All were on their left sides. Four had embedded projectile points. Three additional graves at Ward contained five, six, and nine bodies (Rolingson 1967:338).

We may see at Ward, at 1Ct17, and elsewhere, an Archaic precursor to the Mississippian Xipe Totec–like rite as discussed by Hall (2000). Xipe Totec was a rite of renewal held in the springtime (Miller and Taube 1993:188), a rite of beginnings.

Babies accompanied by shells, whether marine shell modified into "ornaments" or whole freshwater shells, are also potential sacrifices. They are often sprinkled with red ocher that may implicate appeal to a sun deity or the stars (Irwin 1994:216). In historic situations in Mesoamerica, babies were sacrificed as part of a renewal ritual—and were often deposited with marine shell (Miller and Taube 1993:153).

Indian Knoll infant burials 811, 647, 171, and 63 are good candidates for sacrifices in a renewal rite, given that all are associated with shell. Bu811 was also headless, lain on shell, and had an atlatl and shell beads. Bu647 had two large mussel valves included in the grave, and Bu63 had nine pearls. Other sacrificial candidates are Perry Bu53, surrounded by naiad valves and a shell pendant, the two infants at Chiggerville with five or more pairs of bivalves, and the extended newborn and infant at Barrett, both with shell beads. The Kay's Landing group burial of two babies and two children (Bu33, 34, 35, 36), with extensive red ocher, the only shell items found at the site, stone beads and perforated carnivore canines, missing hands, feet, and skull, also is suggestive of sacrifices for a renewal rite. The Anderson site gives us an unburned, ocher-covered infant burial in a rock-lined fire pit (Bu7), which suggests to me a ritual fire, sacrifice, and then, after the fire's extinction, the burial (Dowd 1989). The only infant at the Fennel site on a tributary of the Tennessee River had a mussel valve filled with red ocher. I wonder if the clusters of infants in the deepest levels at Indian Knoll and Carlston Annis were part of place consecration/dedication rites.

A mixture of infant human bone with that of one or more other animals also suggests the earth renewal ceremony in particular. One persistent characteristic of fauna in an offering is the use of immature or very small animals. The most striking representation of an infant in a possible earth renewal deposit might be that found at Bluff Creek (although it may be post-Archaic in age). Bu36, an infant, 2.8'bs, was buried with an ulna awl, shell beads, an ospenis of a carnivore, and an ospenis of a raccoon. Might we call this fertility symbolism? Perry Bu50 was a child, extended, with 10 bone pendants made from leg bones of *Chelydra* sp., a turtle, a common representative of the earth. Infant and child burials 2, 7, 39, and 61 at Big Sandy were buried with animal parts. Bu6, an infant, at Hayes, had a drilled deer ulna. The infant was disarticulated. Anderson's Bu72 was a human infant mixed with a deer fetus, also highly suggestive of a sacrificial rite for renewal.

Winters and others have pondered the meaning (Winters 1969:82) of red ocher in Archaic-period burials. After considering age, violence, sex, quality and quantity of grave goods, and inclusion in multiple burials, Winters concluded that the application of red ocher in the Green and Wabash rivers "was dependent on certain unknown physical conditions at the time of the death of the individual." Here I propose that red ocher is another mark of a ritually killed individual or an individual who died in a particularly auspicious way (such as lightning strike). The ocher-marked individuals in sites of the Green and Wabash valleys amounted to 3.7 percent of the dead and were between the ages of newborn and 37 years. Fifty-three to 100 percent of red ocher burials had grave goods, in contrast to the 25–43 percent of ocherless burials (Winters 1969:81). All of the Green River riverside ceremonial centers had bodies with red ocher, except for Butterfield, while none of the Alabama sites did. Much more analytical work is needed on the use of red ocher during Paleoindian and Archaic times.

Stone as Renewal Offering

Projectile points and knives were the most common type of grave good at several shell-bearing sites and were second to shell beads at other sites. Even outside of burial, the high proportion of points when compared to other tools raises questions about the village label as elucidated in Chapter 6. Blades were often cached in many of the shell heaps as well, and Benton blade production is documented in the Alabama heaps.

There are good ethnographic reasons for suspecting that items of stone were more than just tools when they occurred in burial context and in caches and, as I present below, even when they occur in abundance in the site matrix. Their symbolic meaning and ritual use give further indication of the proposed concern with renewal.

Archaeologists are accustomed to the idea that people would discard old but usable tools and replace them with new tools as an act of renewal. Archaeologists are not so accustomed to thinking of the old tools as *offerings*. In Mesoamerican offerings, spinning, weaving, and grinding tools were commonly given to a deity (e.g., Claassen 2006a, 2006b, Pohl 1983, Schaefer 2002), as were miniatures of these items. Among Plains Indians, arrow offerings were common and were given to/left for spirits or deities living in caves (Sundstrom 2000), in rock shelters (Mallouf 2007), at rock outcrops (Mallouf 2007), and other places of spiritual import. Northeastern Indian stories of Thrown Away Boy/ Spring Boy/Flint indicate that arrows were used to lure deities and spirits out of their cave dens. Stone people such as Flint were the first people on earth (Irwin 1994:223).

Stone, which we think of as dead, was animated and has a renewal role for Indians. "The Buffalo Stone was owned by [Blackfoot] women, and to them alone was the power given to call the buffaloes" (Irwin 1994:222). Absarokee regarded smooth or egg-shaped rocks as female, and pointed rocks as male. When wrapped in a bundle, they could reproduce. Such stones possessed many different kinds of power and could even stimulate hair growth. "A translucent stone symbolized the underwater powers" (Omaha), and for the Lakota, "stone was one of the great powers from which all creation ultimately originated" (Irwin 1994:224–225). Stone was closely associated with lightning. Where lightning struck the ground, thunderstones were created, thought many Plains Indian groups (Irwin 1994:225).

"Flint working was given by spirits to humans such that stone working and flint tools have a sacred quality and origin" (Irwin 1994:192). Of course, the act of flint knapping or fire generation by striking flints together created tiny sparks, making evident to all that lightning lived inside stone and that some individuals were particularly good at calling forth the lightning spirit from stone. Because pure water, rain, and fog resided in caves, lightning and thunder also issued from caves and carried fertility symbolism, so that it is possible that flint knapping at a cave could invoke or attract the spirits responsible for sending rain to the earth. In fact, among Mexican groups, babies were named "the chips, the flakes" of the ancestors (Furst 1995:125). I am reminded of the tens of thousands of flakes recovered at the Austin site (Kentucky) cave mouth (Barker and Breitburg 1992). One could think of these chips as fertility offerings given the association of lightning with fertility and of babies with chips/flakes. (Was this the meaning of the 17kg of flakes in the submound 51 pit at Cahokia [Pauketat et al. 2002], flakes mingled with feasting debris and ritual paraphernalia?) Even the knapping tools were often discarded as caches in the shell-bearing sites, suggesting that they too could be used to petition for fertility/water.

Many New World peoples thought their life forces became solid substances with animating powers, particularly after death (Classen 1993:30, Furst 1995:74, Irwin 1994). Rocky outcrops resembling the human face and profile, gallstones, and kidney stones provided proof for these beliefs (Furst 1995). Two aspects of the soul—one animating, the other carrying personality/ fate—could be held by stone or manifested through stone during and after death (e.g., Furst 1995). The Cahuilla of California believed that the spirit that possessed a priest could manifest as a stone, and the Papago believe that priests have stone crystals inside their hearts. The Wixárika prepare a miniature weaving hung from arrows to wrap the rock crystals that embodied deceased or powerful living family members (Schaefer 2002:45). A rock placed with the corpse to be cremated gave "the detached life force a place to return, anchoring the spirit in the grave and keeping it from haunting the living" (Furst 1995:75). (Woodland-period galena balls in Pickwick burials may reflect similar beliefs, as might the pebble included with Bu1 at Riverton.) The animating soul returns to this world annually as winged beings, as shadowy doubles, as breath, and as gemstone (Furst 1995). In Central America and South America, stone carvings and natural stone human likenesses were soul doubles (Classen 1993:30, Furst 1995). Irwin (1994:35) tells us that "throughout North and Central America . . . stones are regarded as particularly powerful, enduring objects."

The soul-conveying personality entered the fetus through drilling, "much the same way ancient craftsmen worked precious blue or green stones, using a drill with an upright stick" (Furst 1995:71). Breath was blown into the fetus through the drill hole (fontanel). "In Central Mexican belief, stones functioned as the visible [personality] of gods, nobles, rulers, and the self-made men" (Furst 1995:71). Along these lines stone pipes, or sucking tubes, would be reservoirs for the spirit of an evil soul sucked out of a possessed individual (Willoughby 1935:92). Many other relevant characteristics of stone are set forth in Irwin (1994) and in Furst (1995).

Blade caches further suggest the spirit and animas of stone. Blade caches are found in most of the Tennessee and Alabama sites under consideration here. Futato (1983), Johnson and Brookes (1989), and Deter-Wolf (2004) have proposed and illustrated a mortuary ceremony for the Middle Archaic Benton period (people who perhaps created most of the shell heaps on the Tennessee River in Alabama) that was steeped in stone symbolism expressed in oversized, beautifully crafted bifaces placed in caches, which sometimes included ocher (Johnson and Brookes 1989:141). The blades seem unused. Such caches have been recovered at numerous Paleoindian and Archaic sites throughout the southeastern United States (Carr and Stewart 2004). Sassaman et al. (1988) also speak of a stone distribution system in the Savannah valley and of the ceremonial implications. The making of caches, like the making of graves, causes a cavity in the earth, a conceptual cave (see also Brady and Ashmore 1999:135–136), which is the symbol and home of the deities responsible for earth renewal.

In addition to the blade caches found in some graves and in mound matrix that have long been recognized as ceremonial in nature, in these sites there are numerous caches of cores, bifaces, flakes, and heavy groundstone implements. All of these collections could be repositories for souls of the dead person, constitute offerings to particular spirits and culture heroes, or be the equipment of an herbal healer.

Stones are alive—hearing, seeing, storing, reproducing, singing, conveying, and moving. Many Plains Indian groups believed that the hearth stones and sweat house stones were alive (Irwin 1994:179) and could hear. The act of drilling stone is an act of fertility, chips are babies, and stone is of the earth and the Underworld, the source of humans and

TABLE 8.2 Proposed Ritual Killings[1]

Place	Infant	Child	Juvenile	Adult	Notes
Bluff Cr. bu119	1	0	0	4	infant 1's bs
O'Neal bu51-53	0	2	0	2	
O'Neal bu43		2		1	4 in all, one unaged
1Ct17	1	1	1	1	also crem. child's 5 different positions
Perry U1 bu56-60	1	1	0	3	
Perry U1 bu121	2	0	1	4	
Perry U2 bu164	1	0	0	4	fetus buried later?
Perry U2 bu206	0	0	1	3	
Perry U3 bu616-620	0	0	0	4	21 gg
Barrett bu35-38					4 individuals, no ages
Ward bu 323-327	0	0	0	5	2 female, 3 male, 4 with embedded points
Ward bu173-176	0	0	0	4	3 female, 1 male— scalped, stabbed, trophy
Indian Kn. bu611-614	0	0	0	4	3 male + 1unknown
Indian Kn. bu55–58	0	0	0	4	2 male, 2 female, 2 no head
Indian Kn. bu303–308	1	1	0	3	6 in all, 1 no age
Carlston bu146–149	0	1	1	3	
Shell-free mortuaries					
Parrish bu16–19	0	0	0	4	2 with red ocher
Parrish bu45–50	0	0	0	6	1 with red ocher
Parrish bu119–125	0	0	0	7	2 with red ocher
Rosenberger bu1–4	0	2	0	2	lithics, tine
Rosenberger bu33–36	1	0	0	3	
Rosenberger bu115–118	1	0	0	3	

[1]O'Neal (Lubsen 2004), Rosenberger (Wolf and Brooks (1979), others from WPA reports.

food. These beliefs may well have been held by Archaic peoples as they were (are) by modern Indians in this country and in Mexico.

It may be the dense stratum of Ft. Payne chert debitage that best signals the ceremonial nature of the Alabama shell heaps, but these places must have been spiritually significant prior to that work to have been chosen as the sites for cache blade production. It may be the lightning/

fertility association that made lithic production appropriate there and on the tops of earthen mounds in Archaic times and later. The early earthen mound of Watson's Brake, in Louisiana, had abundant microdrills, preforms, and cores made of local materials discarded in the submound stratum. A complete reduction sequence for microdrills was found on the surface of the Stage II mound D (Saunders et al. 2004).

Sites like the East Steubenville bluff top have caused interpretive problems for the study of grave goods because nearly every grave had lithic inclusions. I am proposing that two of the foundational spiritual beliefs in the Archaic were that stones had souls and that important aspects of the human soul were manifested in stone. The archaeological practice of tallying crinoids, stone discs, pebbles, bannerstones, and blocks of pigment may be telling us far more than we have realized, as these "stones" (and perhaps including shells) may represent the different social value of the people, just as the Aztec priests chose different types of stones for august and commoner souls (Furst 1995:71). In this regard I am particularly struck by those bannerstones having butterfly shape and the stacked shell atlatl weights that look like stacked vertebra. Cultures around the world associate the departing soul with a bird or butterfly or other winged being and the departing of breath (Furst 1995). Butterflies and windpipes would serve to expedite a soul's departure, particularly useful at the death of a priest or the sending of a soul to a particular deity.

Although many archaeologists have assumed that these objects were part of hunting equipment placed with dead hunters, the inclusion of points and bannerstones in graves of women, children, and infants means that either those individuals had far more interaction with pointed weaponry and tools than has been allowed by our gender and age stereotypes or that points signify something other than the hunting equipment possessed by the person at the time of death. I think there is evidence here for an Archaic-era belief that the soul became a solid substance upon death, and that flakes and chips could serve a ritualized fertility role and were thus just as much the purpose of lithic manufacturing as was a finished item. I have been delighted to find recently an article by Robert Hall (1983) that has called upon a similar association between stone, water, spirit, flakes, turkey tail points, and fertility to explain aspects of Red Ocher and Glacial Kame ceremonialism.

As public renewal places, the shell heaps were particularly appropriate locations to discard old chipped and groundstone tools, to manufacture new stone tools, to generate debitage, and to cache stone. Stone in block, core, and chip forms may have been brought to these places specifically as offering material, a suggestion recently proposed for Poverty Point as well, where some 70 metric tons of chipped stone artifacts were left (Carr and Stewart 2004:130). "This scenario could include individuals from far-flung regions coming to Poverty Point—but not for trade. These individuals might make the journey . . . for the purpose of some other pilgrimage. As a good guest, one brings a gift of stone" (Carr and Stewart 2004:144). I wonder if stone offerings were made not only by pilgrims attending the ritual events at shell sites, but also by anyone passing a shell mortuary in those centuries and even much later, as has been documented for sacred places on the Plains (Sundstrom 2000).

Rebalancing Rite

Native Americans have probably always been concerned with balance between self and the cosmos as expressed in well-being. Health, wealth, success, luck, and dreaming are the results and manifestations of proper balance. Sickness, infertility, bad luck, curses, and a failure to dream are symptoms of being out of balance. Much individual ritual activity is concerned with maintaining or restoring balance (e.g., Irwin 1994) and priests are an integral part of diagnosis and treatment to effect rebalancing.

Violation of group norms (e.g., murder, incest, theft) or sacred responsibilities (e.g., entering a sacred cave unprepared, mishandling ritual paraphernalia, failing to honor a deity) by either individuals or groups would cause the whole group to suffer and occasion a rebalancing rite by a priest. It is also possible that natural events (e.g., earthquake, eclipse, ash cloud, hurricane, tornado) could bring on a diagnosis of cosmic disfavor and occasion a rebalancing rite. It is also highly likely that a seasonal gathering that included the burial of a number of dead, such as is envisioned for the riverside shell heaps, would require the prevention or curing of corpse sickness, also calling for rebalancing rites. I believe that there are two types of rebalancing rites indicated in these shell-bearing sites. One rite is manifested in the dog burials, the other by the head-twisted human burials. The dog burial rite was enacted fairly frequently, while the head-twisted rite was rare.

As discussed in Chapter 6, and indicated with statistical tests, dog burials are a distinguishing feature of the Green River ceremonial localities specifically, and shell heaps generally. Although it has not been noted in earlier articles, it is apparent from the maps of the Green River sites

produced by Rolingson (1967) and that for Eva/Three Mile component
(Lewis and Lewis 1961: Figures 7, 8) that dog burials are very often
found on the periphery of human burials, in some cases seemingly form-
ing enclosing borders or peripheral midpoints for the area containing
human burials. Dog placement in these sites gives the appearance of
planning. Rolingson's (1967) map of Carlston Annis burials shows dogs
placed in each cardinal direction. There also appear to be two north/
south rows of dog burials, and dog burials on the southern periphery. At
Read, a bluff-top site, dogs are peripheral to the human burials (Figure
8.1) and on the north and southern borders. Dogs in the Kirkland site,
a shell-free mortuary, were mostly located on the eastern side, but two
were found in the center and two on the west side of the site, as well.
Indian Knoll yielded 21 dogs, the majority of which were at the northern
and western peripheries.

Diane Warren (2004), who examined 211 Archaic-aged dogs from
Illinois, Kentucky, Alabama, and Tennessee, found that dogs selected
for burial were of medium size, with significant sexual dimorphism and
overwhelmingly male. Warren concluded that the Kentucky dogs buried with humans had most probably been used as pack animals. These
differences between dogs found with and without humans suggested to
Warren selective killing of dogs for burial with humans.

A closer look at which humans received dog burials is in order, while
keeping in mind that most dogs were *not* buried with humans. Dogs at
Mulberry Creek were most often associated with later sitting burials
and the extended bodies (Webb and DeJarnette 1942:243). The Indian
Knoll human/dog pairs involved three females, two males, and three
children, two ten years old and one five years old (aging and sexing by
Kelley 1980). Four of these human burials were reclining on their right
sides, four on their backs, and two on their faces. One dog was at the
feet of a middle-aged woman, one dog was laid across the head of a
middle-aged woman put face down, and one dog was under the head of
a middle-aged man on his back. The only multiple dog burial at Indian
Knoll was that with a five-year-old child on its face and with at least
one female dog, the only certain female dog found at the site. Six of the
ten dogs with humans, then, were associated with humans who, based
on their body position, possibly died a violent death.

Living dogs appear to have been managed behaviorally, genetically, and
demographically, significant information for our understanding of Archaic
activities and human concerns. However, these concerns may or may not

have been relevant when deciding to bury a dog. If burial of dogs was not motivated by love for a pet, what might the burials be reflecting?

A number of dogs had no skull. The lack of a skull could indicate that they hung from a pole, as was the case in some rituals conducted by some groups, for a period long enough to result in connective tissue disintegration (Hayden 1996:100, James 2006:31).

The identification of Dog with twinning, deformities, and sickness is of great antiquity in the Americas (e.g., James 2006, Miller and Taube 1993:191). Dogs are associated with healing among eastern U.S. groups because they can heal themselves with their saliva (James 2006). Numerous groups in the United States have or had healing rites for a sick individual that required the eating of dog meat, resulting in disarticulated skeletons, which have not been quantified at these shell sites. The Early Archaic dog found in the Ashworth site of Kentucky was disarticulated and had cutting marks (Phil DiBlasi, personal communication, October 2008). Instead, the dogs enumerated were articulated.

In addition to sickness, mythological references to dogs throughout the Americas associated them with death, the Underworld, and the western land of the dead, to which they led the dead (e.g., Iroquois, Huron, Ojibwa, Cherokee, Seminole, Inuit—James 2006:20), and with the night sky, probably because the dog howls at the moon. There were at least two dog stars, and Dog created the Milky Way. Their howling was thought to cause plants to grow (James 2006). In many Eastern Woodland groups, a dog awaited the soul who successfully traversed the Milky Way bridge and came to its fork (James 2006:32). Both the Aztec Xolotl and the Dog of the Cherokee retrieved the bones of humans, or was associated with the bones of humans who repopulated this world (James 2006, Miller and Taube 1993:80, 190). If shell heaps are visualizations of the Underworld and renewal places, then dogs are appropriately buried in them, more so than other places.

Jenny James (2006) gives a detailed explanation of the role of the dog among the Cherokee, also known as the Dog Tribe, which provides much of interest for an interpretation of Archaic dog burials. The sacred dog of the Cherokee 1) reestablishes moral order, balance, wholeness, and harmony in the face of chaos, 2) creates a path to the spirit world and acts as the judge of ethical behavior and correct performance of the hearth rituals, 3) expresses physical and mystical transformation and ensures transformation or punishment of the soul, and 4) protects, guards, and guides humanity and priests on the path to rebirth, including the successful negotiation of a chasm separating this world and the Underworld. (The dog is often cast as a guide across a river dividing the land of the living from that of the dead.) The Green River and the Tennessee River may have been such chasms.

The most likely symbolic uses of dogs during the Archaic appear to be for restoring balance, and for judging and guiding souls. Rebalancing rituals seem to have been particularly appropriate at the hilltop shrines of Baker, Jackson Bluff, Jimtown Hill, East Steubenville, and Read, where the ratios of humans to dogs are 0.6, 0.64, 0.78, 3.0, and 3.6, respectively. That ratio at the riverside shell heaps ranges from 10 to 38 humans per dog. If these bluff-top places were places where body preparation was carried out, then rebalancing rites for corpse handlers would have been particularly relevant and prevalent.

When one or two dogs were buried with a human at a riverside shell heap, that person's death may have been attributed to a violation of religious proscriptions that endangered the community. A priest's soul may also have needed rebalancing at death. A dog might then have been sacrificed to judge and guide that human and to restore balance for the community. Some individuals buried with dogs may have been Priests.

It is interesting that so many dog burials have been found at the edges of human burial areas, as though they form a border or are at the front of the path ready to lead the hundreds of souls out of this place. If burials occurred seasonally at the riverside heaps, and one dog sacrifice occurred at each ritual/feast occasion to rebalance the living and lead the dead, then the number of dog burials at the heaps would indicate the number of seasonal burial events, although no site has been completely excavated. I have already posited that those sites with less or little shell hosted fewer grand aggregations, and the number of dog burials at places like Barrett and Butterfield conform to this prediction. The majority, but not all, of the largest Green River riverside shell heaps have only been tested (DeWeese, Bowles, Haynes), so it is not possible to pursue this potential correlation further. However, the second and fourth largest sites, Carlston Annis and Indian Knoll, do have the predicted rank order of dog burials, 29 and 23, respectively. DeWeese, Bowles, and Haynes should be harboring large numbers of dog burials.

A second indication of rebalancing concerns may be indicated by the head-twisted or torso-twisted burials mentioned in Chapter 6 and burials deposited headfirst. I base this proposal on a passage from Constance Classen (1993:112, 122) referring to Incan cosmology:

The head was thus associated with the past . . . in the Andes; . . . The feet, in turn, were associated with the future, the chaos of the unknown, and with the dead. . . . The trunk of the body corresponds to the living and to the present.

A truly revolutionary event, a pachacute (reversal of space/time), however, could be represented only by the metaphor of the body's turning around and facing the opposite direction (or, on the vertical axis, by being stood on its head). When this occurred the structures of the past would become submerged in the fluidity of the future, and the world would be restructured according to new principles. This is why the Andeans of Haurochiri said of the deity known as Pachakuyuchiq (World Mover) that "when he turns his face [the Earth] moves as well. . . . If he were ever to turn his whole body, the world would end."

Classen also tells us that during the colonial era, there was a native belief that Indians who did not return to ancestral ways and thus violated numerous norms would die and be forced to wander upside down with their feet in the air (1993:134).

Several twisted and headfirst burials were enumerated in Chapter 6. The most dramatic of these burials was that found at Vaughn, a Middle Archaic shell and dirt mound on the Tombigbee River in Mississippi (near the Tennessee River valley). This man's head was twisted 180 degrees and his legs were pulled *over* his head. A second male at this site was also buried with head twisted and covered with shell-bearing soil (Atkinson 1974).

Single cases of head-twisted burial or bodies twisted at the waist are found at Long Branch (Bu81), Anderson (Bu13), Mulberry (Bu86), McCain (Bu3), and Indian Knoll (Moore's Bu93). Three twisted adults were found at Eva (women Bu107, Bu111, and man Bu194). Bodies buried headfirst are infant Bu126 and adult male Bu57 in the Eva/Eva component, and woman Bu102 in the Three Mile component. It could be that the twisted position is included when the Big Sandy field notes say "in many pits head was forced into an unnatural position."

The rarity of these types of burials is in accord with what must have been a rare but severe set of circumstances or event. Events that could seem to reverse time are eclipses and volcanic ash clouds that might darken the daytime sky for as much as a week. Perhaps a storm of tornados, perhaps a large loss of lives in a short period, perhaps a desecration of a mortuary, or an earthquake could also bring about an impression of the reversal of time or space. The head-twisted or upside-down individual may have been a priest who lost the confidence of peers, or a somewhat random sacrificial victim to an Earth Mover deity. This mode of burial should be given close study, for it may signal significant natural or social events. Furthermore, the idea that heads are positioned in the past and feet in the future should be considered in cases when dogs and infants are found buried at either the feet or head of an adult when either a head or feet are missing, and for feet petroglyphs.

Going-to-Water Rites

Water is an integral part of earth renewal, both in the form of rain and as surface water. A concern with water by Archaic peoples is evident in the siting of ceremonial centers by large rivers. The holiest of all water in Mesoamerica, and most probably in North America, was water that flowed from caves (Brady and Ashmore 1999). Several of the caves with Archaic materials in the shell-heap districts have flowing water.

The preparation for and enactment of many historic rites required that the observant bathe, typically in a stream but also in pools, springs, or waterfalls. This going-to-water has been recorded for shamans and priests in purification, healing, and divination activities, and for supplicants needing to purify themselves, such as the sick, violators of sanctions, ballplayers, and attendees at the conclusion of earth renewal rites such as the Busk (Hudson 1976:374). Flowing water, however, could both empower and sap the body. It is important, therefore, that going-to-water be proscribed and supervised. No doubt going-to-water activities were incorporated into the ceremonialism of people camped beside the Harpeth, Duck, Cumberland, Tennessee, Ohio, and Green rivers during the Archaic.

In light of the importance of water, the observation of auditory exostoses on a high number of skulls in a few southern Ohio Valley populations raises several possibilities for ritual practices. According to the data reported by Mensforth (2005:466), 36.4 percent of 88 men at Carlston Annis, 51.6 percent of 254 men at Indian Knoll, 25 percent of 12 Kirkland men, 21.3 percent of 94 Barrett men, and 22.6 percent of 84 Ward men had exostoses. In addition to Kirkland, exostoses appear in individuals in three other shell-free mortuaries. Eva's Big Sandy level has two and Rosenberger has 15 individuals, nine of them male and one an adolescent (Wolf and Brooks 1979:917). One individual at Ensworth presents this pathology. Returning to shell-bearing sites on the Tennessee River, one individual in Eva/Three Mile, one at Long Branch (Lubsen 2004), three at O'Neal (Lubsen 2004), and six at Mulberry Creek

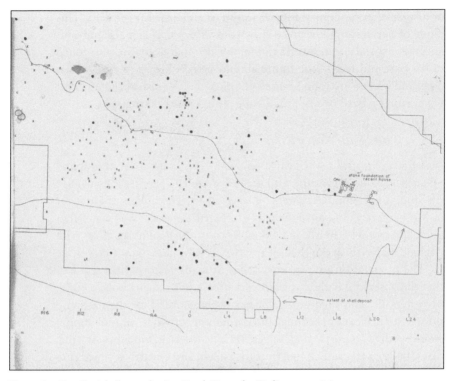

Figure 8.1. Dog Burials (heavy dots) at Read, Kentucky (Rolingson 1967).

(Shields 2003) had auditory exostoses. Finally, 25 percent of the skulls at KYANG, which is located more than a mile from the Ohio River, had exostoses (Phil DiBlasi, personal communication, May 2009). Based on this spotty distribution of auditory exostoses, my shell seasonality study (Claassen 2005), and the seasonal accessibility of shellfish for hand collectors, I cannot embrace Mensforth's idea (2005) that exostoses mean wintertime shellfishing by men.

Interestingly, like dog burials, exostoses are concentrated in Green River burials. It would seem that the Green River, more than any other river in the United States at any other time in prehistory, was particularly sought out for its healing and purification powers. What the Green River offered was its particularly green coloration (Stein 2005a:20)— a color widely associated throughout the Americas with beginning time (Miller and Taube 1993)—its deep water (Stein 2005a:20), and water that presumably passed through, and emerged from, Mammoth Cave and other caves around it. The Underworld was particularly accessible there, and the water of the Green was purified by its passage through the Underworld. Among a number of possible rites are two that I find intriguing: a water-keeper sodality or ritual sweating.

One form of going-to-water might have involved a river-keeper or cave-keeper sodality that came to be centered at Indian Knoll, and that had as its responsibility the cleaning of the cave water and open-air streams and springs in the vicinity. In the Mayan area today, social groups take their identities from springs, water holes, and watery caves (Brady and Ashmore 1999) and have oral accounts of being given the rights to these water sources in exchange for keeping them clean. Men seek cave water when pure water is needed for rituals, and presumably men are the ones who clean the pools and streams (Rissolo 2005:356). It is men with exostoses primarily who are found in the Green River sites, as only 6.9 percent of women in five sites had them (although it should be noted that men have been found to be more susceptible to these growths [Mensforth 2005:466]). If men buried in the Green River heaps were responsible for cleaning the river and pools in Mammoth Cave, where the water would always be cold, or the Green River itself, which drained that cave, or any other streams, falls, pools, and springs that are found in this region, then those activities could account for their exostoses. Such a sodality would appear to be centered at Carlston Annis, at the eastern end of the Green River site distribution, and Indian Knoll, in the middle of the site distribution. Curiously, exostoses are also present in notable numbers at three of the tributary sites in the Green River valley— Kirkland, Ward, and Barrett. Though this distribution may be modified by future examinations of skulls, as of now I offer that this 100-mile stretch of the Green River was tended by river keepers. If more general going-to-water activities were the cause of exostoses, then they should be present in some ears at all of the mortuaries on all of the rivers.

Although frequent water-cleaning activities could account for the exostoses, such growths would also be exacerbated by frequent sweating over several decades. Patricia Lambert (2001) attributes bony ear growths in North Carolina and Virginia skeletal populations to the combination of prolonged steam heat exposure in the sweat followed by the plunge into water that would always be colder than the sweat. Inspection of the ears of 335 individuals from 14 sites in North Carolina and Virginia indicated that 18.2 percent of individuals were affected and from 0 to 52.6 percent of individuals at any one site (Lambert 2001:158). This sweating was practiced differentially at villages across the area, given that some cemetery populations had no one with exostoses. There is a similar spotty distribution in the Archaic sample of sites.

The tremendous amount of fire-cracked rock, fire features, and the shallow basin features found in these sites are suggestive of sweat hut locations as well as graveside fires and cooking fires. Sweating accompanied many historic rituals and birth, for both group and individual needs. Hudson (1976) recorded sweats used for initiates and to treat men exposed to menstruating women. Sweating may also have been prescribed for corpse sickness, as it is today in the Andes.

> [T]he dead could also harm the living, causing them misfortune and disease. This would occur when some aspect of ancestor worship was neglected, but also spontaneously through contact with a corpse or its emanations . . . creating cadaver sicknesses or ancestor wind. It is believed to cause a variety of sicknesses but principally one that starts off as a rash, then enters the bones and destroys the whole body . . . a process of decay similar to that experienced by the corpse. Andeans protected themselves against this contagion . . . through ritual cleansing in a river. . . . The clan comes together with the relatives ten days after a death occurs to accompany the nearest relative to a spring or flowing stream that has been agreed upon, there they duck him three times and wash all the dead person's clothes. (Classen 1993:89)

Surely Archaic burial and feasting at a mortuary would require a similar ritual cleansing as well as a rebalancing rite. Though men may be more susceptible to auditory exostoses, living male heads of households may have been the ones most frequently cleansed at the public mortuary gatherings. However, why would this corpse sickness and treatment be more pronounced at shell-heap mortuaries than at shell-free mortuaries? The concentration of men with exostoses at large riverside shell heaps seems to favor the river-keeper sodality suggestion for the cleansing of the Green River and the upper Tennessee River and their caves.

Summary and Conclusions

During the Archaic era, people began to modify the environment to create places of spiritual power. They began to hold beliefs that required the concentration of ancestors in accessible places, and then venerated their places of rest. These places were constituted as renewal places, manifestations of the Underworld. I have drawn attention in this chapter to large, communitywide rituals that may have been conducted at the various ritual sites in the shell-bearing districts of the southern Ohio Valley. Those rituals proposed were earth renewal ceremonies, rebalancing ceremonies, and going-to-water rites conducted by important priests, in "the role of specialized practitioners in the importation of a complex liturgy" (Brown 2006:476). The events moved annually to a different mound as groups' resources waxed and waned and hosts became guests. The feasts and the kinship ties resulted in enough labor to gather the foodstuffs, ready the gifts, prepare the campsite, repair shrines, and maintain older graves. As places of great numbers of ancestors, great sacrifices, and great feasts, the feasting-with-shell ceremonial centers were no doubt known to strangers and remembered by memory keepers for thousands of years.

Some aspects of the burial ceremonialism will be familiar to scholars of the historic era and, as reconstructed here, can now be said to have great time depth. (In a future publication I will attempt the identification of priest burials and a fuller treatment of Archaic ritual life.) These are sweats for curing sicknesses, graveside fires, earth renewal, rebalancing, the import of the numbers 4, 5, and 6, etc. Other aspects of the proposed rituals, I believe, are equally old yet largely unrecognized by archaeologists—shells as renewal elements, stones as living entities, human sacrifice, and body positions as reflective of cause of death.

After years of ceremonials and feasting, after the lust for vengeance and raiding for sacrifices subsided, and perhaps after the last members of the great families had been melded into newer families, the feasting-with-shellfish ceremonial centers in the Nashville Basin and, later, those on the lower Ohio, were closed. Many of these ceremonial centers were integrated into Woodland and Mississippian ritual life, as well. Pottery, later stone tools, copper, galena, and later burials indicate that these places continued to live in the oral histories and ritual duties. Some Mississippians constructed their sacred mounds nearby (e.g., Annis Mound in the Big Bend and Kroger's Island in Alabama). Visitations to these spiritually important Archaic places continued, perhaps to take medicine there, to dig shells for pottery, to see and honor storied hallowed ground, to venerate the dead and the power of these places, and sometimes to bury their own dead and some of their victims in raiding. In these places, the Mississippians, known for their interest in ancestors, could assert a long-lived greatness that had been held in the collective memory for 3,500 years.

CHAPTER 9
FROM ARCHAIC VILLAGES TO RITUAL CAMPS: THE THEORETICAL LANDSCAPE

A group of these [nomadic] hunters in the early Archaic
period discovered the mussel shoals in the Ohio River near
what is now Steubenville, Ohio, and made their camps on
the hillsides near the shoals. When they wanted food it
was a simple matter to wade out in the shallow water and
gather the shellfish. . . . (F)or the first time, Upper Ohio
Valley man found himself able to settle down in one spot.
No longer did he need to roam the forests tracking game
(Meyer-Oaks 1955a:19).

Although the shell heaps of the Archaic have been dug into for more
than a century, they have been underproblematized. Several decades ago,
I began to question the improbable locations of the Archaic shell heaps
given that shellfish would have been available everywhere and given that
the shells had been hauled to the tops of bluffs, in some cases. These
behaviors and my research on the U.S. freshwater shell button industry
caused me to question others' explanations for the end of shell heap
living in the Ohio Valley. The choices to accumulate shells in only a few
places and to haul them up bluffs were cultural choices, while the most
popular explanations looked to natural causes. Because nature did not
pull these shellfish out of the water and stack them in heaps, cultural
explanations for the disappearance of the riverside and bluff-top shell-
bearing sites are infinitely more appropriate.

Since I first proposed (1988) that these sites were ritual features, the
data and the theory have accumulated in Florida, Georgia, South Carolina, California, and Brazil to strongly support the ritually significant
roles of massive shell accumulations. Yet the heaps and mounds of the

southern Ohio Valley are repeatedly denied such a role or ignored in summations of Archaic ritual life. It is time to put forward a stronger case for the Ohio Valley shell bearing sites as ritual locations and even as accretional burial mounds.

Several hypotheses for both the beginning and the ending of shell heaping have been examined here and others elsewhere (Claassen 1991, 1996). There was no support found for overharvesting of the molluscan resource. The correlation of the Hypsithermal with shellfishing was shown to be particularly poor. There is, in fact, a greater correlation of increased shellfishing with increasing moisture and cooling climate attending the decline of the Hypsithermal and afterward, the opposite situation from that proposed by others. The population growth evident in numbers of sites during the Late Archaic is coincident with, not precedent to, the greater numbers of shell-bearing sites appearing during the Late Archaic.

Fifty-eight shell-bearing sites with differing amounts of shell have figured in this study and compared with that from eleven shell-free mortuary sites of the same time period. This inquiry has revealed that there are several different types of ritually important loci that I have interpreted to constitute sacred site systems: riverside shell-heap mortuary, tributary shell mortuary, bluff-top ritual site, burial-free shell site, and shell-free mortuary. The presence of caches, exotics, dogs, mutilated and shot bodies, babies with marine shell, a high ratio of points to other items, a low ratio of objects to bodies, high incidence of auditory exostoses, site clustering, and site monumentality distinguish the shell ceremonial center where most of the dead of the feasting group were brought. The large quantities of shells were the products of public feasts held for kin and friends when captives and kin were being interred. These burial events may have been part of a large annual fall burial ceremonial, sponsored by a different host group each year that sent invitations to many guest groups. Apart from being a feast byproduct, the shells themselves were important symbols of renewal and often were used to dig the grave, as grave goods, and provided a renewal context for the dead and the living.

The bluff-top sites where public feasting with shell and a ritual including dogs may have taken precedence over human burial was another type of ritual and burial site. One way to honor guests was with a show of labor expenditure that was well demonstrated in these bluff-top settings. A third mortuary setting was the shell-free burial grounds. Here again I think there were social criteria that dictated burial in such a place, ones that would indicate some social distance from those who were buried in the shell heaps. The lack of shells means that public feasting, and perhaps even a scheduled burial event, did not occur at the shell-free burial grounds. In those places bodies were interred "privately." The presence of well-worn teeth, usually attributed to eating shellfish in, for instance, the shell-free Rosenberger cemetery, indicates that those people did consume shellfish even though they did not discard them at these mortuaries.

The ceremonial centers are isolated from domestic camps and are typically found midway up a river. On the Tennessee, Ohio, and Green rivers the shell-bearing sites are found in clusters on alternating banks. The Big Bend cluster has radiocarbon dates that indicate simultaneous use of the heaps, giving rise to the suggestion that here there was a multi-mound mortuary site. Clusters on both banks of these rivers suggest different social groups who met at the river. The bluff-top heaps were interspersed among ceremonial centers on the Green and upriver on the Ohio and on the Wabash. The shell-free mortuaries tend to be found downriver or on tributaries, and to be among the oldest sites.

The chronological data are insufficient at this time to investigate the nuances of changes over time. On a gross scale it seems that the earliest shell-heap creation began at one spot in each river district by people using Morrow Mountain points, although the possibility of Paleoindian shell-fishing has been raised here. Gastropod shell heaps appeared first on the Duck and Harpeth, and a bluff-top tributary site was first in the Green River district. These shell-bearing mortuaries and bluff-top shrines/mortuary camp locations were part of a highly focal set of religious practices that incorporated dog, adult, and infant burials and sacrifices in earth renewal, founding and closing ceremonies, and rebalancing rites, which afforded the opportunity to renew tool kits, and feast in large numbers with friendly groups. This ritual complex seems to have been strongest from 6,500 to 4,000 years ago. It was in these shell-bearing mortuaries where the vast majority of the dead—presumably dwellers of the southern Ohio River valley—were buried during this period. Shell heaping continued unabated on the upper Tennessee, upper Cumberland, and St. Johns rivers long after it ended on the other rivers.

So why was the feasting-with-shell ceremonial center so restricted in space and time if the resource cannot explain its distribution? I have long favored a religious motivation for this phenomenon and find there to be interesting correlations between ceremonial centers and particular features of the natural landscape, such as Mammoth Cave and other caves and major shoals and bluffs. Each shell-heap district has both natural and made places for ritual. But among these venerated places only the shoals are unique within the southern Ohio Valley region. Other regularities are the use of a midway location on a river, and the use of westward- and northward-flowing river segments. Beyond these observations, however, I can offer no explanation for why this phenomenon occurred only in the southern Ohio Valley, unless there was a cosmogram being played out on the scale of the entire eastern United States that placed the land south of the Ohio River in the realm of the Underworld. There is some hint of a familiar cosmogram on the east-west axis, with burial-free shell feasting sites on the Atlantic—the land of the sunrise—and shell mortuaries in the west—the land of the dead.

The demise of shell mounding reflects a demise in large regional feasts and their rituals, a possible end to human sacrifice, and a significant change in where the living wished to bury their dead. Either the motivation to sponsor rituals or the ability to sponsor them dissolved. Far more murdered and mutilated bodies are known from the Late Archaic shell heaps than from earlier or later cultures, indicating a decline in warfare/raiding. Clearly the renewal symbolism associated with shell changed, although it would continue to be carried in the individual marine shell items found with the dead during the Woodland and Mississippian periods. There is also a clear decline in the movement of exotics around the southern Ohio Valley (Goad 1989) during the terminal Archaic and early Early Woodland periods as the need for gifts that would impress guests, and offerings that would impress deities, dissolved.

Theoretical Considerations

The scenario I am offering in this study carries several theoretical implications for topics near and dear to archaeologists. Among these topics, I refer specifically to the concepts of primary forest efficiency, the principle of scarce resources brought about by population growth, and the development of social complexity. I also will offer some thoughts on the continuities between Archaic accretional mortuaries and those of the Adena and the attraction that some Mississippian groups appear to have had for these cemeteries.

Primary Forest Efficiency

The dramatically increased use of shellfish has been interpreted by a generation of archaeologists as part of increasing diet breadth and even latent discovery of their edibleness. The increase in diet breadth was spurred by food stress that came from increasing population coupled with Hypsithermal-linked reductions in prime resources, such as the numbers and the size of deer (Purdue 1991). Joseph Caldwell (1958) linked food awareness and developing processing skills to more efficient forest exploitation, which led to sedentism and then more elaborate treatment of the dead, such as was affected during the Late Archaic in the Ohio Valley.

Asch et al. (1972) defined "efficiency" as the taking of selected foods that are abundant, nutritious, and easily obtained. Naiads were certainly abundant and easily obtained. Their nutritional benefits rival the nuts in protein and croaker and rabbit in calories but fall significantly below other flesh foods in protein, fat, carbohydrates, and kilocalories (Claassen 1998:185). They were no doubt eaten since Paleoindian days and rightly may be part of primary forest efficiency in the late Paleoindian and Early Archaic eras. But what signaled to Caldwell and others both the efficiency and the food stress were the great heaps of the Green and Tennessee rivers and other sites that accumulated primarily in the Late Archaic.

Placing the role of shellfish in a feasting context as I and others have done means that the addition of shellfish in these visible quantities was *not* part of a Middle or Late Archaic dietary strategy adopted for survival in a stingy environment, as expressed by Caldwell's primary forest efficiency (1958) or Jennings's Archaic efficiency (1974). Instead, shellfish utilization in visible accumulations was part of social excess, not human desperation. It may be that mundane or daily consumption of shellfish was no greater in the Archaic than it was in the Paleoindian period. However, feasting needs that developed during the Archaic led to the mass processing and accumulating of shellfish. Like the efficient diet, feasting foods are those that are both abundant and can easily replenish themselves, like shellfish. What drove early Americans to move down the food chain was not primarily daily dietary needs but feasting needs. In the southern Ohio Valley, Florida, and the Atlantic Coast (in Maine, New York, South Carolina, Georgia, and Florida), shellfish were latched upon to fill that role, while seed-bearing plants (that would become domesticates) were the solution in the Midwest, and fish in still other locations.

Jennings (1974:131) wrote that an efficient exploitation would imply technology utilizing many new raw materials and tools that would lead to more leisure time. Did the addition of shellfish lead to more leisure time, he asked? "No," he answered, because he could not see any results of leisure—no "enrichment of life in the areas of religion, aesthetics and other 'finer things.'" How that picture has changed. Rather than facilitating individual leisure, shellfish facilitated group social life. In fact, the increase in socializing evident in the rituals at the shell heaps probably depleted women's and men's leisure time as they prepared the feasts, gifts, the ritual locations, the dead, and the rituals themselves. Sites with visible records of the consumption of shellfish are not where one should anchor the primary forest efficiency interpretation.

Scarce Resources

I am hard pressed to identify a scarce resource that would have driven the creation of territories and complex society. Size and number of deer should have been on the increase after 7,000 years ago during the Middle Archaic, as forage increased with increasing moisture (Purdue 1991). Numerous floral and pollen records, some reviewed in Chapter 5, indicate that the floral communities took on their modern configuration during the Middle Archaic, as did the faunal communities, so no stress should be found there. Shellfish certainly were not scarce and there is a surprising underutilization of other aquatic resources at these sites, all failing to support a picture of food scarcity. We need to stop thinking in terms of limited food supply. The Green River was chosen over others that also had shellfish. In fact, Cypress Creek, a tributary of a tributary of the Green River, was chosen first. Lower-order streams would have offered far lower densities of aquatic foods than would higher-order streams or the Green River itself. There apparently was such an *abundance* of foods and labor that social life could be enlarged during the Archaic and ritual concerns could be elaborated.

Population Growth

Most researchers believe that population increased throughout the Archaic (e.g., Anderson 1996). In a close study of the number and density of sites in the southeastern states, including Kentucky, David Anderson was able to evaluate the demographics of population growth during the Archaic. In both the Early Archaic and Middle Archaic periods, concentrations of sites presumably indicative of greater densities of people were noted on the Cumberland, Tennessee, Duck, and Savannah rivers, with particularly large concentrations on the first two rivers and "lesser concentrations along the Green River and in the upper reaches of the major Gulf-trending drainages like the Chattahoochee, Coosa, Alabama, and Tombigbee" (Anderson 1996:164). As predicted, Middle Archaic shell accumulations are found on the Tennessee and Duck rivers, and at the newly uncovered Panther Rock site on the Cumberland. The shell-bearing burial mound at Vaughn on the Tombigbee is also Middle Archaic in age. But shell mounds and dirt mounds do not show up on the Savannah or the other rivers at this time, yet do appear in a less dense area on the Ohio River.

Overall, Anderson discovered that there was actually a site number decrease during the Middle Archaic. This decrease in sites was particularly noted in the three states of most concern in this study: Alabama, Tennessee, and Kentucky. The number of Archaic sites in the Southeast "suggests that regional population levels may have more or less stabilized fairly early (i.e., in the Early Archaic) and then remained uniform (or even dropped slightly) through the mid-Holocene, with marked growth only coming at the end of the Archaic" (Anderson 1996:158). Though the causal relationship of population growth and ridgetop mounds may hold for Illinois, the focus of Charles and Buikstra, it does not seem to be the stimulus to mortuaries, violence, and the movement of goods in the southern Ohio Valley during the Middle Archaic.

Instead, "considerable landscape filling occurs in the Late Archaic" (Anderson 1996). The most clearly defined concentrations of Late Archaic sites in the Southeast are those of Stallings Island/Atlantic Coast, St. Johns, Green River, and Poverty Point/Jaketown (Anderson 1996:166). Three of these four cultures were shell-accumulating cultures and the fourth was an earth-heaping culture. All other Late Archaic cultures in the Southeast—Wheeler, Norwood, Elliott's Point, Cedarland/Claiborne, Catahoula, O'Bryan Ridge—had fewer and less dense sites (Anderson 1996:166).

Cemeteries, mounds, and villages do increase in number and bulk during the Late Archaic, no doubt linked to greater numbers of people on the landscape in this region. In fact, there is a greater apparent association between increased population and shell piling during the Late Archaic than there is between the Hypsithermal or population growth and any of these features in the Middle Archaic, but the Late Archaic is too late to explain the beginning of shell-heaping, mounds, cemeteries, violence, and "exchange."

What we have in the case of these shell-bearing sites are monuments without complex social organization. There are numerous cases of monumental construction bringing together large numbers of people otherwise scattered across the landscape much of the time (Cobb and Nassaney 2002). In most areas, however, there is little or no evidence for large nucleated settlements, or sedentary communities at least until well into the Woodland period. . . . Complexity in ritual but not in social organization is inferred, although something greater than band level organization is either implicit or explicit in most arguments. (Anderson 2002:258)

Anderson's solution is tribal organization but not complex tribes (2002:258).

We have, in the number of dead included in this study, a fair estimate of the number of people who lived during the Late Archaic. If we consider the estimate of 17,938 dead in the shell-bearing sites and assume that all of them were buried from 6,000 to 4,000 years ago (which, of course, they were not), we have but 8.97 people buried per year in these places. If we assume that in all of the undug and unestimated bodies in shell heaps there are another 18,000 people, we still have but 18 people buried per year. If we triple the number of bodies in the shell-free sites to 2,000 and again assume they were all buried in this same 2,000-year period, we now have 38,000 people, or 19 buried per year in the southern Ohio Valley.

These few deaths a year in an area that spreads from the Ohio River to the Tennessee River raises two suggestions: the population levels were too low to sustain complex society or there were significant numbers of people—more than 18,200—who were not buried in shell-bearing sites, or buried at all. This situation is highly possible and would further emphasize the specialness of the shell mounds and the dead they contain.

I have also raised the point in Chapter 6 that if one insists that these large sites were villages, then one must be prepared to explain what happened at the end of the Archaic period, when populations were increasing in size and thus density, to cause people to *abandon* the village way of life and return to the nomadism that marked the Early and Middle Woodland groups in the region, *abandoning* the most secure foodstuff in their environment. Under the sacred place and feasting scenario, the disappearance of shells owed not to the complete cessation of shellfishing but to the end of shell accumulation.

Sedentism: The Necessary Precondition for Cemeteries, Territories, Mounds, Violence, and Exchange Networks

Undergraduate students learn that increasing population leads at some point in the Archaic to immobility or sedentism, resulting in the birth of territories and resource ownership within that territory. The features of social life most often discussed as being caused by population growth and thence sedentism are villages, mounds, and cemeteries (Fagan 2000). For authors such as Doug Charles and Jane Buikstra (e.g., 1983), mounds and cemeteries are indicative of the development of corporate groups or socially complex groups by the Late Archaic, a process that began in the Middle Archaic. Charles and Buikstra (1983:124) assert that formal cemetery areas are associated with corporate lineal inheritance of crucial and restricted resources and that both cemeteries and mounds signal this land ownership and the move to complex social organization. The violence so in evidence during the Archaic was resorted to in defense of the key foodstuffs where they were found. Winters (1974: xi, xii, xx), as well as Meindl et al. (2001) and Mensforth (2001, 2005), explicitly connects Archaic violence to a presumed scarcity of resources or to the patchiness of shellfish.

The sedentism of the Middle and Late Archaic was evident to archaeologists in the shell-heap villages. But if the shell heaps are not villages, as I have argued here, and no other candidates for villages are apparent, then sedentism was not the precursor to cemeteries and monumental architecture. They were not corporate groups as such. Though corporate groups do indeed have territories, cemeteries, villages, monuments, etc., what the Archaic shell-bearing mounds and dirt mounds show us is that complex social organization is not a prerequisite for these developments—nor is sedentism (Anderson 2002:269, Gibson 2004:264).

Villages

Although there are some candidates for Middle Archaic villages, such as Koster in the Illinois River valley and the shell-free Black Earth site, there is a striking lack of shell-heap/village pairs in the southern Ohio Valley during both the Middle and Late Archaic periods. Given the prevailing theoretical orientation that these Archaic societies were complex and that complex societies live in villages, the failure to identify any other villages has led some to reason that the shell heaps must be villages (e.g., Marquardt and Watson 2005a, 2005c). Instead, I am proposing that there were cemeteries and violence without villages, without sedentism.

Mounds

Mounds and visible mortuaries were appropriate once a society moved beyond concern with the near dead, largely the work of women at the household level, to veneration of the long dead, directed by men and conducted away from the household (Marcus 1999). Gibson and Carr (1999) proposed four antecedent factors for hunter-gatherers to build mounds: an intensifiable food, a missing resource, networking that concentrated power in the hands of a few at least occasionally, and balanced reciprocity (Gibson and Carr 1999, cited in Brooks 2004:112). In this case, the intensifiable food was shellfish, the missing resources were those that carried symbolic meanings creating "exchange to move sacred artifacts with power into areas" and into the hands of priests (Brooks 2004:112), and the balanced reciprocity came in the form of movable rituals and feasts. Anderson (2002:268), too, envisioned a priest-based authority that was centralized but pronounced only when people aggregated.

For the people of central and southern Mexico, mounds were and are sacred mountains. Mountains contain caves and springs, both portals to the Underworld, and are sources of abundance. Mounds mark out safe space and are power points in a sacred landscape (Bassie-Sweet 1996). Mounds are about well-being, renewal, and powers from other worlds.

In northern North America some archaeologists have emphasized that mounds in the Woodland period (Byers 1998) and Historic period (Gibson 1998:25, Knight 1986:68, Swanton 1931:37) were used in purification/renewal rites and that mounds were "regarded as microcosmic earth mothers" (Gibson 1998:25, 2004:262) and gifts from the Great Spirit. Mounds of later cultures were places of renewal, just as I am proposing for the Archaic. We can now say that this practice began throughout the eastern Mississippi River watershed in the Middle Archaic. Unlike the Gulf coastal plain dirt mounds, mortuary monuments of the southern Ohio Valley were possibly accidental mounds. And unlike the more southerly mounds, which Gibson says (2004:263) were always multimound groupings, those to the north were single mounds, although founded within a multimound ritualized landscape. Even in the case of multiple mounds, complex society was not needed to build these monuments (Gibson 2004:262-265).

Feasting

I am proposing that in the prehistoric situation under study here, feasting occurred in the context of religious observance among multiple groups of foragers. The frequency and size of the public feasts of the past are evident in the mollusks accumulated at riverside sites.

Two situations are curious in the feasting behavior of the Late Archaic in the southern Ohio Valley. One is the lack of domesticates in the heaps, the other is the lack of pottery. Both of these phenomena have been attributed to feasting needs.

Pottery was adopted in feasting settings around 4,500-4,000 years ago in the Stallings and Orange cultures (Sassaman 1993a, 2006), later in the biographies of shell heaps in Alabama, and never in the feasting sites on the Ohio, Green, and Cumberland rivers. Even the late Late Archaic Green River sites of Bowles and Read and the Cumberland River sites of Robinson and Penitentiary Bluff failed to yield fiber-tempered pottery. The spread of pottery from the shell-bearing rings, heaps, and mounds of the coast to the shell-bearing mounds of the Tennessee River surely occurred within the context of feasting. But why did pottery not then spread to the Cumberland, Green, Wabash, and upper Ohio rivers? Were the feasts on the Tennessee River not attended by the more northerly folks after 3,700 years ago, when pottery appeared on the Tennessee? Why, when pottery did appear on the Ohio River, was it not first found in these feasting localities?

The situation for domesticated plants is the same as for pottery. The social needs for foodstuffs at feasts have been cited as the principal motivation for domesticating plants (e.g., Hayden 2001:24), yet here we have a case where the earliest domesticates do not appear in feasting context but rather in rock shelters. Though ceramics may have been too late for the feasts held on the Green River, domesticated squash, sunflower, sumpweed, and maygrass appeared much earlier and were used by people in central Tennessee and in Illinois (Crawford 2005).

Crawford (2005) had occasion to consider the plant remains from Carlston Annis, Bowles, and Peter's Cave in different segments of the Green River. Referring only to the flotation samples from the two riverside heaps, Crawford found that the changes in relative abundance of species and the taxa composition were similar, as was the dominance of plant foods by nuts and fleshy fruits. Cucurbits were recovered at both sites and AMS dated to 5740+640 rcy at Carlston Annis (not calibrated here owing to the large standard deviation) and 5033–3907 BP at Bowles

(Crawford 2005:196). Surprisingly, the domesticate *Iva annua,* in use in the Illinois River valley at the time, was absent in both shell heaps (Crawford 2005:204), while wild rice was found at Bowles. There were no domesticates recovered in flotation samples from East Steubenville (5848–3462 BP), either.

Horticulture appeared earlier in the Illinois River valley, central Tennessee, and in the Ozarks than in the Green/Wabash/upper Ohio area, casting an aura of conservatism over these shell mounders, as pointed out by Crawford. Domestic plants are, however, present in the debris recovered at Penitentiary Branch (4270–2068 BP), Robinson (3612–2336 BP), and Riverton (4230–2985 BP), which overlap in radiocarbon dating with later activities at Carlston Annis and Bowles, suggesting that domesticates came to be included in the feasts sometime after 4,000 years ago. Inexplicably (for now), the Green River folks rejected domesticated plants as part of their feast menu and ultimately abandoned the floodplain locations favored for horticulture.

Mortuary Behavior

Much of what I have proposed in this study significantly circumvents the standard theoretical discussions of mortuary behavior, and even contradicts them. For instance, articulations of theory by Binford (1971) and Saxe (1970) argue that the status relationships held in life would be reflected in burial treatments. Their focus is on the lived life of the dead individual. A person treated differently in death was treated differently in life, according to these authors (and others).

Accordingly, the Indian Knoll population appears to have had ascribed status because exotic grave goods were included with infants who could not have earned these items. That there were no items included with infants at Bluegrass or Rosenberger, and that infants at Rosenberger were found in reused pits, means these communities must have had a different social organization from that at Indian Knoll, an interpretation offered by Driskell (1979:774).

Instead, I believe that it was not the life lived but the most basic variables related to the circumstances of death—when, where, and how—that are the key to understanding the Archaic mortuary aspects presented here. There seem to be two kinds of death, "normal" and "abnormal," with all minority burial treatments relegated to the abnormal deaths. Hofman (1985) made a proposal along these lines suggesting that cremation was related to circumstances of the family at the time of death—distance and time from an aggregation place/event, specifically.

In a religious system of multiple deities, spirits, and culture heroes, the need for suitable offerings specific to these classes of Other World entities probably had more to do with the items included as grave goods and the motivation for the procurement of exotics and production of pigments and fine crafts than did any desire to distinguish oneself or one's family. As indicated in the text, I think that marine shells were often used as part of an offering to a rain deity, red ocher for a sun deity, stones to hold a soul or represent its departure, naiad shells to indicate rebirth, etc.

Were the Shell Mound Users Complex Hunter-Gatherers?

Sassaman (2004) has situated the debate of the past two decades over the meaning of these Archaic shell heaps clearly into a larger debate about the origins of social complexity among hunter-gatherers. When surveyed at the continental scale, it would seem that the regionalized mortuary expressions indicate the growth of social complexity beyond a doubt. Maritime Archaic, Glacial Kame, Old Copper Culture, Riverine Archaic or SMA, the lower Illinois Valley, Classic Stallings, have long been recognized as significant social and geographical expressions of mortuary behavior. They, and now the mound builders of the lower Mississippi Valley, Orange Culture, and the numerous shell-ring builders of the coast, clearly indicate that social forces and individuals were working to honor their deities and their dead in new ways, if not their kin group or even living individuals. Ridgeline cemeteries covered by low mounds visible to anyone on the floodplain below are argued to reflect corporate groups marking off fixed and restricted foodstuffs in the lower Illinois Valley.

I think it is safe to say that we can see in all of these regional expressions, at least, religious cults, directed by priests, whose clearest manifestation is found in the treatment of the dead. In addition to the regional differences, there are several striking differences evident throughout the Ohio Valley in more general treatments of the dead that are apparent in the Middle Archaic but were absent earlier. These are 1) a move away from cremation (if indeed that was the usual method for disposing of the dead) to flesh burial in the greater region, 2) the move to group the dead together into burial loci, if not cemeteries, and 3) the move to mark the burial locus in ways that were evident to others of the era and to descendants. It seems that most communities in the Archaic came to need the ancestors in ways tangible. The living even came to recognize that they were to be the ancestors of their descendants as they worked to mark for posterity the location of the bodies of their own kin. For the first time during the Middle Archaic, people artificially made focal points of worship, elaborating on the natural places available. They began to create places where spiritual powers would become concentrated. And these powers were cajoled, summonsed, begged, and thanked in greatly elaborated ways.

I propose that the stimulus for the translocation of animals, plants, minerals, and other natural substances in the Archaic was the desire to acquire objects for offerings, and then their movement to the point of offering. Offerings, both material and immaterial, were required. The movement of goods increased in intensity during the Archaic as greater numbers of people encountered spirits in greater numbers of settings and then established greater numbers of places where those spirits could be and should be honored. With the growing populations and constraint on movements seen in the Late Archaic, these items of worship had to be gotten through social relationships that either allowed the penitent to pass into the territory of others to fetch the materials needed or convinced the occupants of other territories to provide the raw materials and finished products.

How complex were the creators and users of the southern Ohio Valley shell-feasting sites of the Middle and Late Archaic? Social complexity is commonly assayed using a trait list of situations that are opposed to (our) conceptions of equality among adults (specifically meaning men), known as egalitarianism. Listed traits are high population densities, sedentism for at least the majority of the year, large resident group size, focal harvest of one high-ranking foodstuff, food storage, resource ownership, inherited status, occupational specialization, warfare, ritual feasting complexes, territories with defended boundaries, standardized valuables, and prestige goods (Sassaman 2004).

The social groups of the Ohio Valley who employed shell-bearing mortuaries present a complicated picture when held against this trait list. Arguing as I have that the occupation of the shell-bearing sites was, at most, for a month or two at a time and were domestic camps, not villages, there are no apparent village sites in the Green River or Ohio River watersheds. Recent excavations at Whitesburg Bridge provide a clear example of shell heap with associated village, but this pairing is uncommon outside the Tennessee River valley. This lack of visible Archaic domestic sites suggests low population density of mobile foragers, the situation proposed for the Adena (Clay 1998) and Hopewellians (Brown 2006, Carr 2006), as well.

Food storage evidence is also essentially lacking in the Archaic sites (notable exceptions can be found at Mims Point) unless a portion of the huge numbers of mollusks consumed were dried. Drying is quick in the open air and their storage would require nothing more than a ristrolike arrangement. Shellfish harvest, as intensive as it was, does not qualify as a high-ranking foodstuff. Shellfish were not in short supply or limited in distribution and would not have engendered feelings of ownership. I am willing to grant that the people who established shell heaps at the three significant shoals found at Louisville, Muscle Shoals, and Stallings Island may have exerted ownership rights in those setting but ownership of the shoals, a sacred place. I do wonder if there was ownership of dogs and dog-breeding places, but was this resource sufficient to underwrite transegalitarianism in the Middle Archaic? No, nor does it seem to have been sufficient for a Late Archaic trigger. If the number of dogs is the clue to resource ownership and intensification, then there were only about five groups with sufficient dogs to qualify. Would this be enough people to drive an exchange system (if it is an exchange system) or differential burial treatments? Again, the answer seems to be no, negating Hayden's belief that dog breeding must have begun among complex hunter-gatherers (Hayden 1994:101).

Several of the items have been viewed as prestige goods, to which we might add dogs. I am arguing that rather than reflecting inherited status or prestige, the items included in graves and the burial treatments have far more to do with the circumstances surrounding the death of these individuals than any birth status or acquired social status during life, and are most correctly viewed as offerings. I do agree that there is some occupational information imparted by some of the grave goods, particularly the role of priest, indicating that these individuals were recognized during life for their activities. Perhaps ritual leader was an occupational specialty as the trait list would require, but only that occupation seems identifiable. Brown (2006) suggests that rich burials may well be those priests who orchestrated Hopewell ritual life; perhaps the same explanation could be applied to the richest Archaic burials. In Alabama shell sites where Benton blade production was obvious and intense in deep levels, it is easy to imagine that a small set of individuals undertook the production of these blades, but there is nothing particular about the grave goods to link anyone to that craft specialization. And though I have found it fairly easy to identify victims of violence/ raiding, the identification of valiant warriors escapes me. They are possibly marked by the inclusion of extra bodies or trophy part bones from other people in their graves. Maybe they have marine shell beads.

Marine shell, certain cherts, atlatls, and foreign animals are candidates for prestige goods in Middle Archaic and earlier Late Archaic burials, but the status that would evoke these goods is not obvious. All are found spread among every age and gender as well as burial position, facts that suggest a relevance other than high social status. For example, I have suggested that shell beads placed with infants mark rain sacrifices. Coal, *Leptoxis* shell beads, marine shell beads in general, carved bone pins, and perhaps dogs may indicate "ethnic" differences. New grave goods introduced into very late Late Archaic burials were copper, galena, pearls, and new forms of shell items, all of which will come to seemingly mark social differences in Adena and Hopewell cultures (or perhaps just differences among ritual specialists [Brown 2006]) but whether they do in the Late Archaic remains to be seen. Of course the pursuit of this topic is seriously hampered by the lack of radiocarbon dated skeletons with grave goods.

Once again, I call attention to the offerings used in Archaic rituals. Offerings have, at a minimum, two types of value: aesthetic value (the feeling evoked by the item) and use value (satisfying a need). These two values are the source of the power contained in the item. The extent to which that raw material is then modified by humans, in the production of offerings, introduces the possibility that labor and the social relations of that labor figure into an exchange value. Once there is esteem or aesthetic value, use value, and exchange value, a commodity has been created. These three values are socially ascribed values that are historically relevant. Exchange value is quantifiable and standardized—so many of item X equal so many of item Y or a service (Orser 1992).

The common conceptualization of the exchange network that began during the Middle Archaic and was greatly elaborated upon and then abandoned during the Late Archaic/Early Woodland (Goad 1989) seems to imply that the quest for offerings had morphed into an exchange of commodities by the Late Archaic. Commodities are instruments of status differentiation and class formation, meaning that marked social statuses would seem to have been developing. The logic of this evolutionary track is sound, but I do not see strong evidence for either an exchange system in the classic economic sense or commodities during the Archaic of the southern Ohio Valley. The quantity of goods is not so great nor the distances so great that mechanisms other than exchange were precluded necessarily.

Marine shell beads are the most evident of these items. There is only one case of marine shell bead production in the Green River district, and that was found with Bu610 of Indian Knoll (Watson 2005:561). From the period 7,000 to 3,500 years ago come 18,443 probable Busyconid shell beads in six river valleys (11,891 Green River, 2,113 Savannah River, 2,261 Tennessee River, 1,013 Harpeth River, 20 Cumberland River, 25 Wabash River, 20 Cumberland River, 6 Duck River). Of course the number of beads that can be cut from a *Busycon* sp. shell depends on the size of shell and the skill of the artisan, making a count of individual shells very difficult. Using a random number of 50 beads per shell would require 367 shells. The number of columella items, large pieces of lips, and nearly complete shells suggests fewer than an additional 100 whole Busyconid shells, for a total of 467 animals. Even if this number was more accurately 4,670 shells, when divided over the probable 1,000 years of most intensive use, the harvest is miniscule and need not depend on trading relationships (Claassen 2008).

The *Leptoxis* beads are local to the Tennessee River and probably the Ohio and Green. Coal seems to have moved very infrequently beyond the Green River valley. The martin, swan, and goose bones are also too few to *require* trading. Ft. Payne chert has a regional distribution, with various groups substituting various other regional cherts (Deter-Wolf 2004).

Individuals could have fetched these items in raw or finished form from other people and places at some distance as part of their pledge to host a ritual, or on their way to make offerings at a sacred site, or these items could have been gifted at these great feasts held on the Atlantic Coast and Tennessee, Ohio, and Green rivers (and surely were). Furthermore, if these items were commodities, they should be appearing in contexts other than burials.

From the trait list of social complexity, we are left with only three positive occurrences: raiding, feasting complexes, and bounded territories. The evidence for raiding is unequivocal and is greater during the Archaic in this region than it is during the Woodland or Paleoindian period. The point of this study has been to demonstrate the feasting complexes.

We have, then, social life in the southern Ohio Valley during most of the Archaic that has a few elements of social complexity. Throughout the time shell heaping was practiced, social differences were those between priests and their groups, not within groups. Those group differences and elements of social differentiation found within cemeteries were derived from and based on ritual practice and practitioners, not individual ambition. Hayden (1996) has offered that while all societies had/have individuals with personalities eager to distinguish themselves, in early societies these individuals' activities and proclivities were direct at, absorbed by, ritual requirements. The groups under examination in this study are an excellent example of just such a ritual system that worked to downplay individual aggrandizing while driving the making of powerful places.

Others have also questioned if corporate groups and ownership were evident in the Ohio Valley at all before Mississippian times. George Crothers (2004) doubts that the Green River folks even lived in communities. He imagines the heaps on the Green River to have functioned somewhat like hotels with supermarkets nearby. Family parties came and went at their whim, attracted to the places when they needed or wanted shellfish. Neither the resources nor the place was owned, and if someone in the party died while resident there, the living simply left the body there. Crothers bases this view of people engaged in what he calls the "foraging mode of production" on the lack of mixing in the deposits, the randomly placed burials, the lack of houses, the low proportion of debitage to finished tools, and, of course, the fecundity of the environment. Crothers is focused on the food potential of the environment. If these people were anything but fully mobile, they would have begun to conceptualize ownership—of territory and resources, which clearly they had not, he asserts. I should think that the evidence I have presented in Chapter 6 for the number of dead in these heaps, and the initial burial of victims, should negate such a simple subsistence-based existence. Would 18,000 people have died while tarrying in these places for a few months? Though I disagree with Crother's vision I do agree with his conclusion that these foragers were highly mobile and did not live in villages.

In another very interesting proposal, Berle Clay (1998:16–17), writing about the later Adena, questioned the idea that mortuary sites would be used exclusively by one corporate group:

> There is a strong tendency on our part as contemporary observers to unhesitatingly view burial mounds as symbols of corporate identity to which a social group was drawn by respect for its dead, much in the manner of a family cemetery. . . . Given what we know of Adena archaeology, a more appealing scheme either shifts the ritual centers to the edges of corporate group territories, or makes territorial boundaries irrelevant to location of the ritual sites (Clay 1991). As such, these centers shift from being the central places of group territories to loci between different groups that served as hinges between them. Expressive of Brose's emphasis upon cooperation between groups, they represent the architectural expressions of negotiations between groups.

When the possibility of multiple intergroup cooperation is considered, the ritual settlement becomes an increasingly complicated pattern of overlapping territories and interacting corporate groups. As ritual sites, because of that interaction, mounds and circles occurred seemingly in isolation. At the same time, they also clustered, reflecting the complexity of intergroup relations in specific and scattered contexts.

I have stated elsewhere that I think the pattern of clusters of shell heap mortuaries on alternating banks indicates two different moieties who meet at the river. Granger (1988:162) also thought that "several local bands [in the Falls district] possibly share a mortuary activity site . . . where rituals concerning the dead happen."

The creators of the shell heaps were not stimulated by stressful population growth. There were no scare resources. Nevertheless, they began a ritual and feasting cycle, created places to hold the rituals and bury their dead, killed others, and procured exotic items. The creators did these things while living as foragers (an assignment confirmed by Crothers 2004). They had no villages to speak of, or if they did, those villages lay well beyond the reaches of the southern Ohio Valley. The sacred places created may have been used by multiple groups; social boundaries may not have existed at these rivers, only sacred ones.

This situation of shared but isolated ritual centers among hunter-gatherers undermines the various arguments of ownership and complex/corporate group social organization during the Archaic, a situation that continued unabated in the Early and Middle Woodland, as well. Clay has made this case for Adena culture and a similar situation for Hopewell culture has been argued by Brown (2006) and Carr (2006). Brown has presented a case for the Hopewellians living in a priest-dominated culture, rather than one of aggrandizing individuals with a social hierarchy. They had priests, not chiefs. We can then envision the entire Ohio Valley from 7,000 years ago until about 1,200 years ago supporting foragers with ephemeral habitations being directed by priests in activities of a ritual nature that occupied the bulk of their "free" time and energy and created fixed ritual locations of monumental proportions.

I imagine small groups foraging in somewhat bounded territories, who kept their dead until such time as the stars, moon, and/or sun positions became auspicious for the burial rites and a runner or visitor announced the date and place of the annual aggregation. I imagine that this event was under the direction/coordination of a loosely formed group of elders and priests and perhaps a sodality, and was to some degree sponsored by a leading family of that place. I imagine that one to five captives were taken either in preparation for the annual renewal celebration or that the aggregation was called as a result of such a capture. Both kin and potential or actual allies were issued an invitation. The dead were collected and transported to the meeting grounds (or to a mortuary camp first), camps were established, rituals were conducted, feasts were held, and tool kits were culled and renewed, all generally similar to the later Huron Feast of the Dead. The climax of the gathering was the sacrifice of one or more captives for a renewal/fertility purpose. These sacrifices were performed for the benefit of all. The promises of peace and safe passage were made for everyone assembled. Rebalancing rituals were performed for the benefit of all. The feasting was for food and the building of social ties and the creation of fictive kin. The final burial was made for the benefit of all and for that of the next-of-kin. Perhaps moieties were involved, with members of one moiety mourning and members of the other moiety preparing the bodies for final disposal.

Crothers (2004) asked the question, "Did Green River peoples live in societies?" I say yes. I base my perception of their society on the evidence of contact between groups, on the large numbers of bodies gathered into a few places, the preparation for feasts, in the acts of sacrifice. I see sociality in the specialists who had to be solicited to produce the finely made cache blades, and in the rites that required rattles and medicine bags, in the sweats, in the labor needed to bury four to seven people simultaneously, or conduct a cremation or a sacrifice. I envision a sodality of water/cave keepers centered in the Green River as well as a dog burial rite centered at Read and the Green River in general, and at Perry. In fact, it seems to me that the events that transpired at the shell heaps required more society than those that went on at Archaic earthen mounds, which may well be the product of a small group of people for a small group of people and did not involve burial. Within the clusters of shell heaps and the mounds opposite one another across a river will be found evidence of friction or alliance, although it seems that the preferred situation was not to overlap mounds along a river and to minimize overlap within a cluster by regular spacing. When overlapping did happen, it was generally at the ends of a mound cluster.

Whether the objects once intended for offerings had become commodities by the Middle Woodland is debatable, but I think that the use of offerings first for deities and places in Paleoindian times and then the accumulation of the same substances and forms with individuals as grave goods in the Archaic reflect religious roles (as priests, as healers, as offerings) for those individuals, and indicates beyond a doubt that the path to social complexity in the eastern United States was through the ascendancy of ritual directors over others before Mississippian times. Clay (1998:15) has opined that the dispersal of groups around the landscape, evident in the separate ritual centers, signaled a lack of tribal development. "Prior to this era [AD 400], tribal identity was stymied by mortuary ritual not enhanced by it. Settlement nucleation 'may be the single most visible archaeological correlate of more complex tribal organization'" (Clay 1998:15 quoted in Anderson 2002:258). In other words, village life is the correct place to look for indications of complexity, but villages did not exist in the Archaic in the southern Ohio Valley or the Southeast in general. Instead, throughout the Southeast from 10,000 to 1,100 years ago there was an annual pattern of dispersed population, then nucleated for a short time, then dispersed again. "Authority was centralized only when nucleated, a priest-based system most likely" (Anderson 2002:268).

Clay found support for this interpretation of priest-led, rather than chief-led, foraging societies in the biodistance study of Taxman (1994:84). Taxman found that the nonmetric traits of Adena skeletons from two widely separated Kentucky counties were highly similar:

> For Kentucky, these are exactly the sort of population samples that might be expected if the mounds represent communal efforts. The conclusions from this exercise are that from a broad regional perspective, there were different Adena "breeding populations," for example north and south of the Ohio River. . . . More importantly, Taxman sees his data as supporting my suggestion that the accretional burial mounds represent the cemeteries of composite, exogamous, and not corporate groups. If the latter were the case, biological distance between mounds, and certainly between mound clusters, would be expected. (Clay 1998:16)

Although the necessary biodistance work among the Archaic skeletal populations of the Ohio Valley districts discussed here has not been done, this Woodland situation seems relevant to the Archaic groups of the southern Ohio Valley, as well.

A picture of individual differentiation rather than group differentiation seems to be developing for the shell-mound builders of Florida and the Atlantic Coast rings. Like the southern Ohio Valley groups, within a feasting context (but apparently without sacrifices) group differences were asserted, it has been proposed, through the temporary occupation of mounds of different height at multimound sites and by shell-heap shape and differential shell heights within individual shell arcs (Russo 2004). But the shell arcs and rings seem to have had their aggrandizers as well. These domestic feasting locations have exotics even though there are no burials that are found distributed according to the presumed status of the individual or family occupying the prime parts of the shell arc, either the center or the ends (Russo 2004).

Archaic-Woodland Continuity

Given that I have argued that the shell heaps were monumental ritual centers, they presage the ritual centers of Adena and Hopewell, also located in the Ohio Valley. The shared geography is no doubt relevant to the question of continuity of practices. Dragoo (1959:213–214) posited long ago that the Panhandle Archaic was the precursor for Early Woodland in the upper Ohio Valley. If the shell heaps were ritual facilities, they offer an origin for the Early Woodland mounds (Berle Clay, personal communication, November 2001). In fact, this predecessor role for the shell heaps is strengthen by the essential elements of Adena ceremonialism as outlined by Clay in 1998, which in turn have helped me identify just what those relevant elements of Archaic mortuary practice were.

Clay typifies Adena mortuary practice as "low cost," particularly in the one-time use of sealed graves but even with the log crypts that were meant to be reused. The Adena mortuary facilities (mounds and paired-post circles) were isolated from domestic locations and the evidence of social complexity was diametrically opposed in the two settings. In fact, there were no domestic sites of any significance anywhere near Adena mounds. Mortuary sites were frequently clustered at a riverbank and multiplied in number with repeated use of the location. Mounds grew accretionally as both bodies and an underworld substance—either shells or dirt—were added with each ceremony. It is assumed that not everyone was buried at an Adena mortuary site. The riverside mortuaries contained "domestic debris" and were located at the borders of territories. They were also vacant ceremonial centers except during the time of the ceremony.

Each of these aspects of Adena ritual practice I consider to characterize the ritual practice of the Ohio Valley Archaic shell heapers, and together they seem sufficient to demonstrate a continuity in at least the nature of ritual practice, if not in some of the actual beliefs and conduct. Furthermore, I have long been struck by the similarity between the focus of Archaic shell heapers on but a few rivers and the same behavior by Hopewellians, who chose even fewer rivers beside which to site their mortuary facilities. Sacred places were isolated and enhanced in ways very different from the later Mississippian practice of siting ritual facilities.

> In fact, the superimposition of Adena mortuary structures on Archaic cemeteries at the William Davis Mound (Seeman 1986:570) in Ohio and the Cotiga Mound (46Mo1) (Frankenberg and Henning 1994; Wall 1994) [as well as at Half Moon] in West Virginia can hardly be coincidental, and suggests that the Archaic-Woodland spatial similarities may be more complex than simply the products of parallel patterns of exchange. Despite the apparent change in mortuary customs, there may have been a strong ritual continuity between the periods (Clay 1998:15).

The role of the Ohio River in this phenomenon and its place in the later Adena and Hopewell social systems strongly suggests that the Archaic feasting-with-shellfish ceremonial centers and related bluff-top ceremonial sites and shell-free mortuaries were actually ancestral to the Woodland-period features. Both cultures had ritual practice directed by priests. But unlike the Archaic worshippers who focused on north-flowing rivers, the Woodland folks preferred south-flowing rivers, a transition that began with the choice of the Wabash late in the Late Archaic sites.

Of course there are important differences in ritual, as well—in the use of freshwater shells, bluff tops, dogs and atlatls, burial of mutilated bodies, the obviously large feasts held during the Archaic, and the use of log tombs, paired-post structures, earthworks, and pearls during the Woodland, among many other differences both significant and insignificant. Although it may be that earthen mounds distinguish the two religious systems, it could be that the shell-free capping "midden" of many of the Green River shell sites and possibly others as well is, in fact, nascent earthen-mounding behavior covering shell-bearing mortuaries. Clay pointed out that Adena earthen mounds could cap and replace Adena paired-post circles, indicating permitted substitution of ritual features in later religious practice.

Other elements of continuity between the two periods have been identified. Brose (1979) said that the exchange system of the Late Archaic formed the basis of the Woodland-period exchange system. Domesticated plants seem to have played little to no part in the respective subsistence systems and certainly supported neither religious system. Marine shell continued to be important as offering material. Finally, the genetics indicated a significant correlation between Indian Knoll and Chiggerville people and the Kentucky Adena people (Wyckoff 1977).

Substitution of Archaic ritual features by later ritual features is also seen in the Tennessee Valley and in Florida. Dirt mounds cover shell heaps in Alabama. Sand mounds apparently were constructed regularly at the sites of older shell mounds in Florida (Homsey 1999). Copena burials and characteristic artifacts are found in the tops of many of the older shell heaps, and Copena people continued to use the same caves and rock shelters in the immediate Tennessee River valley. We may even see the co-occurrence of shell mounding and dirt mounding at Vaughn Mound and in the newly discovered dirt mound at Whitesburg Bridge.

Memory

In the history of these shell places, we can see both fine-scale memories and grand-scale memories. Fine-scale memory is demonstrated in the superpositioning of clay floors, of pits and fire features, and in the low level of disturbance of burials, even in the reuse of these places. The removal of skulls and limbs well after burial indicates memory. Caches are memory makers and expressions. Over the course of 500 to 2,000 years, these places were remembered by Archaic peoples.

All of the districts discussed here had sites that were visited by Woodland peoples, judging from their pottery and, in some cases, burials. There was Mississippian interest in Archaic shell heaps, as well. Altogether there is much indication of a collective memory of these Archaic places. Later people placed mounds near Archaic heaps (e.g., Annis mound 15Bt2, Wright Mounds 1Lu63), incorporated Archaic shell deposits into their own mounds (e.g., McKelvey 40Hn1), placed bodies into Archaic mortuaries (e.g., Perry 1Lu25, Union Hollow 1Lu72), built buildings upon them (e.g., Ward 15McL11), and rejuvenated the use of marine shell (Ottesen 1979).

Mississippian religion has been characterized as, among other things, ancestor worship (Fagan 2005:463). The use of Archaic shell heaps on the Tennessee River by Mississippians (Webb offered they were the residents of Moundville) is one expression of that concern with ancestors. Not only were some Mississippian dead transported to these once great places of ritual and human sacrifice, but often these bodies, like those of the Archaic, had been mutilated or were interred as part of a group, with at least one member evincing a violent death (e.g., reports in Webb and DeJarnette 1942). It seems as if these past activities and the very places where these great events had occurred had been kept alive for 4,000 years and were being claimed by leaders seeking a holy alliance. War captives and victims were brought to various burial mounds where earlier captives and victims and the valiant and the blessed had also been buried. I suspect that it was more than oral history that kept the locations and the activities of these ancestors alive. I suspect that these places had never been forgotten and had been accumulating power throughout the millennia by continued pilgrimages to them, offerings left at them, shells used from them, and rites that were conducted at them.

Directions and Questions for Future Work

The amount of basic research still undone relevant to the Archaic shell accumulators and ritual site users is overwhelming. Excavation of more sites, the publication of tardy site reports, and "absolute" dating are the primary deficiencies facing those of us who are interested in this phenomenon. The easiest challenge to address of these three that would also provide the most pertinent data the quickest is a significant radiocarbon dating program.

Dating

Throughout this study, I have stressed that the radiocarbon dates available are far too few and far too unfocused to be very useful for the tasks at hand. The most visible of all of the activities recorded in these sites, that of shellfishing, has not been dated, yet shellfishing is the definitional base of this site type and cultural expression, as well as the basis for arguing primary forest efficiency, sedentism, and village life. Importantly, we do not know the extent to which Paleoindians concentrated shells or Woodland and Mississippian peoples added shells to these piles, or used them to temper their pottery. We do not know the extent to which human burials intruded into shell and substrata predating and postdating shellfishing. We do not know if multiple shell concentrations at single sites, such as the spatially divided shell deposits at Read and Ward, were amassed simultaneously or sequentially. We do not know when activities at Read and Ward changed from that of bluff-top–like camps to major ceremonial centers.

Efforts are being made to improve the usefulness of freshwater shell as a dating medium. Among these efforts is the isolation of proteins from calcium carbonate, allowing the circumvention of old carbon (Dr. Tull, University of Arizona Radiocarbon Lab, personal communication, March 2009). Others are constructing reservoir correction values for freshwater shell (Peacock 2006; Jonathan Lothrop for Ohio River shells, personal communication, April 2004). Published corrections for California (Culleton 2006) and for Lake Michigan and Lake Huron (Moore et al. 1998) are instructive as well as useful for those regions.

The other two readily apparent activities at these shell-bearing sites—human burial and dog burial—are also yet to be directly dated in any meaningful way, although human burials have received some dates. Unfortunately, very few of the dated burials had grave goods, leaving us virtually no information about innovation in the burial programs. All burial treatments are also in need of a focused dating program. Are sitting burials particularly late in time? Are all burials with copper and galena equally as late as sitting burials? When did the dog burial activities begin at shell-bearing sites and when did they end? Are large numbers of dogs at Perry post-Archaic?

Several sites have suspect dates or dates based on outmoded techniques and need to be replaced, such as Parrish, Ward, Kirkland, Eva, Perry, and many of the Falls heaps. Though recent excavation and research have begun to give us more significant suites of dates at individual sites, many more such programs are needed in order to understand the use histories of individual sites, of site clusters, and of rivers. Knowledge of the contemporaneity of clusters and sites within clusters is needed. At a minimum, all heaps in at least two adjacent clusters need to be dated multiple times. We need dates for paired sites. We need sequences of site founding across the region and within a district. What are the temporal relationships between tributary sites and river sites such as 15Oh98 on a tributary of the Rough River, itself a tributary of the Green?

Site Reports

There is a great need for the analysis and reporting of the shell-bearing sites excavated in earlier decades, particularly those in central Tennessee, on the upper Tennessee River, and on the Ohio River around the Falls. Kentucky, Tennessee, and Alabama nonburial WPA photos have been put online, as have Tennessee field notes and maps (visit McClung Museum Web site). These projects should be fodder for many master's and doctoral candidates.

Excavation/ Lab Analysis

The total excavated square meters in these districts cannot yet be calculated for lack of field reports. However, at least 31,243 sq. m. have been explored by archaeologists. About 67 percent of those square meters (21,461 sq. m.) come from Green River sites, and considerably less is contributed by the Tennessee River sites, 6,749 sq. m. The Ohio River value should be in between those two values if we knew the areas excavated in the earlier projects (Appendix I). Sites in central Tennessee and on the Wabash have under 1,100 sq. m. uncovered, combined. Clearly we need much larger sample sizes in all of these areas. Excavations are needed at Tennessee River sites during any drawdown of the lake levels, and at sites on the Cumberland River.

In addition to sampling these sites for more information on mound construction, activity areas, and features, excavations are needed to address questions of differences and similarities between sites within the same cluster and between opposing sites on a river and between clusters. Modern excavations are needed at unsampled Green River sites, especially those in clusters 1, 2, and 5, and those stray sites elsewhere in the drainage. Clusters and mounds opposite one another across the river are the logical places to look for evidence of friction or alliance. I have often wondered what archaeologists who are familiar with mound construction in Florida shell-bearing sites would see in the Green River or Ohio River sites?

There is likewise a pressing need for the analysis of burial fauna. This is a large arena for the expression of beliefs that is virtually untapped. Caches and pit fill also need to be examined for potential information on offerings.

Expanding the Scope of the Inquiry

There are other shell-bearing Archaic-aged sites north of the Ohio River that have not been incorporated into this study for a lack of literature on them. I am thinking specifically of sites in Ohio and Indiana on the White River, sites such as DuPont with shells and at least two victims of violence, the older sites on the lower Wabash, and the cluster of shell sites on the Cumberland between Robinson and Penitentiary Branch. There may be sites of relevance on the Ouachita in Arkansas and on other north-flowing tributaries of the Tennessee.

I have also proposed that the northern Atlantic shell heaps—in Maine and on the Hudson River—were feasting localities, like the southern

Atlantic shell-feasting arcs/rings and mounds. What evidence beside acres and meters of shells is there to support such an interpretation?

Skeletal Analyses

All of the skeletons implicated in this study should have been examined recently for basic biological data, as directed by NAGPRA. One notable exception is the bodies curated by the Museum of Anthropology at the University of Alabama, where the 1940s–1950s analyses were submitted for NAGPRA. Often additional observations have been recorded, such as that about grave goods, extraneous animal and human bones, and trauma. This information needs to be made widely available to researchers.

Biodistance studies are needed for several reasons. We need to know more about the social relationships between clusters on one river and between rivers, and between people buried in shell-bearing sites and those buried in shell-free sites. Are the people buried on either side of the river indistinguishable from one another? Are those people buried in a flexed position on one side—the purported locals of a shell heap—genetically different from those people buried in extended, stacked, or kneeling positions, in groups, or with missing body parts—the possible foreigners? Are the initial burials foreigners? Are isolated skulls collected from local or foreign people? Are there any genetic differences between people buried in shell and those buried in shell-free settings within one site or when comparing site types? Are there genetically linked traits such as Wormian bones, or enlarged and extended canines that can be traced across the Ohio Valley?

Biodistance studies of the dogs would also provide very useful information about the possible radiation of dogs from central points, such as Read and Perry. Can Read and Perry dogs be isolated? Are the dogs found in Dust Cave related to those dogs buried at Perry and elsewhere in the Alabama district?

Bone chemistry work is needed. If the samples for biodistance are too small, tooth and bone chemistry could address the questions of geographical distances between purported victims and locals. Can marriage patterns be uncovered through trace element analysis of teeth or bone? Will differences in human diet be correlated with differences in burial treatment at other sites, as was found at Rosenberger (Collins and Lannie 1979)? Bone chemistry on dogs could also be employed to address the hypothesis that dogs were being bred at Read and Perry and moving out from there. Can sequences of burial be worked out with flouride studies?

Most Archaic human skeletal collections need to be examined for evidence of trauma—broken bones, scalping, patterned missing body parts. We are only just beginning to comprehend the extent to which violence occurred during the Middle and Late Archaic and the extent to which it did not occur in other eras and areas.

Burial positioning and depth offer much promise for their potential information about gender and rituals, as proposed here. These data were often not reported and even still are rarely reported, even if recorded in the field notes or on burial forms. More attention needs to be paid to burial depths, to the richest burials, and to the first burials. A systematic study of a topic such as head orientation or side down could move us well along in our understanding of Archaic ritual practices.

Specific Propositions Presented Herein for Testing

Finally, there are many propositions put forth in this study that need greater refining, testing, and data. While it is my hope that I have offered solutions to the various problems of explaining the history of the so-called Shell Mound Archaic, it is even more important to me to have stimulated more creative and engaging thought about this era, phenomenon, and geography. A partial listing of those propositions follows:

- Offerings drove the earliest movement of goods and materials.
- Feasting was the motivation for intensive shellfishing and aggregation of shells.
- There were no "villages" among Archaic shellfishers, at least in the immediate region.
- There was a subset of the population among the dead in shell heaps.
- Unusual burial position or treatment reflects cause of death.
- Adult burials on the face, extended, stacked, or in groups indicate sacrifices and foreigners.
- Dog rituals were centered at Perry, Read, and bluff-top locations.
- Bluff-top sites are distinctive from floodplain sites.
- Bluff-top sites are mortuary processing camps.

- There was a lack of corporate groups in this region.
- The Big Bend shell heaps (Green River) represent a single multimound mortuary site.
- Clusters of sites on alternating banks were the creations of different social groups that cooperated in burial ritual.
- Skeletal and artifactual remains found in nearby caves and rock shelters were derived from the same people using nearby shell heaps and shell-free mortuaries.
- Natural places, riverside shell-heap mortuaries, riverside shell-heap non-mortuaries, bluff-top sites, and shell-free mortuaries constitute different types of sites in a ritual landscape.
- The differences in grave goods between types of sites—shell-free mortuary, riverside shell mortuary, bluff-top shell mortuary—will provide a better understanding of the social landscape than will differences between individuals in one site or one type of site.
- Archaic shell-bearing mortuary sites were located away from domestic settings.
- There is more continuity than difference between southern Ohio Archaic renewal ritual and Adena/Hopewell renewal ritual.
- Dirt cappings on shell-heaps represent the start of earthen mound building in the southern Ohio Valley.
- The reuse of Archaic shell heaps by Mississippians for mortuaries represented a political statement and is a part of ancestor worship.
- Some shell tempering was derived from Archaic shells.

It is possible that some of the shell accumulations occurred at what might be longer-term habitation areas than the short-term (one-month) ritual camps that I have imagined. Few of these propositions must be correct in every instance for the thesis to stand that the monumental sites with burials were aggregation camps for annual rituals, feasts, and burials; that the bluff-top and knoll sites were ritual loci, and that the burial-free shell sites or shell-free burial sites were also ritual places.

Conclusions

Was there a Shell Mound Archaic "culture"? No. Instead, the shell heaps were mortuary places for the geographically widespread groups who foraged in this region, and perhaps elsewhere, and who hosted renewal rites with grand feasts and gift giving. Because significant population growth did not begin in the Middle Archaic or earlier, each of the notable features of Late Archaic life must have been generated by something other than population growth. I believe that the social and material needs of religious practice during the Archaic can explain all of the elements of the so-called Shell Mound Archaic, as well as the other regional manifestations of the time. These elements are the violence, the exotics, the monuments, the cemeteries, and the clustering of those cemeteries on but a few rivers, as well as the beginning and end of shell heaping in the upper southern Ohio Valley.

Rather than scarce resources leading to aggression and defense, raiding to acquire sacrificial persons was the motivation behind the violence in evidence at these sites, most probably orchestrated by religious practitioners. The rites for which the sacrifices were needed and the accompanying feasts were performed at the shell heaps and possibly the blufftop sites directed by priests. That there were far greater numbers of murder victims buried in the shell-bearing than in the non–shell-bearing mortuaries was demonstrated. Perhaps the earliest places were founded through village activities, but by 7,500 years ago the shell mound mortuary appeared. Largely accretional in growth, the mound/cemeteries were located at spiritually important places in the landscape—on islands, at major shoals, near caves, and on a river that arguably drained or caused a deep and intricate cave system. Some heaps grew to substantial sizes, reflecting a long history of ritual performance and regionwide feasting. The foreign objects found in some burials and in caches in the general matrix at the shell heaps were emplaced primarily as offerings during the rituals at the shell heaps and caves, given as gifts to guests at the feasts, and left at spiritually charged places. The domestic "refuse" was generated through short-term encampments, renewal of tools, and burial. These rituals were focused on renewal, continuation, rebalancing, and abundance. The ancestors and their living descendants were the actors in these rituals. The abundance of the ancestors and favor of the deities were elicited by the priest and were obvious in the size of the monument.

I believe that the strongest hypothesis for explaining the end of the sacred site systems as found in the various districts outlined here was a change in ritual beliefs and practices. The most striking change in all the districts was the closure of shell-bearing mortuaries. Possibilities for relevant causes that I have entertained here are the end of a river- or cave-keeper sodality and the end of the regionwide renewal rites that required human sacrifice. They, in turn, drove the raiding and need for possible alliance feasts. As the ritual gatherings dissolved, the need for the exotic goods and the large feasts also dissolved. There are numerous examples in history of major religious cults starting, spreading, and stopping among Native Americans with great rapidity, often governed simply by the dream or vision of an individual woman or man. It could be that the entire karstic region between the Ohio and the Tennessee rivers was believed to be the origin place of humans, with groups coming from outside that area into the various river valleys to conduct renewal rituals.

Crothers (2004) wondered if the Archaic dirt mounds of the lower Mississippi Valley figured differently in that social setting than did the shell heaps in the Ohio Valley. He pointed out that the dirt mounds usually lacked bodies (Vaughn on the Tombigbee is an exception). I think that both types of monuments were similar in that the people were creating sacred places on the landscape using Underworld substances (shell and dirt) for renewal, but significantly different in how they expected renewal to be ensured. The rituals performed at the two types of constructed places surely were very different in elements, in the deities appealed to, in their frequency, in the act of feasting, and in their scale, even if not in their goal of earth and family renewal. There is the possibility that the shell-mound mortuary users also held rituals at the earthen mounds of the Gulf plain. An important aspect of future work will be to understand the implications of a recently reported earthen mound at Whitesburg Bridge (Gage and Sherwood 2008).

This book has been about the sacred world of Archaic peoples. Whether I have persuaded the reader or not as to the sacred roles of these shell-bearing sites, it must be admitted that professional interest in the sacred world these people perceived has been inadequate. The shell mounds, the dirt mounds, and the natural landscape offer significant portals for us to explore both the sacred and the political dimensions of these Middle and Late Archaic societies.

APPENDIX
SITE DATA

Site #		Excavated Sq. Meters	# Burials	Burial/ Sq. Meter	Marine Shell	Dog Burials	Dogs with Humans
Big Sandy	40Hy18		59		x	11	3
Cherry	40Bn74	435	69	1/6.3	x	7	4
Kays Lndg.	40Hy13		76		o	1	o
Eva/Eva	40Bn12	297	17	1/17.4	o	o	o
Eva/3 mi.	40Bn12	297	102	1/2.9	o	15	3
Long Branch	1Lu67	185	94	1/1.9	x	3	1
Bluff Creek	1Lu59	446	114	1/2.5	x	2	o
O'Neal	1Lu61	251	43	1/4.1	x	1	o
Mulberry Cr.							
Mulberry Cr. MA	1Ct27	402	11	1/36.5	o	2	2
Mulberry Cr. LA	1Ct27	402	73	1/5.5	x	17	1
Little Bear Cr.	1Ct8	460	136	1/3.4	x	6	o
Perry all	1Lu25	2,322	708	1/3.3	x	75	11
Perry Unit 1							
Lu86	1Lu86	223	26	1/8.6	x	o	o
Whitesburg Br.	1Ma10	985	117	1/8.4	x	10	o
Fennel	1Ct130	44.1	15	1/2.9	x	o	o
Tenn. River Total		6,749	1,660			150	25
Ervin	40Mu174	18	8	1/2.3	x		o
Hayes	40Ml139		6			6	1
Mizzell	40Wm255		22			o	o
Anderson	40Wm9	139	74	1/1.8	x	1	o
Hart	40Wm14		588			15	o
Hermitage Sp.	40Dv551		339		x	9	4
Robinson	40Sm4	288	51	1/4.5	1	2	o
Penitentiary	40Jk25	378	20	1/19	o	o	o
Cent. Tenn. Total		823	1,108			33	5

(cont.)

Bifaces	Bifaces/Non-Infant	Number of Features	Feature/Sq Meter	Burials with Exostoses	% of Graves with Goods	Ave. # Grave Goods	Author Saw C=Coll F=File
					40	3.1	c,f
		44	1/10		40	2.4	c
					24	3.1	c,f
204	14.6	3	1/99	0	29	1.0	c,f
136	1.7	6	1/50	1	24	2.0	c,f
311	3.9	7	1/26	1	24	5.1	c,f
284	1.7	13	1/34		15	5.5	c
210	4.4	17	1/15	3	17	2.8	c
297	2.7	23	1/17				c
				1	27		c
				5	18		c
442	3.4	54	1/9		21	3.4	c
7,282	10.28	195	1/12				c
					39	3.1	
					11	1.0	
1,030	>8.8	29	1/34		36		
163	12.5	17	1/3		44	3.1	
10,359		408		11	27.3	3.0	
					50	18.0	
		4			71	3.0	f
238		347					
1,356	23.8	48	1/3	0	38	5.4	c
				0	44	2.6	
508	11	77	1/4	0	18	2.8	
294	17.3	131	1/3	0	0	0.0	
2,396		607		0	36.8	5.3	

(cont.)

Site #		Excavated Sq. Meters	# Burials	Burial/ Sq. Meter	Marine Shell	Dog Burials	Dogs with Humans
Ward	15McL11	1,507	433	1/3.5	x	27	7
Barrett	15McL4	1,358	412	1/3.3	x	14	2
Butterfield	15McL7	2,278	153	1/14.8	o	8	1
Bowles	15Oh13	149	24	1/6.2	x	2	?
Jimtown Hill	15Oh19	2,322	14	1/166	o	10	o
Indian Knoll	15Oh2	5,580	880	1/6.3	x	23	11
Jackson Bluff	15Oh12	1,236	7	1/176	o	10	o
Chiggerville	15Oh1	826	114	1/7.2	x	12	5
Baker	15Mu12	399	6	1/66.5	o	12	o
Read	15Bt10	3,846	247	1/15.6	x	65	o
Carlston Annis	15Bt5	1,960	390	1/5	x	29	4
Green River Total		**21,461**	**2,680**			**212**	**30**
DuPont			28			1	
McCain		186	24	1/7.5	o	o	o
Bono	12Lr194						
Panther Rock	15Cl58	50	1	1/50	o	1	o
Old Clarksville	12Cl1	35	x		o		
Clark's Pt.	12cl3	4.5	1+	na	o		
Miller	12Hr5	4.4	?		o		
Ferry Lndg.	12Hr3		x		o		
Hoke	12Hr103		?		o		
Breeden	12Hr11	2	na	na	o		
Bluegrass	12W162		82			2	2
KYANG	15Jf267	159	37	1/3.9	o	o	o
Lone Hill	15Jf10		300+		o	x	
Minor's Lane	15Jf36		x		o		
Hornung	15Jf60	56	14+	1/4	o	3	1
Crib (Raaf)	12Sp2		1,000+				
Paddy's West	15Fl46		1-2				
Reid	12Fl1	2.3	o	na	o	o	o
Globe Hill	46Hk34	23	o	na	o	o	o

(cont.)

Bifaces	Bifaces/ Non-Infant	Number of Features	Feature/ Sq Meter	Burials with Exostoses	% of Graves with Goods	Ave. # Grave Goods	Author Saw C=Coll F=File
481	1.4	61	1/25	22	12	2.2	c,f
253	0.6	32	1/42	25	26	2.0	c,f
252	1.8	34	1/67		11	3.8	c,f
		17	1/9		10	10.0	c,f
197	15	22	1/105		0	0.0	c,f
9,424	15.3	10		148	31	3.6	c,f
50	7.1	30	1/41		29	1.0	c,f
300	3.6	53	1/16		31	2.6	c,f
		9	1/44		50	2.5	c,f
565	2.6	168	1/23		30	3.1	c,f
2,101	6.6	129	1/15	40	55	2.5	c,f
13,623		565		235	25.9	3.0	
255	12.8				13	3.3	
		136	1/0.37	0			
							c
15	na	3	1/1.5	na	na	na	
							c
							c
10	na	4					
434		132		x	34	2.8	
		28		10	8	1.0	c
							c
							c
							c
							c
193	0	1	1/23.0	na	na	na	

(cont.)

Site #	Excavated Sq. Meters	# Burials	Burial/ Sq. Meter	Marine Shell	Dog Burials	Dogs with Humans
East Steubenville	46Br31	7,424	6	1/1237	0	2	0
New Cumberland	46Hk1						
M&M							
Fish Run	46Mr118						
Ohio River Total		7,946	1,488			9	3
Robeson Hills	12Lw1	28	9	1/3	0	0	0
Swan Island	12Cw319	12	x	na	0	0	0
Riverton	12Cw170	211	6	1/35	0	0	0
Wabash River Total		261	15			0	0
Vaughn			300+		x		
Other Total			300+			0	0
Total All Shell Sites	61 sites	31,243	7,656			419	67
Shell-Free Mortuary Sites							
Meyer	12Sp1082	84	27	1/3		1	0
Little Pigeon Cr.	12Sp		31				
Shadow Wood	15Jf674		15		0		
Rosenberger	15Jf18	6,424	230	1/28	0	1	0
Railway Museum	15Jf630		17		0	x	?
Habich	15Jf550		27		0	0	0
Parrish	15Hk45	917	133	1/6.7	0	2	0
Kirkland	15McL12	1,042	70	1/14.8	x	11	0
Eva/Big Sandy	40Bn12	297	60		0	3	1
Ensworth	40Dv184	5,525	64	1/15	0	1	0
Shell-Free Total	10 sites	14,289	616			19	1

(cont.)

Bi-faces	Bifaces/ Non-Infant	Number of Features	Feature/ Sq Meter	Burials with Exostoses	% of Graves with Goods	Ave. # Grave Goods	Author Saw C=Coll F=File
383	63.0	74	1/101		0	0.0	
1,290		378		10	13.7	1.8	
46	5.1				11	1.0	
					0	0.0	
161	40.3				17	2.4	
207					9.3	1.1	
27,875		1,956		256			
		96					
		32					
706	4.2	149	1/43		53	2.6	c
		50					c
587	4.4	53	1/17		41	2.6	c
70	1.6	8	1/130		6	2	c,f
132	2.9	1			36	2	c,f
271	4.9	271	1/20		25	3.7	
1,766		660			32.2	2.6	

References Cited

ABEL, TIMOTHY, DAVID STOTHERS, AND JASON KORALEWSKI
2001   The Williams Mortuary Complex: A Transitional Archaic Regional
        Interaction Center in Northwestern Ohio. In *Archaic Transitions in
        Ohio and Kentucky Prehistory*, edited by O. Prufer, S. Pedde, and R.
        Meindl, pp. 290–327. Kent State University Press, Kent, Ohio.

ALEXANDER, H.
1963   The Levi Site: Early Man Near Austin, Texas. *American Antiquity*
        28(4):510–528.

AMICK, DANIEL
1985   Buried Late Holocene Terrace Site Testing in the Central Duck River
        Basin. In *Exploring Tennessee Prehistory*, edited by T. Whyte, C.
        Boyd, and B. Riggs, pp. 23–38. Report of Investigations, No. 42.
        Anthropology, University of Tennessee, Knoxville.

ANDERSON, DAVID
1996   Approaches to Modeling Regional Settlement in the Archaic Period
        Southeast. In *Archaeology of the Mid-Holocene Southeast*, edited
        by K. Sassaman and D. Anderson, pp. 157–176. University Press of
        Florida, Gainesville.

2002   The Evolution of Tribal Social Organization in the Southeastern
        United States. In *The Archaeology of Tribal Societies*, edited by W.
        Parkinson, pp. 246–278. International Monographs in Prehistory,
        Archaeological Series 15, Ann Arbor, Michigan.

ANGST, MICHAEL
1998   Archaeological Salvage Excavation at the Reid Site (12Fl1), Floyd
        County, Indiana, Reports of Investigation 50. Archaeological Re-
        sources Management Services, Ball State University.

ANSLINGER, C. MICHAEL
1986   The Riverton Culture: Lithic Systems and Settlement Parameters.
        Master's thesis, Washington State University.

ARNOLD, JEAN
1996   The Archaeology of Complex Hunter-Gatherers. *Journal of Arch-
        aeological Method and Theory* 3:77–126.

ASCH, NANCY, RICHARD FORD, AND DAVID ASCH
1972   Paleoethnobotany of the Koster Site: The Archaic Horizons. Illinois
         Valley Archaeological Program, Research Papers, Vol. 6, Illinois
         State Museum, Springfield.

ATEN, LAWRENCE
1999   Middle Archaic Ceremonialism at Tick Island, Florida: Ripley
         Bullen's 1961 Excavation at the Harris Creek Site. *Florida Anthro-
         pologist* 52(3):131–200.

ATHENS, WILLIAM
2000   Phase I Cultural Resources Survey and Archaeological Inventory of
         a 17.7 km long Proposed Levee Project for U.S. Fish and Wildlife
         Service. Goodwin and Associates, Savannah, Georgia.

ATKINSON, JAMES R.
1974   Appendix A: Test Excavations at the Vaughn Mound Site. In *Arch-
         eological Survey and test excavations in the upper-central Tombig-
         bee River Valley: Aliceville—Columbus Lock and Dam and Im-
         poundment Areas, Alabama and Mississippi.* Mark Rucker, author.
         Anthropology, Mississippi State University.

BADER, ANNE
2005   Why Dig Yet Another Late Archaic site in the Falls of the Ohio
         River region? Insights into corporate identity through an exam-
         ination of mortuary behavior at the KYANG site, Jefferson County,
         Kentucky, and the Meyer site, Spencer County, Indiana. Paper de-
         livered at the annual Kentucky Heritage Conference meeting, in
         press.

2006   Do Not Stand Beside My Grave and Weep. Paper presented at the
         annual meeting of the Midcontinental Archaeology Conference,
         Dayton, Ohio.

2007   Phase III Data Recovery and Construction Monitoring of the Lone
         Hill Site (15Jf562/15Jf10), Jefferson County, Kentucky. AMEC
         Earth and Environmental.

2009   Archaeological Background. In Phase III Archaeological Mitigation
         of the Panther Rock Site (15Cl58), Carroll County, Kentucky,
         compiled by Richard Stallings, pp. 20–55. AMEC Earth and
         Environmental.

BAERREIS, DAVID
2005   Terrestrial Gastropods at the Carlston Annis Site, 15Bt5: Their
         Habitat and Climatic Implications. *Archaeology of the Middle
         Green River Region, Kentucky,* edited by W. Marquardt and P.
         Watson, pp. 243–256. Institute of Archaeology and Paleoenviron-
         mental Studies, Monograph 5, Florida Museum of Natural History,
         University of Florida, Gainesville.

BAILLOU, CHARLES
1968   Notes on Cherokee Symbolism. *Southern Indian Studies* 20:12–16.

BARKER, GARY, AND EMANUEL BREITBURG
1992   Archaic Occupations at the Austin Site (40Rb82). Paper read at the annual meeting of the Southeastern Archaeological Conference, Little Rock, Arkansas.

BASSIE-SWEET, KAREN
1996   *At the Edge of the World: Caves and Late Classic Maya World View.* Norman, University of Oklahoma Press.

BECKER, MARSHALL
1988   Caches as burials, burials as caches: the meaning of ritual deposits among the Classic period lowland Maya. In *Recent Studies in Pre-Columbian Archaeology,* edited by N. Saunders and O. de Montmollin, pp.117–142. BAR International Series 421, Oxford, England.

BELLIS, JAMES
1981   Test Excavation Conducted at the Breeden Site 12 Hr11, in Harrison County, Indiana. Paper presented at the annual meeting of the Indiana Academy of Science.

BINFORD, LEWIS
1971   Mortuary Practices: Their Study and Their Potential. In *Approaches to the Social Dimensions of Mortuary Practices,* edited by J. Brown, pp. 6–29. Memoirs of the Society for American Archaeology, No. 25. Washington, D.C.

BLITZ, JOHN
1983   Locust Beads and Archaic Mounds. *Mississippi Archaeology* 28(1): 20–43.

BLITZ, JOHN, AND PATRICK LIVINGOOD
2004   Sociopolitical Implications of Mississippian Mound Volume. *American Antiquity* 69(2):291–303.

BLUM, MICHAEL, AMY CARTER, TRACY ZAYAC, AND RON GOBEL
2002   Middle Holocene Sea Level and Evolution of the Gulf of Mexico Coast. *Journal of Coastal Research,* Special Issue 36:65–80.

BRADY, JAMES, AND WENDY ASHMORE
1999   Mountains, Caves, Water: Ideational Landscapes of the Ancient Maya. In *Archaeologies of Landscape: Contemporary Perspectives,* edited by W. Ashmore and A. Knapp, pp. 124–145. Blackwell Publishers, Oxford, England.

BRENDEL, SHIRLEY
1972   Tennessee River Valley Archaic Shell Mound People: A Review of their Physical Characteristics. *Tennessee Anthropologist* 28:49–59.

BRIDGES, PATRICIA, JOHN BLITZ, AND MARTIN SOLANO
2000   Changes in Long Bone Diaphyseal Strength with Horticultural Intensification in West-Central Illinois. *American Journal of Physical Anthropology* 112:217–238.

BROCK, OSCAR, AND MARGARET CLAYTON
1966   Archaeological Investigations in the Mud Creek–Town Creek Drainage Area of Northwest Alabama. *Journal of Alabama Archaeology* 12(2):71–132.

BROOKS, SAMUEL
2004   Cultural complexity in the Middle Archaic of Mississippi. In *Signs of Power*, edited by J. Gibson and P. Carr, pp. 97–113. University of Alabama Press, Tuscaloosa.

BROSE, DAVID
1979   A Speculative Model of the Role of Exchange in the Prehistory of the Eastern Woodlands. In *Hopewell Archaeology*, edited by D. Brose and N. Greber, pp. 3–8. Kent State University Press, Kent, Ohio.

BROWN, JAMES
1983   Summary. In *Archaic Hunters and Gatherers in the American Midwest*, edited by J. Phillips and J. Brown, pp. 5–10. New York, Academic Press.

2006   The Shamanic Element in Hopewellian Period Ritual. In *Recreating Hopewell*, edited by D. Charles and J. Buikstra, pp. 475–488. University Press of Florida, Gainesville.

BROWN, LINDA
2005   Planting the Bones: Hunting Ceremonialism at Contemporary and Nineteenth-Century shrines in the Guatemalan Highlands. *Latin American Antiquity* 16(2):131–146.

BUCK C. E., J. A. CHRISTEN, AND G. JAMES
1999   BCal: an on-line Bayesian Radiocarbon Calibration Tool. *Internet Archaeology* 7.

BUIKSTRA, JANE, DOUG CHARLES, AND GORDON RAKITA
1998   *Staging Ritual: Hopewell Ceremonialism at the Mound House Site, Greene County, Illinois.* Studies in Archeology and History, No. 1. Center for American Archeology, Kampsville, Illinois.

BURDIN, RICK
2008   Archaeological Investigations of the Overflow Pond Area in Harrison County, Indiana: The 2007 Survey and Excavations at the Breeden (12Hr11) and Overflow Pond (12Hr12) Sites. University of Kentucky, Anthropology, Lexington.

BYERS, A. MARTIN
1998   Is the Newark Circle-Octagon the Ohio Hopewell "Rosetta Stone"? A Question of Archaeological Interpretation. In *Ancient Earthen*

Enclosures of the Eastern Woodlands, edited by R. Mainfort and L. Sullivan, pp.135–153. University Press of Florida, Gainesville.

CALDWELL, JOSEPH
1958   *Trend and Tradition in the Prehistory of the Eastern United States.* Memoir of the American Anthropological Association, No. 88. Menasha, Wisconsin.

CAMERON, CATHERINE
2002   Sacred Earthen Architecture in the Northern Southwest: The Bluff Great House Berm. *American Antiquity* 67(4):677–696.

CARLANDER, HARRIET
1954   A History of Fish and Fishing in the Upper Mississippi River. Upper Mississippi River Conservation Commission, Davenport, Iowa.

CARR, CHRISTOPHER
2006   Salient Issues in the Social and Political Organizations of Northern Hopewellian Peoples. *In Gathering Hopewell: Society, Ritual, and Ritual Interaction,* edited by C. Carr and D. Case, p.73–118. Springer, New York.

CARR, CHRISTOPHER, AND TROY CASE (EDS.)
2005   *Gathering Hopewell: Society, Ritual and Ritual Interaction.* Springer, New York.

CARR, PHILIP, AND LEE STEWART
2004   Poverty Point Chipped-Stone Tool Raw Materials: Inferring Social and Economic Strategies. In *Signs of Power,* edited by J. Gibson and P. Carr, pp. 129–145. University of Alabama Press, Tuscaloosa.

CARSTENS, KEN, AND PATTY JO WATSON (EDS.)
1996   *Of Caves and Shell Mounds.* University of Alabama Press, Tuscaloosa.

CECI, LYNN
1989   Tracing Wampum's Origins: Shell Bead Evidence from Archaeological Sites in Western and Coastal New York. In *Proceedings of the 1986 Shell Bead Conference: Selected Papers,* edited by L. Ceci, pp. 17–24. Rochester Museum and Science Center Research Records, No. 20.

CHARLES, DOUGLAS, AND JANE BUIKSTRA (EDS.)
2006   *Re-creating Hopewell,* edited by D. Charles and J. Buikstra. University Press of Florida, Gainesville.

CHARLES, DOUGLAS, AND JANE BUIKSTRA
1983   Archaic Mortuary Sites in the Central Mississippi Drainage: Distribution, Structure, and Behavioral Implications. In *Archaic Hunters and Gatherers in the American Midwest,* edited by J. Phillips and J. Brown, pp. 117–145. Academic Press, New York.

CLAASSEN, CHERYL (ED.)

1995   *Dogan Point: A Shell Matrix Site in the Lower Hudson Valley.* Occasional Publications in Northeastern Anthropology 14.

CLAASSEN, CHERYL

1988   New Hypotheses for the Demise of the Shell Mound Archaic. Paper presented at the annual meeting of the Southeastern Archaeological Conference, New Orleans.

1991   Gender, Shellfishing, and the Shell Mound Archaic. In *Engendering Archaeology: Women and Prehistory,* edited by J. Gero and M. Conkey, pp. 276–300. Blackwell, London.

1994   Washboards, Pigtoes, and Muckets: Historic Musseling Industries in the Mississippi Watershed. *Historical Archaeology* 28(2):1–164.

1996   A Consideration of the Social Organization of the Shell Mound Archaic. In *Archaeology of the Mid-Holocene Southeast,* edited by K. Sassaman and D. Anderson, pp. 235–258. University Press of Florida, Gainesville.

1998   *Shells.* Cambridge University Press, Cambridge.

2005   An Analytical Study of Shellfish from the DeWeese Mound, Kentucky. In *Archaeology of the Middle Green River Region, Kentucky,* edited by W. Marquardt and P. Watson, pp. 279–294. Institute of Archaeology and Paleoenvironmental Studies, Monograph 5, Florida Museum of Natural History, University of Florida, Gainesville.

2006a   Putting the Sacred Back into Eastern U.S. Caves. Paper read at the annual meeting of the Kentucky Heritage Council.

2006b   A Tradition of Cave Rituals. Paper read at the annual meeting of the Society for American Archaeology, San Juan, Puerto Rico.

2007   Newt Kash Rockshelter: A Menstrual Retreat? Paper presented at the annual meeting of the Society for American Archaeology, Austin, Texas.

2008   Shell Symbolism in Pre-Columbian North America. In *Early Human Impact on Megamolluscs,* edited by Andrzej Antczak and Roberto Cipriani, pp. 231–236. British Archaeological Reports S1865.

CLASSEN, CONSTANCE

1993   *Inca Cosmology and the Human Body.* University of Utah Press, Salt Lake City.

CLARK, CLARENCE

1971   Management of Naiad Populations in Ohio. In *Rare and Endangered Mollusks (Naiads) of the U.S.,* pp. 26–33. U.S. Department of the Interior, Fish and Wildlife Service, Washington, D.C.

CLARK, JOHN, AND DENNIS GOSSER

1995   Reinventing Mesoamerica's First Pottery. In *The Emergence of Pottery,* edited by W. Barnett and J. Hoopes, pp. 209–221. Smithsonian Press, Washington, D.C.

CLAY, BERLE

1991   Adena Ritual Development: An Organizational Type in a Temporal Perspective. In *The Human Landscape in Kentucky's Past*, edited by C. Stout and C. Hensley, pp. 30–39. Kentucky Heritage Council, Frankfort.

1998   The Essential Features of Adena Ritual and Their Implications. *Southeastern Archaeology* 17(1):1–21.

CLENCH, WILLIAM

1974   Mollusca from Russell Cave. In *Investigations in Russell Cave*, edited by John Griffin, pp. 86–90. National Park Service, U.S. Department of the Interior, Washington, D.C.

COBB, CHRISTOPHER, AND MICHAEL NASSANEY

2002   Domesticating Self and Society in the Woodland Southeast. In *The Woodland Southeast*, edited by D. Anderson and R. Mainfort, pp. 525–539. University of Alabama Press, Tuscaloosa.

COKER, ROBERT

1919   *Fresh-water Mussels and Mussel Industries of the United States.* Bulletin of the U.S. Bureau of Fisheries for 1917–1918. Washington, D.C.

COLLINS, MICHAEL, AND DONNA LANNIE

1979   Carbon Isotope Ratios. In *Excavations at Four Archaic Sites in the Lower Ohio Valley, Jefferson County, Kentucky*, Vol. II, edited by M. Collins and B. Driskell, pp. 946–947. Anthropology, University of Kentucky, Lexington

CORKRAN, DAVID

1969   Alexander Longe's Journal. *Southern Indian Studies* 21:3–49.

CRAWFORD, GARY

2005   Plant Remains from Carlston Annis (1972, 1974), Bowles, and Peter Cave. In *Archaeology of the Middle Green River Region, Kentucky*, edited by W. Marquardt and P. Watson, pp. 181–212. Institute of Archaeology and Paleoenvironmental Studies, Monograph 5, Florida Museum of Natural History, University of Florida, Gainesville.

CRIDLEBAUGH, PATRICIA

1986   Penitentiary Branch: A Late Archaic Cumberland River Shell Midden in Middle Tennessee. *Report of Investigations 4*. Nashville, Tennessee Department of Conservation, Division of Archaeology.

CRITES, GARY

1987   Middle and Late Holocene Ethnobotany of the Hayes Site (40Ml139): Evidence from Unit 99ON918E. *Midcontinental Journal of Archaeology* 12(1):3–32.

CROTHERS, GEORGE

1999   Prehistoric Hunters and Gatherers, and the Archaic Period Green River Shell Middens of Western Kentucky. Ph.D. dissertation, Anthropology. Washington University, St. Louis.

2004   The Green River in Comparison to the Lower Mississippi Valley during the Archaic: To Build Mounds or Not to Build Mounds? In *Signs of Power,* edited by J. Gibson and P. Carr, pp. 86–96. University of Alabama Press, Tuscaloosa.

2005   Vertebrate Fauna from the Carlston Annis Site. In *Archaeology of the Middle Green River Region, Kentucky,* edited by W. Marquardt and P. Watson, pp. 295–314. Institute of Archaeology and Paleoenvironmental Studies, Monograph 5, Florida Museum of Natural History, University of Florida, Gainesville.

CULLETON, BRENDAN
2006   Implications of a freshwater radiocarbon reservoir correction for the timing of late Holocene settlement of the Elk Hills, Kern County, California. *Journal of Archaeological Science* 33:1331–1339.

CURREN, CAILUP
1974   An Ethnozoological Analysis of the Vertebrate Remains, Little Bear Creek Site (1Ct8). *Journal of Alabama Archaeology* 20(2):127–182.

DANGLADE, ERNEST
1922   *Kentucky River and Its Mussel Resources.* U.S. Bureau of Fisheries, Document 934. Washington, D.C.

DEAN, WALTER, THOMAS AHLBRANDT, ROGER ANDERSON, AND J. PLATT BRADBURY
1996   Regional aridity in North America during the middle Holocene. *The Holocene* 6(2):145–155.

DEBOER, WARREN
2005   Colours for a North American Past. *World Archaeology* 37(1): 66–91.

DEJARNETTE, DAVID, EDWARD KURJACK, AND JAMES CAMBRON
1962   Stanfield-Worley Bluff Shelter Excavations. *Journal of Alabama Archaeology* 8(3).

DELCOURT, PAUL, AND HAZEL DELCOURT
1980   Vegetation Maps for Eastern North America: 40,000 Yr B.P. to the Present. In *Geobotany II,* edited by Robert Romans, pp. 123–166. Plenum Press, New York.

DENNISTON, R. F., L. A. GONZÁLEZ, Y. ASMEROM, R. G. BAKER, M. K. REAGAN, AND E. A. BETTIS
1999   Evidence for increased cool season moisture during the middle Holocene. *Geology* 27(9):815–818.

DESELM, H. R., B. E. WOFFORD, MAX E. MEDLEY, AND ROBERT R. HAYNES
1997   Western and Central-Southeastern Elements in the Flora of the Southern Ridge and Valley. In *Proceedings of the Seventh Symposium on the Natural History of Lower Tennessee and Cumberland*

River Valleys, edited by A. Scot, S. Hamilton, E. Chester, and D. White, pp. 214–242. Center for Field Biology, Austin Peay State University, Clarksville, Tennessee.

DETER-WOLF, AARON

2004   The Ensworth School Site (40DV184): A Middle Archaic Benton Occupation Along the Harpeth River Drainage in Middle Tennessee. *Tennessee Archaeologist* 1(1):18–35.

DETER-WOLF, AARON, SEAN NORRIS, MARC WAMPLER, AND JOSH TUSCHI

2004   The Ensworth School Project: Archaeological Investigations at Site 40Dv184, Davidson County, Tennessee. TRC Nashville. Report on file, Tennessee Department of Environment and Conservation, Nashville.

DONOVAN, TIMOTHY

1979   The Unionid Mussels of Ft. Gibson Reservoir, Oklahoma Population Estimates, and the Impact of Commercial Harvesting. Manuscript on file, Oklahoma Department of Wildlife Conservation, Oklahoma City.

DOWD, JOHN

1989   *The Anderson Site: Middle Archaic Adaptation in Tennessee's Central Basin.* Miscellaneous Paper, No. 13, Tennessee Anthropological Association.

DRAGOO, DON

1959   Archaic Hunters of the Upper Ohio Valley. *Annales of the Carnegie Museum* 35:139–245.

DRISKELL, BOYCE

1979   The Rosenberger Site (15Jf18). In *Excavations at Four Archaic Sites in the Lower Ohio Valley, Jefferson County, Kentucky,* Vol. II, edited by M. Collins and B. Driskell, pp. 697–803. Anthropology, University of Kentucky, Lexington.

1994   Stratigraphy and Chronology at Dust Cave. *Journal of Alabama Archaeology* 40:17–34.

DRISKELL, BOYCE, HENRY GRAY, JOHN BASSETT, DONNA DEAN LANNIE, STEVEN SMITH, AND MICHAEL COLLINS

1979   Background. In *Excavations at Four Archaic Sites in the Lower Ohio Valley, Jefferson County, Kentucky,* Vol. II, edited by M. Collins and B. Driskell, pp. 7–37. Anthropology, University of Kentucky.

DYE, DAVID

1980   Primary Forest Efficiency in the Western Middle Tennessee Valley. Ph.D. dissertation, Washington University, St. Louis.

1996   Riverine Adaptation in the Midsouth. In *Of Caves and Shell Mounds,* edited by K. Carstens and P. J. Watson, pp. 140–158. University of Alabama Press, Tuscaloosa.

ELDRIDGE, JOHN
1914   *The Mussel Fishery of the Fox River.* U.S. Bureau of Fisheries Document 804. Washington, D.C.

FAGAN, BRIAN
2000   Ancient North America: The Archaeology of a Continent. 3rd edition. Thames and Hudson, New York.
2005   Ancient North America: The Archaeological of a Continent. 4th edition. Thames and Hudson, New York.

FAIRBANKS, CHARLES
1942   The Taxonomic Position of Stalling's Island, Georgia. *American Antiquity* 3:223–231.

FISH, SUZANNE, MARIA GASPAR, PAULO DEBLASIS, AND PAUL FISH
2006   A Multi-scale perspective on shell mound complexes of southern coastal Brazil. Paper read at the annual meeting of the Society for American Archaeology, San Juan, Puerto Rico.

FITZGIBBONS, PHILLIP, JONATHAN LOTHROP, AND DAVID CREMEENS
2004   Archaeology and Geoarchaeology of the East Steubenville Site, Northern West Virginia. Poster presented at the annual meeting of the Society for American Archaeology, Montreal.

FOWLEY, J. PHILIP, AND KENNETH LONG
1997   Harlansburg Cave: The Longest Cave in Pennsylvania. *Journal of Cave and Karst Studies* 59:106–111.

FRANKENBERG, SUSAN, AND GRACE HENNING
1994   Phase III Data Recovery Investigations of the Cotiza Mound, Mingo County, West Virginia. Report. GAI Consultants, Monroeville, Pennsylvania. Submitted to the West Virginia Department of Transportation, Division of Highways.

FUNKHOUSER, WILLIAM, AND WILLIAM WEBB
1928   Ancient Life in Kentucky. *Kentucky Geological Survey,* Series 6, Geologic Reports V. 34.

FURST, JILL
1995   The Natural History of the Soul in Ancient Mexico. Yale University Press, New Haven, Connecticut.

FUTATO, EUGENE
1983   Archaeological Investigations in the Cedar Creek and Upper Bear Creek Reservoirs. University of Alabama Office of Archaeological Research, Report of Investigations, No. 3, Tuscaloosa.
2002   Middle and Late Archaic Settlement at the Perry Site, 1Lu25, Lauderdale County, Alabama. *Journal of Alabama Archaeology* 48:80–92.

GAGE, MATTHEW, AND SARAH SHERWOOD
2008   The Whitesburg Bridge Mound: A Late Archaic Earthen Mound in the Middle Tennessee Valley. Paper presented at the annual meeting of the Southeastern Archaeological Conference, Charlotte.

GAI
2007   *Panhandle Archaic Americans in the Upper Ohio Valley: Archaeological Data Recovery at the East Steubenville (46Br31) and Highland Hills (46Br60) Sites WV Route 2 Follansbee-Weirton Road Upgrade Project Brooke County, West Virginia.* Technical Report, 2 Vols. West Virginia Department of Transportation, Division of Highways.

GERMAINE, GEORGE
1986   Lithic Debitage Analysis of the East Steubenville Site. Master's thesis, Catholic University of America.

GIBSON, JON
1998   Broken Circles, Owl Monsters, and Black Earth Midden: Separating Sacred and Secular at Poverty Point. In *Ancient Earthen Enclosures of the Eastern Woodlands*, edited by R. Mainfort and L. Sullivan, pp. 135–153. University Press of Florida, Gainesville.
2004   The Power of Beneficent Obligation in First Mound-Building Societies. In *Signs of Power: The Rise of Cultural Complexity in the Southeast*, edited by J. Gibson and P. Carr, pp. 254–269. University of Alabama Press, Tuscaloosa.

GIBSON, JON, AND PHILIP CARR (EDS.)
2004   *Signs of Power: The Rise of Cultural Complexity in the Southeast.* University of Alabama Press, Tuscaloosa.

GIBSON, JON, AND PHILLIP CARR
1999   Signs of Power: why early mounds are southern and other thoughts. Paper presented at the annual meeting of the Southeastern Archaeological Conference, Pensacola, Florida.

GLORE, MICHAEL
2005   Zooarchaeological Analysis of Bt5, Operation C. In *Archaeology of the Middle Green River Region, Kentucky,* edited by W. Marquardt and P. Watson, pp. 315–338. Institute of Archaeology and Paleoenvironmental Studies, Monograph 5, Florida Museum of Natural History, University of Florida, Gainesville.

GOAD, SHARON
1989   Patterns of Late Archaic Exchange. *Tennessee Anthropologist* 5:1–16.

GRANGER, JOSEPH
1988   Late/Terminal Archaic Settlement in Falls of the Ohio River Region of Kentucky: An Examination of Components, In *Paleoindian and Archaic Research in Kentucky,* edited by C. Hockensmith, D. Pollack, and T. Sanders, pp. 153–204. Kentucky Heritage Council, Frankfort.

GRIFFIN, JOHN
1974   Investigations in Russell Cave, Russell Cave National Monument, Alabama. National Park Service Publications in Archaeology 13, U.S. Department of the Interior, Washington, D.C.

HAAG, WILLIAM
1942   Early Horizons in the Southeast. *American Antiquity* 7(3):209–222.
1948   An Osteometric Analysis of some Aboriginal Dogs. University of Kentucky Reports in Anthropology, No. 73. Lexington.

HALL, C., D. AMICK, W. TURNER, AND J. HOFMAN
1985   Columbia Archaeological Project Archaic Period Radiocarbon Dates. In *Exploring Tennessee Prehistory: A Dedication to Alfred K. Guthe,* edited by T. Whyte, C. Boyd, and B. Riggs, pp. 61–79. University of Tennessee, Anthropology, Report of Investigations, No. 42.

HALL, ROBERT
1983   A Pan-Continental Perspective on Red Ocher and Glacial Kame Ceremonialism. In *Lulu linear punctuated: essays in honor of George Irving Quimby,* edited by R. Dunnell and D. Grayson, pp. 75–108. Anthropological Papers, University of Michigan, Museum of Anthropology, no. 72. Ann Arbor.
1997   *An Archaeology of the Soul: North American Indian Belief and Ritual.* University of Illinois Press, Urbana.
2000   Sacrificed Foursomes and Green Corn Ceremonialism. In *Mounds, Modoc, and Mesoamerica: Papers in Honor of Melvin L. Fowler,* edited by S. Ahler, pp. 245–253. Illinois State Museum Scientific Papers, Vol. 28. Springfield.

HALPERIN, CHRISTINA, SERGIO GARZA, KEITH PRUFER, AND JAMES BRADY
2003   Caves and Ancient Maya Ritual Use of Jute. *Latin American Antiquity* 14:207–219.

HARIOT, JOHN
1951   *A Brief and True Report of the New Found Land of Virginia.* His-
[1588] tory Book Club, New York.

HAYDEN, BRIAN
1996   *Pithouses of Keatley Creek.* Harcourt Brace College Publishers, Ft. Worth, Texas.
2001   Fabulous feasts: A Prolegomenon to the Importance of Feasting. In *Feasts: Archaeological and Ethnographic Perspectives on Food, Politics, and Power,* edited by M. Dietler and B. Hayden, pp. 23–64. Smithsonian Institution Press, Washington, D.C.

HAYNES, C. VANCE
1976   Late Quaternary Geology of the Lower Pomme de Terre Valley. In *Prehistoric Man and His Environments: A Case Study in the*

Ozark Highland, edited by R. Wood and B. McMillan, pp. 47–61. Academic Press, New York.

HENSLEY, CHRISTINE

1989   The Green River Archaeological Study: Preliminary Report. Paper presented at the Southeastern Archaeological Conference, Tampa.

1991   The Middle Green River Shell Mounds: Challenging Traditional Interpretations Using Internal Site Structure Analysis. In *The Human Landscape in Kentucky's Past: Site Structure and Settlement Patterns*, edited by C. Stout and C. Hensley, pp. 78–97. Kentucky Heritage Council, Frankfort.

1994   The Archaic Settlement System of the Middle Green River Valley, Kentucky. Ph.D. dissertation, Anthropology, Washington University, St. Louis.

HERRMANN, NICHOLAS

1990   The Paleodemography of the Read Shell Midden, 15Bt10. Master's thesis, Washington University, St. Louis.

2004   Biological Affinities of Archaic Period Skeletal Populations from West-Central Kentucky and Tennessee. Ph.D. dissertation, University of Tennessee.

HILLER, ERNEST

1939   Houseboat and River Bottoms People: A Study of 683 Households in Sample Localities Adjacent to the Ohio and Mississippi Rivers. *Illinois Studies in the Social Sciences* 24(1). University of Illinois Press, Urbana.

HOCKENSMITH, CHARLES, THOMAS SANDERS, AND DAVID POLLACK

1983   National Register of Historic Places Inventory—Nomination Form. USDOI, NPS. On file at the Kentucky Heritage Council.

HOFMAN, JACK

1984   Radiocarbon dates from Ervin: A Mid-Holocene shell midden on the Duck River in Middle Tennessee. *Tennessee Anthropological Association Newsletter* 9:2.

1985   Middle Archaic Ritual and Shell Midden Archaeology: Considering the Significance of Cremations. In *Exploring Tennessee Prehistory*, edited by T. Whyte, C. Boyd, and B. Riggs, pp. 1–22. Report of Investigations, No. 42. Anthropology, University of Tennessee, Knoxville.

1986   Hunter-Gatherer Variability: Toward an Explanatory Model. Ph.D. dissertation, University of Tennessee.

HOMSEY, LARA

1999   Differing Geographical Expressions of the Shell Mound Archaic: A Regional Perspective from Florida. Manuscript in possession of author.

HUDSON, CHARLES
1976   *The Southeastern Indians.* University of Tennessee Press, Knoxville.
IRWIN, LEE
1994   *The Dream Seekers: Native American Visionary Traditions of the Great Plains.* University of Oklahoma Press, Norman.
JACKSON, ED, AND SUSAN SCOTT
2001   Archaic Faunal Utilization in the Louisiana Bottomlands. *Southeastern Archaeology* 20 (2):187–196.
JAMES, JENNY
2006   The Dog Tribe. *Southern Anthropologist* 32(1/2):17–46.
JANZEN, DONALD
1977   An Examination of Late Archaic Development in the Falls of the Ohio River Area. In *For the Director,* edited by C. Cleland, pp. 123–143. Anthropology Papers, Museum of Anthropology, University of Michigan, No. 61. Ann Arbor.
JEFFERIES, RICHARD
1996   The Emergence of Long-Distance Exchange Networks in the Southeastern United States. In *Archaeology of the Mid-Holocene Southeast,* edited by K. Sassaman and D. Anderson, pp. 222–234. University Press of Florida, Gainesville.
1997   Middle Archaic Bone Pins: Evidence of Mid-Holocene Regional-Scale Social Groups in the Southern Midwest. *American Antiquity* 62(3):464–487.
2006   Death Rituals at the Tunacunnhee Site. In *Re-creating Hopewell,* edited by D. Charles and J. Buikstra, pp. 161–177. University Press of Florida, Gainesville.
JEFFERIES, RICHARD, AND BRIAN BUTLER (EDS.)
1982   The Carrier Mills Archaeological Project: Human Adaptation in the Saline Valley, Illinois. Southern Illinois University at Carbondale, Center for Archaeological Investigations, Research Paper, No. 33.
JENNINGS, JESSE
1974   *Prehistory of North America,* 2nd edition. Mayfield Publications, Mountain View, California.
JOERSCHKE, BONNIE
1983   The Demography, Long Bone Growth, and Pathology of a Middle Archaic Skeletal Population From Middle Tennessee: The Anderson Site (40Wm9). Master's thesis, University of Tennessee.
JOHNSON, JAY, AND SAMUEL BROOKES
1989   Benton Points, Turkey Tails, and Cache Blades: Middle Archaic Exchange in the Midsouth. *Southeastern Archaeology* 8(2):134–145.

KAY, MARVIN (ED.)

1982   *Holocene Adaptation within the Lower Pomme de Terre River Valley, Missouri.* Report submitted to the U.S. Army Corps of Engineers, Kansas City District.

KELLEY, M.

1980   Disease and Environment: A Comparative analysis of three early American skeletal collections. Ph.D. dissertation, Anthropology, Case Western University, Cleveland, Ohio.

KELLY, LUCRETIA ,AND JOHN KELLY

2007   Swans in the American Bottom during the Emergent Mississippian and Mississippian. *Illinois Archaeology* 15&16:112–141.

KENNEDY, MARY

1996   Radiocarbon Dates from Salts and Mammoth Cave. In *Of Caves and Shell Mounds,* edited by K. Carstens and P. J. Watson, pp. 48–81. University of Alabama Press, Tuscaloosa.

KING, JASON, AND JANE BUIKSTRA

2006   Rituals of Renewal in the Lower Illinois River Valley: Evidence from the Mound House Site. Poster presented at the annual meeting of the Society for American Archaeology, San Juan, Puerto Rico.

KLIPPEL, WALTER, AND DARCY MOREY

1986   Contextual and Nutritional Analysis of Freshwater Gastropods from Middle Archaic Deposits at the Hayes Site, Middle Tennessee. *American Antiquity* 51(4):799–813.

KLIPPEL, WALTER, G. CELMER, AND JAMES PURDUE

1978   The Holocene naiad record at Rodgers Shelter in the western Ozark highland of Missouri. *Plains Anthropologist* 23:257–271.

KNEBERG, MADELINE

1952   The Tennessee Area. In *Archaeology of Eastern United States,* edited by J. Griffin, pp. 190–198. University of Chicago Press, Chicago.

KNIGHT, JAMES

1986   The Institutional Organization of Mississippian Religion. *American Antiquity* 51:675–685.

KNIGHT, VERNON

2001   Feasting and the Emergence of Platform Mound Ceremonialism in Eastern North America. In *Feasts: Archaeological and Ethnographic Perspectives on Food, Politics, and Power,* edited by M. Dietler and B. Hayden, pp. 311–333. Smithsonian Institution Press, Washington, D.C.

LAMBERT, PATRICIA

2001   Auditory Exostoses: A Clue to Gender in Prehistoric and His-toric Farming Communities of North Carolina and Virginia. In

Archaeological Studies of Gender in the Southeastern United States, edited by J. Eastman and C. Rodning, pp. 152–172. University Press of Florida, Gainesville.

LEWIS, T. N., AND MADELINE LEWIS
1961   *Eva: An Archaic Site.* University of Tennessee Press, Knoxville.

LEWIS, THOMAS, AND MADELINE KNEBERG
1959   The Archaic Culture in the Middle South. *American Antiquity* 25 (2):161–183.

1970   *Hiwassee Island: An Archaeological Account of Four Tennessee Indian*
[1946] *Peoples.* University of Tennessee Press, Knoxville.

LINDSTROM, BRUCE, AND KENNETH STEVERSON
1987   Lithic Artifacts from the Anderson Site, 40Wm9. *Tennessee Anthropologist* 12(1):1–50.

LITTLE, KEITH
2003   Late Holocene Climate Fluctuations and Culture Change in Southeastern North America. *Southeastern Archaeology* 22:9–32.

LOCKHART, JAMI, GEORGE SABO III, AND JERRY HILLIARD
2007   Ritual Use of Caves and Rock Shelters in Ozark Prehistory. Paper presented at the annual meeting of the Society for American Archaeology, Austin, Texas.

LUBSEN, KYLE
2004   What Trauma in Skeletal Remains Can Tell Us About Subsistence Activities During the Archaic: An Examination of the Burials at the Long Branch (1Lu67) and O'Neal (1Lu61) Sites. Master's thesis, University of Alabama.

LUBY, E., AND M. GRUBER
1999   The dead must be fed: Symbolic meanings of the San Francisco Bay area. *Cambridge Archaeological Journal* 9:95–108.

LUND, JENS
1983   Fishing as a Folk Occupation in the Lower Ohio Valley. Ph.D. dissertation, Department of Folklore, University of Indiana, Bloomington. University Microfilms, Ann Arbor, Michigan.

MAGENNIS, ANN
1977   Middle and Late Archaic Mortuary Patterning: An Example from the Western Tennessee Valley. Master's thesis, University of Tennessee.

MALLOUF, ROBERT
2007   Indicators of Ritual Behavior in Rockshelters of the Davis Mountains. Paper presented at the annual meeting of the Society for American Archaeology, Austin, Texas.

MARCUS, JOYCE
1999   Women's Ritual in Formative Oaxaca: Figurine Making, Divination, Death, and the Ancestors. Memoirs of the Museum of Anthropology, University of Michigan, Ann Arbor.

MARQUARDT, WILLIAM
2005   Lithic Artifacts in the Middle Green River Area. In *Archaeology of
         the Middle Green River Region, Kentucky,* edited by W. Marquardt
         and P. Watson, pp. 351–430. Institute of Archaeology and Paleo-
         environmental Studies, Monograph 5, Florida Museum of Natural
         History, University of Florida, Gainesville.

MARQUARDT, WILLIAM, AND PATTY JO WATSON (EDS.)
2005   *Archaeology of the Middle Green River Region, Kentucky.* Institute
         of Archaeology and Paleoenvironmental Studies, Monograph 5,
         Florida Museum of Natural History, University of Florida, Gainesville.

MARQUARDT, WILLIAM, AND PATTY JO WATSON
1983   The Shell Mound Archaic of Western Kentucky. In *Archaic Hunter
         and Gatherers in the Midwest,* edited by J. Phillips and J. Brown, pp.
         323–340. Academic Press, New York.

2004   The Green River Shell Mound Archaic: Interpretive Trajectories. In
         *Aboriginal Ritual and Economy in the Eastern Woodlands: Papers
         in Memory of Howard Dalton Winters,* edited by A. Cantwell,
         L. Conrad, and J. Reyman, pp. 113–122. Illinois State Museum,
         Scientific Papers 30. Springfield, Illinois.

2005a   Green River Shell Mound Archaic: Conclusions. In *Archaeology
         of the Middle Green River Region, Kentucky,* edited by William
         Marquardt and Patty Jo Watson, pp. 629–649. Institute of Archae-
         ology and Paleoenvironmental Studies, Monograph 5, Florida Mu-
         seum of Natural History, University of Florida, Gainesville.

2005b   Regional Survey and Testing. In *Archaeology of the Middle Green
         River Region, Kentucky,* edited by W. Marquardt and P. Watson, pp.
         41–70. Institute of Archaeology and Paleoenvironmental Studies,
         Monograph 5, Florida Museum of Natural History, University of
         Florida, Gainesville.

2005c   SMAP Investigations at the Carlston Annis Site,15Bt5. In *Archae-
         ology of the Middle Green River Region, Kentucky,* edited by W.
         Marquardt and P. Watson, pp. 87–120. Institute of Archaeology
         and Paleoenvironmental Studies, Monograph 5, Florida Museum of
         Natural History, University of Florida, Gainesville.

MASLOWSKI, ROBERT, CHARLES NIQUETTE, AND D. WINGFIELD
1995   The Kentucky, Ohio, and West Virginia Radiocarbon Database.
         West Virginia Archeologist 47:1–2.

MAYER-OAKES, WILLIAM
1955a   *The Globe Hill Shell Heap.* West Virginia Archeological Society,
         Publication Series No. 3, Moundsville, West Virginia.

1955b   Prehistory of the Upper Ohio Valley; An Introductory Archeological
         Study. Anthropological Series No. 2. Annals of Carnegie Museum,
         Pittsburgh.

MAYES, LEIGH
1997   The Bluegrass Site (12W162): Bioarchaeological Analysis of a
        Middle-Late Archaic Mortuary Site in Southwestern Indiana.
        Master's thesis, University of Southern Mississippi, Hattiesburg.

MCCAA, ROBERT
2003   Paleodemography of the Americas from Ancient Times to Colo-
        nialism and Beyond. In *The Backbone of History,* edited by R. Steckel
        and J. Rose, pp. 94–125. Cambridge University Press, Oxford.

MCGRAW, BETTY, AND WILLIAM HUSER
1995   Preliminary Report of Phase III Investigation of the Hedden Site, a
        Late Archaic Habitation and Mortuary Site in McCracken County,
        Kentucky. Paper presented at the Annual meeting of the Kentucky
        Heritage Council, Richmond.

MCKNIGHT, JUSTINE
2004   Mid-Holocene Landscapes and Plant Use at the East Steubenville
        Site. Poster presented at the annual meeting of the Society for
        American Archaeology, Montreal.

MCNUTT, CHARLES
2008   The Benton Phenomenon and Middle Archaic Chronology in Ad-
        jacent Portions of Tennessee, Mississippi, and Alabama. *South-
        eastern Archaeology* 27(1):45–60.

MEEKS, SCOTT, SARAH BLANKENSHIP, HEATHER WELBORN, AND
    JEREMY SWEAT
2007   Tennessee's Past and Present Environments. Paper read at the annual
        meeting of the Southeastern Archaeological Conference, Knoxville.

MEINDL, RICHARD, ROBERT MENSFORTH, AND HEATHER YORK
2001   Mortality, Fertility, and Growth in the Kentucky Late Archaic: The
        Paleodemography of the Ward Site. In *Archaic Transitions in Ohio
        and Kentucky Prehistory,* edited by O. Prufer, S. Pedde, and R.
        Meindl, pp. 87–109. Kent State University Press, Kent, Ohio.

MENSFORTH, ROBERT
2001   Warfare and Trophy Taking in the Archaic Period. In *Archaic Tran-
        sitions in Ohio and Kentucky Prehistory,* edited by O. Prufer, S.
        Pedde, and R. Meindl, pp. 110–137. Kent State University Press,
        Kent, Ohio.

2005   Paleodemography of the Skeletal Population from the Carlston
        Annis Site, 15Mt5. In *Archaeology of the Middle Green River
        Region, Kentucky,* edited by W. Marquardt and P. Watson, pp.
        453–488. Institute of Archaeology and Paleoenvironmental Studies,
        Monograph 5, Florida Museum of Natural History, University of
        Florida, Gainesville.

2007   Human Trophy Taking in Eastern North American During the Archaic Period: Its Relationship to Warfare and Social Complexity. In *The Taking and Displaying of Human Body Parts as Trophies by Amerindians*, edited by R. Chacon and D. Dye, pp. 218–273. Springer Verlag, New York.

MILLER, MARY, AND KARL TAUBE
1993   *An Illustrated Dictionary of the Gods and Symbols of Ancient Mexico and the Maya.* Thames and Hudson, London.

MILLER, REX
1941   *McCain Site, Dubois County, Indiana.* Prehistory Research Series: Indiana Historical Society 2(1).

MILNE, COURTNEY
1995   *Sacred Places in North America: A Journey into the Medicine Wheel.* Stewart, Taboir and Chang, New York.

MILNER, GEORGE, AND RICHARD JEFFERIES
1998   The Read Archaic Shell Midden in Kentucky. *Southeastern Archaeology* 17(2):119–132.

MIRES, ANN MARIE
1991   Sifting the Ashes: Reconstruction of a Complex Archaic Mortuary Program in Louisiana. In *What Mean These Bones? Studies in Southeastern Bioarchaeology*, edited by M. Powell, P. Bridges, and A. Mires, pp. 114–130. University of Alabama Press, Tuscaloosa.

MOCAS, STEVE
1985   Lawrence Site. *Tennessee Archaeologist* 10(1):76–91.
2009   Radiocarbon Dates. In *Phase III Archaeological Mitigation of the Panther Rock Site (15Cl58), Carroll County, Kentucky*, compiled by Richard Stallings, pp. 116–118. AMEC Earth and Environmental.

MOHNEY, KENNETH
2002   Steubenville Projectile Points, Social and Technological Functions in the Panhandle Archaic of the Upper Ohio River Valley. Ph.D. dissertation, Anthropology, University of Pittsburgh.

MOORE, CHRISTOPHER
2008   A Macroscopic Investigation of Technological Style and the Production of Middle to Late Archaic Fishhooks at the Chiggerville, Read, and Baker Sites, Western Kentucky. Paper presented at the annual meeting of the Southeastern Archaeological Conference, Charlotte.

MOORE, CLARENCE
1916   Some Aboriginal Sites on Green River, Kentucky. *Journal of the Academy of Natural Science,* Second Series, No. 16. Philadelphia.

MOORE, T. C., DAVID K. REA, AND HOLLY GODSEY
1998   Regional variation in modern radiocarbon ages and the hard-water effects in Lakes Michigan and Huron *Journal of Paleolimnology* 20:347–351.

Morey, Darcy, and George Crothers

1998   Clearing Up Clouded Waters: Paleoenvironmental Analysis of Freshwater Mussel Assemblages from the Green River Shell Middens,
Western Kentucky. *Journal of Archaeological Science* 25:907–926.

Morey, Darcy, George Crothers, Julie Stein, James Fenton, and
Nicholas Herrmann

2002   The Fluvial and Geomorphic Context of Indian Knoll, an Archaic
Shell Midden in West-Central Kentucky. *Geoarchaeology* 17(6):
521–553.

Morrison, J. P. E.

1942   Preliminary Report on Mollusks Found in the Shell Mounds of
the Pickwick Landing Basin in the Tennessee River Valley. In *An
Archeological Survey of Pickwick Basin in the Adjacent Portions
of the States of Alabama, Mississippi and Tennessee,* by W. Webb
and D. DeJarnette, pp. 341–392. U.S. Government Printing Office,
Washington, D.C.

Morse, Dan

1967   The Robinson Site and Shell Mound Archaic Culture in the Middle
South. Ph.D. dissertation, University of Michigan.

1977   A human femur tube from Arkansas. *Arkansas Archeologist*
16–17–18:42–44.

Muto, Guy, and Joel Gunn

1981   A Study of Late-Quaternary Environments and Early Man along the
Tombigbee River, Alabama and Mississippi. Report submitted to the
National Park Service, Atlanta. Blair and Affiliates, Oklahoma City.

Nance, Jack

1986   Archaic Culture in the Lower Tennessee-Cumberland-Ohio Region.
Paper read at the annual meeting of the Southeastern Archaeological
Conference, Nashville.

O'Brien, Michael

2001   Archaeology, Paleoecosystems and Ecological Restoration. In *The
Historical Ecology Handbook,* edited by D. Egan and E. Howell, pp.
35–44. Society for Ecological Restoration, Island Press, Washington,
D.C.

O'Brien, Michael, and W. Raymond Wood

1998   *Prehistory of Missouri.* University of Missouri Press, Columbia.

Orser, Charles

1992   Beneath the Material Surface of Things: Commodities, Artifacts, and
Slave Plantations. *Historical Archaeology* 26(3):95–104.

Ortmann, Arnold

1927   The Naiades of the Green River Drainage in Kentucky. *Annales of
the Carnegie Museum* 17(1):167–188.

OSBORN, ROBIN
2004   Hoards, votives, offerings: the archaeology of the dedicated object. *World Archaeology* 36(1):1–10.

OTTESEN, ANNE
1979   Acquisition of Exotic Raw Materials by Late Woodland and Mississippian Peoples. Ph.D. dissertation, Anthropology, New York University.

PARKER, MALCOLM
1974   Owl Creek People 6660BC: The Hart Site at Nashville 1972–1974. Manuscript on file at the Tennessee Department of Environment and Conservation, Division of Archaeology, Nashville.

PATCH, DIANE
2005   The Freshwater Molluscan Fauna: Identification and Interpretation for Archaeological Research. In *Archaeology of the Middle Green River Region, Kentucky*, edited by W. Marquardt and P. Watson, pp. 257–278. Institute of Archaeology and Paleoenvironmental Studies, Monograph 5, Florida Museum of Natural History, University of Florida, Gainesville.

PAUKETAT, TIM, LUCRETIA KELLY, GAYLE FRITZ, NEAL LOPINOT, SCOTT ELIAS, AND EVE HARGRAVE
2002   The Residues of Feasting and Public Ritual at Early Cahokia. *American Antiquity* 67(2):257–280.

PEACOCK, EVAN
2002   Shellfish Use During the Woodland Period in the Middle South. In *The Woodland Southeast*, edited by D. Anderson and R. Mainfort, pp. 444–460. University of Alabama Press, Tuscaloosa.

2006   AMS Dating of Shell-Tempered Pottery and the Reservoir Effect. Paper presented at the 10th International Council on Archaeozoology, Mexico City.

2009   Freshwater Mussel Shell. In *Phase III Archaeological Mitigation of the Panther Rock Site (15Cl58), Carroll County, Kentucky*, compiled by Richard Stallings, pp. 189–195. AMEC Earth and Environmental.

PEDDE, SARA, AND OLAF PRUFER
2001   The Kentucky Green River Archaic as Seen from the Ward Site. In *Archaic Transitions in Ohio and Kentucky Prehistory*, edited by O. Prufer, S. Pedde, and R. Meindl, pp. 59–86. Kent State University Press, Kent, Ohio.

PHILLIPS, PHILIP, AND JAMES BROWN (EDS.)
1983   *Archaic Hunters and Gatherers in the American Midwest*. Academic Press, New York.

PIPES, MARIE
2007   Faunal Analysis. In Panhandle Archaic Americans in the Upper
        Ohio Valley: Archaeological Data Recovery at the East Steuben-
        ville (46Br31) and Highland Hills (46Br60) Sites WV Route 2
        Follansbee-Weirton Road Upgrade Project Brooke County, West
        Virginia. Technical Report, Vol. 1, pp. 388–416. West Virginia
        Department of Transportation, Division of Highways.

POHL, MARY
1983   Maya Ritual Faunas: Vertebrate Remains from Burials, Caches,
        Caves, and Cenotes in the Maya Lowlands. In *Civilization in the
        Ancient Americas: Essays in Honor of Gordon R. Willey*, edited by
        R. Leventhal and A. Kolata, pp. 55–104. University of New Mexico
        Press and Peabody Museum of Archaeology and Ethnology, Harvard
        University, Cambridge, Massachusetts.

POWELL, JOSEPH
1995   Dental variation and biological affinity among Middle Holocene
        human populations in North America. Ph.D. dissertation, Texas
        A&M University, College Station.

PRICE, T. DOUGLAS, AND JAMES BROWN (EDS.)
1985   Prehistoric Hunter-Gatherers: The Emergence of Cultural Complex-
        ity. Academic Press, New York.

PURDUE, JACK
1991   Dynamism in the Body Size of White-tailed Deer from Southern Illi-
        nois. In *Beamers, Bobwhites, and Blue-Points: Tributes to the Career
        of Paul W. Parmalee*, edited by J. Purdue, W. Klippel, and B. Styles,
        pp. 277–283. Scientific Paper 23. Illinois State Museum, Springfield.

RANDALL, ASA, AND KENNETH SASSAMAN
2005   St. John's Archaeological Field School 2003–2004: Hontoon Island
        State Park. Technical Report 6, Laboratory of Southeastern Archae-
        ology, Anthropology, University of Florida, Gainesville.

RANKIN, TOM
1982   Taped Interview with T. J. Whitfield, 9 September. Tape on file,
        Nathan Bedford Forrest Folklife Museum, Camden, Tennessee.

REID, KENNETH
1983   The Nebo Hill Phase: Late Archaic Prehistory in the Lower Missouri
        Valley. In *Archaic Hunters and Gatherers in the American Midwest*,
        edited by J. Phillips and J. Brown, pp. 11–40. Academic Press, New
        York.

REILLY, KENT, AND JAMES GARBER (EDS.)
2007   *Ancient Objects and Sacred Realms: Interpretations of Mississippian
        Iconography.* University of Texas Press, Austin.

RISSOLO, DOMINIQUE
2005   Beneath the Yalahua: Emerging Patterns of Ancient Maya Ritual
        Cave Use from Northern Quintana Roo, Mexico. In *In the Maw
        of the Earth Monster: Mesoamerican Ritual Cave Use*, edited by J.
        Brady and K. Prufer, pp. 342–372. University of Texas Press, Austin.

RITCHIE, WILLIAM
1965   *The Archaeology of New York State*. Natural History Press, Garden
        City, New York.

ROLINGSON, MARTHA
1967   Temporal Perspective on the Archaic Cultures of the Middle Green
        River Region, Kentucky. Ph.D. dissertation, Anthropology, Univer-
        sity of Michigan.

ROLINGSON, MARTHA, AND DOUGLAS SCHWARTZ
1967   *Late Paleo-Indian and Early Archaic Manifestations in Western Ken-
        tucky*. University of Kentucky, Lexington.

ROLLINS, HAROLD, AND LISA DUGAS
2007   Shell Analysis. In Panhandle Archaic Americans in the Upper Ohio
        Valley: Archaeological Data Recovery at the East Steubenville
        (46Br31) and Highland Hills (46Br60) Sites WV Route 2 Follansbee-
        Weirton Road Upgrade Project Brooke County, West Virginia. Tech-
        nical Report, Vol. 1, pp. 375–416. West Virginia Department of
        Transportation, Division of Highways.

ROSS-STALLINGS, NANCY
2009   Fauna and Bone Tools. In *Phase III Archaeological Mitigation of the
        Panther Rock Site (15Cl58), Carroll County, Kentucky*, compiled by
        R. Stallings, pp. 134–189. AMEC Earth and Environmental.

ROTHSCHILD, NAN
1979   Mortuary Behavior and Social Organization at Indian Knoll and
        Dickson Mounds. *American Antiquity* 44(4):658–675.

RUSSO, MICHAEL
1994a   A Brief Introduction to the Study of Archaic Mounds in the Southeast.
        Southeastern Archaeology 13(2):89–92.

1994b   Why We Don't Believe in Archaic Ceremonial Mounds and Why We
        Should: The Case from Florida. *Southeastern Archaeology* 13(2):
        93–108.

2004   Measuring Shell Rings for Social Inequality. In *Signs of Power: Rise
        of Cultural Complexity in the Southeast*, edited by J. Gibson and P.
        Carr, pp. 26–70. University of Alabama Press, Tuscaloosa.

SASSAMAN, KENNETH
1993a   *Early Pottery in the Southeast: Tradition and Innovation in Cooking
        Technology*. University of Alabama Press, Tuscaloosa.

1993b   *Mims Point 1992.* Savannah River Archaeological Research Papers 4, South Carolina Institute of Archaeology and Anthropology, Columbia.

2004   Complex Hunter-Gatherers in Evolution and History: A North American Perspective. *Journal of Archaeological Research* 12(3): 227–280.

2005   Hontoon Dead Creek Mound. In *St. Johns Archaeological Field School 2003–2004: Hontoon Island State Park,* edited by A. Randall and K. Sassaman, pp. 83–106. Technical Report 6, Laboratory of Southeastern Archaeology, Anthropology, University of Florida, Gainesville.

2006   *People of the Shoals: Stallings Culture of the Savannah River Valley.* University Press of Florida, Gainesville.

SASSAMAN, KENNETH, AND ASA RANDALL
2006   Shell Mounds of Middle St. John's Basin, Northeast Florida. Paper delivered at the annual meeting of the Society for American Archaeology, San Juan, Puerto Rico.

SASSAMAN, KENNETH, GLEN HANSON, AND TERRY CHARLES
1988   Raw Material Procurement and Reduction of Hunter-Gatherer Range in the Savannah River Valley. *Southeastern Archaeology* 7:79–94.

SASSAMAN, KENNETH, AND MICHAEL HECKENBERGER
2004   Crossing the Symbolic Rubicon in the Southeast. In *Signs of Power: Rise of Cultural Complexity in the Southeast,* edited by J. Gibson and P. Carr, pp. 214–233. University of Alabama Press, Tuscaloosa.

SAUNDERS, JOE
2004   Are We Fixing to Make the Same Mistake Again? In *Signs of Power,* edited by J. Gibson and P. Carr, pp. 146–161. University of Alabama Press, Tuscaloosa.

SAUNDERS, JOE, ROLFE MANDEL, GARTH SAMPSON, CHARLES ALLEN, THURMAN ALLEN, DANIEL BUSH, AND JAMES FEATHERS
2004   Watson Brake, A Middle Archaic Mound Complex in Northeast Louisiana. *American Antiquity* 70(4):631–668.

SAUNDERS, REBECCA
2004   The Stratigraphic Sequence at Rollins Shell Ring: Implications for Ring Function. *Florida Anthropologist* 57(4):249–270.

SAXE, ARTHUR
1970   Social Dimensions of Mortuary Practices. Ph.D. dissertation, Anthropology, University of Michigan.

SCARPINO, PHILIP
1985   *Great River: An Environmental History of the Upper Mississippi, 1890–1950.* University of Missouri Press, Columbia.

SCHAEFER, STACY
2002   To Think with a Good Heart: Wixárika Women, Weavers, and Shamans. University of Utah Press, Salt Lake City.

SEBRING, EDWARD
1985   Documentary on Mussel Fishing Debuts. Vincennes Sun-Commercial, 14 October:1, 5. Vincennes, Indiana.

SEEMAN, MARK
1986   Adena "Houses" and their implications for Early Woodland settlement models in the Ohio Valley. In Early Woodland Archeology, edited by K. Farnsworth, pp. 564–580. Center for American Archaeology, Kampsville, Illinois.

SHERWOOD, SARAH, AND JEFFERSON CHAPMAN
2005   The Identification and Potential Significance of Early Holocene Prepared Clay Surfaces: Examples from Dust Cave and Icehouse Bottom. Southeastern Archaeology 24(1):70–82.

SHIELDS, BEN
2003   An Analysis of the Archaic Human Burials at the Mulberry Creek (1CT27) Shell Mound, Colbert County, Alabama. Master's thesis, University of Alabama, Tuscaloosa.

2007   Negotiating Archaic Period Social Scripts: Mortuary Practices at Mulberry Creek, Alabama. Paper presented at the annual meeting of the Southeastern Archaeological Conference, Knoxville, Tennessee.

SIMEK, JAN, SARAH BLANKENSHIP, AND ALAN CRESSLER
2007   Prehistoric Ceremonial Use of Caves in Southeastern North America. Paper presented at the annual meeting of the Society for American Archaeology, Austin, Texas.

SMITH, HUGH
1898   The Mussel Fishery and Pearl-Button Industry of the Mississippi River. Bulletin of the U.S. Fisheries Commission 18, Washington, D.C.

SMITH, MARIA
1993   A probable case of decapitation at the Late Archaic Robinson Site (40SM4), Smith County, Tennessee. Tennessee Anthropologist 18: 131–142.

1995   Scalping in the Archaic Period: Evidence from the Western Tennessee Valley. Southeastern Archaeology 14:60–68.

1996   Biocultural Inquiry into Archaic Period Populations of the Southeast: Trauma and Occupational Stress. In Archaeology of the Mid-Holocene Southeast, edited by K. Sassaman and D. Anderson, pp. 134–156. University Press of Florida, Gainesville.

2003   Beyond Palisades: The Nature and Frequency of Late Prehistoric Deliberate Violent Trauma in the Chickamauga Reservoir of

East Tennessee. *American Journal of Physical Anthropology* 121:303–318.

SMITH, PHILIP

1965   Recent Adjustments in Animal Ranges. In *The Quaternary of the United States,* edited by H. Wright and D. Frey, pp. 633–642. Princeton University Press, Princeton, New Jersey.

STANSBERY, DAVID

1970   Eastern Freshwater Mollusks: The Mississippi and St. Lawrence River Systems. *Malacologia* 10:9–22.

1971   Comments. In *Rare and Endangered Mollusks of the U.S.,* edited by S. Jorgenson and R. Sharp, p. 72. U.S. Department of the Interior, Fish and Wildlife Service, Bureau of Sport Fisheries and Wildlife, Washington, D.C.

STEIN, JULIE

2005a   Environment of the Green River Sites. In *Archaeology of the Middle Green River Region, Kentucky,* edited by W. Marquardt and P. Watson, pp. 19–39. Institute of Archaeology and Paleoenvironmental Studies, Monograph 5, Florida Museum of Natural History, University of Florida, Gainesville.

2005b   Formation Processes of the Carlston Annis Shell Midden. In *Archaeology of the Middle Green River Region, Kentucky,* edited by W. Marquardt and P. Watson, pp. 121–152. Institute of Archaeology and Paleoenvironmental Studies, Monograph 5, Florida Museum of Natural History, University of Florida, Gainesville.

STOCKARD, S.

1904   History of Lawrence, Jackson, Independence and Stone Counties, Arkansas. *Arkansas Democrat,* Little Rock.

SUNDSTROM, LINEA

2000   Blind Encounters: Archaeologists and Sacred Sites in the Northern Plains. Paper presented at the annual meetings of the Plains Anthropological Conference, Saint Paul.

SURFACE-EVANS, SARAH

2006   Visualizing Social Complexity: The Role of Landscape on Shell Mound Archaic Settlement Patterns in the Central Ohio River Valley. Paper read at the annual meeting of the Society for American Archaeology, San Juan, Puerto Rico.

SWANTON, JOHN

1931   Source Material for the Social and Ceremonial Life of the Choctaw Indians. Bureau of American Ethnology, Bulletin 103, Washington, D.C.

TAÇON, PAUL

1999   Identifying Ancient Sacred Landscapes in Australia: From Physical to Social. In *Archaeologies of Landscape: Contemporary Perspectives,* edited by W. Ashmore and A. Knapp, pp. 33–57. Blackwell Publishers, Oxford, England.

TAXMAN, STEVEN
1994   Nonmetric Trait Variation in the Adena Peoples of the Ohio River Drainage. *Midcontinental Journal of Archaeology* 19(1):71–98.

THANZ, NINA
1977   A Correlation of Environmental and Cultural Changes in Northeastern Florida During the Late Archaic. *Florida Journal of Anthropology* 2(1):3–22.

TOLL, H. WOLCOTT
2001   Making and Breaking Pots in the Chaco World. *American Antiquity* 66:56–78.

TURNER, JAMES
2006   An Investigation of Violence-Related Trauma at Two Sites in the Pickwick Basin: Dust Cave and the O'Neal Site. Master's thesis, Mississippi State University.

WAGNER, GAIL
2005   Anthropogenic Changes at the Carlston Annis Site. In *Archaeology of the Middle Green River Region, Kentucky,* edited by W. Marquardt and P. Watson, pp. 213–242. Institute of Archaeology and Paleoenvironmental Studies, Monograph 5, Florida Museum of Natural History, University of Florida, Gainesville.

WALKER, RENEE, AND PAUL PARMALEE
2004   A Noteworthy Cache of Goose Humeri from Late Paleoindian Levels at Dust Cave, Northwestern Alabama. *Journal of Alabama Archaeology* 50(1):18–35.

WALKER, RENEE, DARCY MOREY, AND JOHN RELETHFORD
2005   Early and Mid-Holocene Dogs in Southeastern North America: Examples from Dust Cave. *Southeastern Archaeology* 24(1):83–92.

WALL, ROBERT
1994   Phase III Archaeological Data Recovery Sub-Mound Component at Cotiga Mound, 46Mo1, Mingo County, West Virginia. Draft report, West Virginia Department of Transportation, Division of Highways.

WALLACE, ANTHONY
1972   *Death and Rebirth of Seneca.* Vintage Press, New York.

WALTHALL, JOHN
1990   *Prehistoric Indians of the Southeast: Archaeology of Alabama and the Middle South.* University of Alabama Press, Birmingham.

WARD, STEVEN
2005   Dental Biology of the Carlston Annis Shell Mound Population. In *Archaeology of the Middle Green River Region, Kentucky,* edited by W. Marquardt and P. Watson, pp. 489–503. Institute of Archaeology

and Paleoenvironmental Studies, Monograph 5, Florida Museum of Natural History, University of Florida, Gainesville.

WARREN, DIANE

2004   Skeletal Biology and Paleopathology of Domestic Dogs from Prehistoric Alabama, Illinois, Kentucky, and Tennessee. Ph.D. dissertation, Anthropology, Indiana University, Bloomington.

WARREN, ROBERT

1975   Prehistoric Unionacean Utilization at the Widows Creek Site (1JA305), Northeast Alabama. Master's thesis, University of Nebraska.

WATSON, PATTY JO

2005   WPA Excavations in the Middle Green River Region: A Comparative Account. In *Archaeology of the Middle Green River Region, Kentucky,* edited by W. Marquardt and P. Watson, pp. 515–628. Institute of Archaeology and Paleoenvironmental Studies, Monograph 5, Florida Museum of Natural History, University of Florida, Gainesville.

WEBB, WILLIAM

1939   *An Archaeological Survey of Wheeler Basin on the Tennessee River in Northern Alabama.* U.S. Government Printing Office, Washington, D.C.

1950a   *Carlston Annis Mound, Site 5, Butler County, Kentucky.* University of Kentucky, Reports in Anthropology 7(4). Lexington.

1950b   *The Read Shell Midden.* University of Kentucky, Reports in Anthropology 7(5). Lexington.

1951   *The Parrish Village Site.* University of Kentucky Press, Lexington.

1974   *Indian Knoll.* University of Tennessee Press, Knoxville.

WEBB, WILLIAM, AND DAVID DEJARNETTE

1942   *An Archeological Survey of Pickwick Basin in the Adjacent Portions of the States of Alabama, Mississippi and Tennessee.* BAE Bulletin 129.

1948a   *The Flint River Site, Ma48.* Geological Survey of Alabama, Museum Paper 23, Alabama Museum of Natural History.

1948b   *Little Bear Creek Site Ct 8.* Museum Paper 26, Alabama Museum of Natural History.

1948c   *The Perry Site Lu25, Units 3 and 4, Lauderdale Co., Alabama.* Geological Survey of Alabama, Museum Paper 25, Alabama Museum of Natural History.

1948d   *The Whitesburg Bridge Site Ma10.* Museum Paper 24, Alabama Museum of Natural History.

WEBB, WILLIAM, AND WILLIAM FUNKHOUSERS

1932   Archaeological Survey of Kentucky. *Reports in Archaeology and Anthropology,* Vol. 2. University of Kentucky, Lexington.

WEBB, WILLIAM, AND WILLIAM HAAG

1939   *The Chiggerville Site 1, Ohio County, Kentucky.* Publications of
Department of Anthropology and Archaeology, University of Kentucky, Lexington 4(1).

1940   *Cypress Creek Villages.* Reports in Anthropology 4(2). University of
Kentucky, Lexington.

1947   *Archaic Sites in McLean County, Kentucky.* Reports in Anthropology
7(1). University of Kentucky, Lexington.

WEBB, WILLIAM, AND CHARLES SNOW

1974   *The Adena People.* University of Tennessee, Knoxville.

WEBB, WILLIAM, AND CHARLES WILDER

1951   *An Archaeological Survey of Guntersville Basin on the Tennessee
River in Northern Alabama.* University of Kentucky Press,
Lexington.

WEISS, DENNIS

1974   Late Pleistocene Stratigraphy and Paleoecology of the Lower
Hudson River Estuary. *Geological Society of America Bulletin*
85:1561–1570.

WENDLAND, WAYNE

1978   Holocene Man in North America: The Ecological Setting and Climatic Background. *Plains Anthropologist* 23:273–287.

WHEELER, RYAN, CHRISTINE NEWMAN, AND RAY MCGEE

2000   A New Look at the Mount Taylor and Bluffton Sites, Volusia County,
with an Outline of the Mount Taylor Culture. *Florida Anthropologist* 53(2–3):132–157.

WHITE, ANDREW

2002   *Survey and Excavations in the Nugent East Area, Clark County,
Indiana, 1998–1999.* Reports of Investigations 206. IPFW Archae-
ological Survey, Fort Wayne, Indiana. Submitted to Nugent Sand
Company.

2004   Excavations at the Clark's Point Site (12-Cl-3), Clark County, Indiana. IPFW Archaeological Survey Reports of Investigations 302.

WIDMER, RANDOLPH

2004   Explaining Sociopolitical Complexity in the Foraging Adaptations
of the Southeastern United States: The Roles of Demography, Kinship, and Ecology in Sociocultural Evolution. In *Signs of Power,*
edited by J. Gibson and P. Carr, pp. 234–253. University of Alabama
Press, Tuscaloosa.

WILLIAMS, JOHN

1969   *Mussel Fishery Investigations, Tennessee, Ohio and Green Rivers:
Final Report. Report* [Project No. 4-19-R]. Prepared by Murray

State University Biological Station, Murray, Kentucky. Submitted to Kentucky Department of Fish and Wildlife Resources, Frankfort.

WILLOUGHBY, CHARLES
1935   *Antiquities of the New England Indians, with notes on the ancient cultures of the adjacent territory.* Peabody Museum, Harvard University.

WILSON, CHARLES, AND H. WALTON CLARK
1914   *The Mussels of the Cumberland River and Its Tributaries.* U.S. Bureau of Fisheries Document 781. Washington, D.C.

WINTERS, HOWARD
1969   *The Riverton Culture.* Illinois State Museum, Report of Investigations 13. Illinois Archaeological Survey.
1974   Introduction. In *Indian Knoll,* pp. v–xxvii. W. Webb, author. Knoxville, University of Tennessee Press.

WOLF, DAVID, AND ROBERT BROOKS
1979   The Prehistoric People of the Rosenberger Site. In *Excavations at Four Archaic Sites in the Lower Ohio Valley, Jefferson County, Kentucky,* Vol. II, edited by M. Collins, pp. 899–945. Anthropology, University of Kentucky, Lexington.

WYCKOFF, LARRY M.
1977   Biological Relationships and Growth. (Chiggerville). Master's thesis, Western Michigan University, Kalamazoo.

YERKES, RICHARD
2005   Bone Chemistry, Body Parts, and Growth Marks: Evaluating Ohio Hopewell and Cahokia Mississippian Seasonality, Subsistence, Ritual, and Feasting. *American Antiquity* 70(2):241–266.

YU, Z.
1997   Middle Holocene dry climate caused by changes in atmospheric circulation patterns: Evidence from Lake levels and stable isotopes. *Geology* 25:251–254.

INDEX

Page numbers in **boldface** refer to illustrations.

Feasting with Shellfish in the Southern Ohio Valley was designed and typeset on a Macintosh computer system using InDesign software. The body text is set in 10/13 Sabon and display type is set in Sabon. This book was designed and typeset by Chad Pelton, and manufactured by Thomson-Shore, Inc